ADVANCE PRAISE FOR
FACTS & FURY

"In this important book, Bill Kuhn spells out in a clear, easily accessible and well-researched manner the depth and breadth of the damage the Republican Party and the rest of the far-Right has done to the American people and American democracy in recent decades. *Facts &Fury* makes a valuable contribution to our understanding of why our country has gone so far off track."

—LINCOLN MITCHELL, Columbia University

"*Facts & Fury* by Bill Kuhn is an incisive and witty look at the greatest (I mean worst) moments in recent Republican Party history. Kuhn weaves together American political, religious, and economic trends since FDR's New Deal to explain how we ended up with Trump. It's a not-so-pretty must-read for anyone who cares about Democracy."

—MARY SHANNON LITTLE, writer and lawyer

"We are lucky to have Bill Kuhn out there in the trenches fighting for a better America. Now, he has written a powerful, timely, and much-needed analysis of how the Republican party went off the rails, abandoned its mandate, and embraced extremism. It's a scary book, but still manages to be hopeful."

—AJ JACOBS, *New York Times* bestselling
author of *The Year of Living Biblically*

"No matter which side of the aisle you're on, Bill Kuhn's *Facts & Fury* is an indispensable guide to America's troubled electoral system. It is at once a playbook for the remarkable Republican game plan and a call to action for those afraid of the consequences. When the votes are counted this book will be required reading for anyone who wants to know what's really going on—and why."

—JONATHAN WALD, TV News Executive and former adjunct,
Columbia University Graduate School of Journalism

FACTS & FURY

FACTS &
FURY

AN UNAPOLOGETIC PRIMER
ON HOW THE GOP HAS DESTROYED
AMERICAN DEMOCRACY

BILL KUHN

GREENLEAF
BOOK GROUP PRESS

Published by Greenleaf Book Group Press
Austin, Texas
www.gbgpress.com

Distributed by Greenleaf Book Group

For ordering information or special discounts for bulk purchases, please contact Greenleaf Book Group at PO Box 91869, Austin, TX 78709, 512.891.6100.

Design and composition by Greenleaf Book Group
Cover design by Greenleaf Book Group and Kim Lance
Cover image: ©iStock/Getty Images Plus/Sergio Lacueva

Publisher's Cataloging-in-Publication data is available.

Print ISBN: 978-1-62634-954-4
eBook ISBN: 978-1-62634-955-1

Part of the Tree Neutral® program, which offsets the number of trees consumed in the production and printing of this book by taking proactive steps, such as planting trees in direct proportion to the number of trees used: www.treeneutral.com

Printed in the United States of America on acid-free paper

22 23 24 25 26 27   10 9 8 7 6 5 4 3 2 1

First Edition

I dedicate this book to my mother and father.
Your strength and toughness encouraged me every day.

ACKNOWLEDGMENTS

TO JOHN NEWSOME, my cofounder at Fight for a Better America. You're a damn fine leader and an inspiration to me and everyone who works with our organization. And to Russell Hamilton, Linda Goldman, Matt O'Connor, Molly Lindsay, and Kimberly Wicoff. Thanks for your partnership and putting in those long hours. It was worth it. To all the super volunteers, co-hosts, and donors who helped us win back the House in 2018 and the presidency and Senate in 2020 and 2021. To my family, Tom, Stacy, Nick, Rachel, and Miles. Frank, Emily, Peter, Bernie, and your significant others and children/grandchildren. And to my wife, Chiti. In these dark times, you spark the light of laughter and love. Thank you.

To the brilliant authors, journalists, and researchers who have taught me so much, and to the think tanks, foundations, and donors who have provided critical funding for the work that keeps our democracy alive: E. J. Dionne, Jacob Hacker, Paul Pierson, Kim Phillips-Fein, Chris Mooney, Norm Ornstein, Thomas Mann, Kevin Kruse, John Dean, Gary Clabaugh, Alex Hertel-Fernandez, Cary Coglianese, Adam M. Finkel, Christopher Carrigan, Michael Lewis, Mariana Mazzucato, Jane Mayer, Tom Nichols, Gabriel Sherman, Heather Cox Richardson, Brookings Institution, Kaiser Family Foundation, Commonwealth Fund, and the many others from whom I gained valuable perspective for this book.

To my wonderful editors, Toby Lester, Lincoln Mitchell, Rebecca Sacks, and Jeremy Townsend, and the entire Greenleaf team. Thanks for your advice and patience.

CONTENTS

SECTION 3

SECTION 4

SECTION 7

SECTION 8

SECTION 9

INTRODUCTION

IN FEBRUARY OF 2021, after having incited the January 6 coup attempt at the Capitol, during which five people died, former President Trump went on trial in the United States Senate. This was not his first but his second impeachment—and thanks to the Republicans in the Senate, he was acquitted for a second time, despite overwhelming evidence of his guilt.

That alone is appalling. But there is so much more. A group of right-wing Rambos not long ago hatched a detailed plan to kidnap and murder the governors of Michigan, Virginia, and Ohio—a plan replete with decoy strategies and pipe bombs—and nearly carried out that plan.[1] Moreover, as I write this, we are living through a pandemic in which, until very recently, more than four thousand people were dying every day, and yet we've been fighting over mask-wearing and other basic health protections.

Even after the January 6 insurrection, during which their own lives and staffs were at risk, more than 150 congressional Republicans officially objected to the Electoral College results of the November election, which had been certified by each of the states and their attorneys general.

Many have pointed the finger at Donald Trump for orchestrating all this. And it's true that in his four years in office, he stoked hatred and violence among his supporters and labeled anyone he didn't like or agree with an enemy. Obviously, he's contributed to our present predicament, in which the institutions of our democracy are weakening and public trust in government is fraying. But Trump is only the gallon or two of gasoline poured on a conflagration that's been burning for forty-plus years. As the renowned conservative scholar Norman Ornstein puts it, "The Republicans waged a three-decade war on government. They got Trump."

I won't mention Trump much in this book, because we all know what a colossal failure he was. Let's save our outrage for the conditions that allowed him to take power. How were voters effectively conditioned—through decades of corruption, fearmongering, and destructive policy—to put a guy like him up as a candidate? How was he able to win? How was he allowed to wreck the executive branch and make the legislative branch look like whimpering children? He had lots of powerful enablers. Did you see Lindsey Graham perform his impression of a lapdog for four years?

So how did we get here? Do you ever wonder why government is always portrayed as dysfunctional? Why you hear the phrase "nothing gets done" ad nauseam? Why Obamacare is mostly hated but its primary provisions are cherished? Where all the conspiracy theories started? Why we don't have good access to health care and why education isn't funded properly? How about taxes? Why do the rich keep winning? Why is it that senators representing 10 percent of the population can block any major legislation that helps the other 90 percent?

If you're asking yourself those sorts of questions, this is the book for you. There are a lot of great scholarly works, both conservative and liberal, that address such questions, but you probably haven't read them, because you don't have the time or would rather not spend your nights with a five-hundred page tome about the evolution of conservatism. I can probably name fifty amazing and knowledgeable researchers and academics who have studied this topic intensely for several years, or even decades. But most readers will never read them.

Everything I say in this book is based on the work that these scholars have done—work that proves that our current moment is the result of a decades-long siege on American democracy and the American people, led by congressional Republicans, Republican presidents, and their wealthy benefactors. But I have used these scholars' work to write a different kind of book, one organized as a series of short, engaging chapters that are designed to educate and entertain readers who have been on the sidelines but have a sense that something has gone deeply wrong. I've devoted each chapter to a different idea, and in each case, I frame it with my own outraged commentary. Sometimes I curse, because I can't help myself.

WHO AM I TO WRITE SUCH A BOOK?

Primarily, I am a concerned citizen—very concerned. The havoc and destruction wreaked upon our political system keep me up at night. I can no longer stand by as our institutions continue to buckle under the weight of one party's greed and disdain for the people it claims to serve. The truth is, our system wasn't built to cope with the Republican Party of the last forty years, and everyone needs to be concerned about it.

But I'm more than just a concerned citizen. I'm also a passionate political organizer.

I grew up in a political household. My mother was a key fundraiser for the Democratic Party, most notably for Walter Mondale during his 1984 presidential run against Ronald Reagan. My stepfather served as a lawyer on the Judiciary Committee during President Nixon's impeachment, and as White House counsel to President Clinton. Politics and the Washington experience were the air I breathed during my formative years.

Early in my career, I worked in investment banking. But ultimately that didn't sit well with me—I was a privileged White male, after all, benefiting from conservative economic policies at the expense of others whom I believed deserved more from our system. So after Trump's election in 2016, I cofounded an organization called Fight for a Better America, a 501(c)(4) dedicated to voter engagement and grassroots organizing.

Fight for a Better America raises money to invest in key battleground districts and states through the US, with the goal of either flipping them blue or maintaining a Democratic incumbent. Through my travels with the organization, I have made hundreds of contacts with folks in local civic and Democratic clubs throughout the country, primarily in California, Pennsylvania, New York, Florida, and New Jersey, and I've organized hundreds of volunteers on the ground. I've had thousands of conversations with voters and prospective volunteers about the issues that affect them the most.

I'm also a teacher who understands the learning process. For the past eight years, I've also been teaching high school at all grade levels, and I know just how difficult it can be to get ideas across. People who are fairly new to political history are like the students in my classrooms. They often need help engaging with the material. They need some humor and entertainment. They need visuals. They need emotion. Drawing on my skills as a teacher, I've provided all of that in this book. The chapters are all brief, and each breaks down the works of expert researchers and academics into enjoyable chunks. Very deliberately, each begins with a *What?* and a *Why?* so that you'll always know at the outset of each what I'm talking about and why it matters.

I should say that this book does not absolve congressional Democrats and past Democratic presidents of blame. They've been part of the problem, of course. But the fact is, they're a thousand times saner and more committed to the public good than Republicans, and they don't tend to collapse the economy or unilaterally start wars over commodities. I should also say that there are plenty of Republicans who don't approve of their party. When I talk about Republicans in this book, I mean primarily members of Congress, the conservative media ecosystem, and a group of elite financial backers.

For too long, we've allowed corporate interests and those representing them to cast government in a bad light. John Dewey said, "As long as politics is the shadow cast on society by big business, the attenuation of the shadow will not change the substance."[2] Indeed, our government functions more like a shadow than an entity. Government is supposed to mitigate the harmful consequences of private industry, not make those consequences worse. Government is supposed to level the playing field for people who are left behind, not make it less level. Government is supposed to help those who suffer needlessly with no private source of assistance to turn to. Government is supposed to be progressive in its response to our rapidly changing society.

So why doesn't our government do that? Because, beginning in earnest in the 1980s, the Republican Party has devoted itself to waging war on government, deploying a whole range of tactics to weaken public institutions and erode the public's trust in them. They've committed themselves to breaking our government, condemning its brokenness, and then claiming that only they can fix the problems that they've created.

How have they gotten away with this? Well, in part by developing a highly sophisticated propaganda machine to cover their lily-white butts. Remember, politics is a highly complex process, with millions of moving parts and not a great deal of transparency. It's easy to blame the *other guy* for something for which you are entirely at fault. Nothing is ever clear cut. With the right tools, it's possible to fool a lot of people, at least for a while.

But no longer. After forty years of this irresponsibly destructive behavior, millions of us are now outraged by their behavior. They have been exposed—and as I hope this book will convince you, it's now time to do something about it.

STRUCTURE OF THE BOOK

Unlike most books on politics and government, I'm not trying to impress academic colleagues or the Pulitzer committee. I'm not trying to win favor among pundits, journalists, and campaign veterans. Rather, I'm trying to inform and entertain the average voter.

As I've said, this book is broken down into a series of relatively short entries that detail various conservative attacks on democracy. I've written each to stand alone—you can read them in order to get a full picture of our current reality, or you can just pick the ones you're most interested in. I open each chapter with a damning quote or two, present the *What?* and the *Why?* and then dive into the meat and potatoes—lots of research from brilliant academics who've been studying the problem in question for decades. My paraphrasing of their work is colorful and exasperated, because I can't believe Republican chicanery has been going on right in front of our noses for this long.

More generally, I've organized this book into nine thematic sections:

In the first section, I discuss the far-reaching effects of conservatives' attitude toward government during the past forty-plus years and how it's shaped our politics and way of life. Let's just say that their attitude has been one of . . . antagonism. They hate government. As the prominent conservative activist with that most unlikable of faces Grover Norquist crowed in 2012, they want to shrink government down to the size where they "can drown it in the bathtub."[3]

In the second section, I'll discuss Republicans' unhealthy obsession with private enterprise. I'm sure you have a relative and/or friend in your life who blathers on about the saintly ethos of "free markets" and how they should never be trampled on. If you don't, consider yourself lucky. These ideologues believe first and foremost that there are actually such things as totally free markets—and that there's nothing that the government should do about the ridiculous inequality in this country, because that would be *socialism*. In this section I'll make clear, first, that markets are never free (their rules are made up by the people who create them) and, second, that government plays a vital role in protecting people's rights, alleviating poverty, and, most importantly, ensuring capitalism works for all. If we deny these truths, we will only make our present predicament worse. And that's not good for anyone, including the rich.

In the sections of the book that follow, I'll discuss all sorts of other enraging subjects, including:

- How the GOP has been able to keep or come within a slim majority in the House and Senate for so long through artificial electoral advantages that are downright fascist.

- How congressional conservatives, spurred on by corporate money, have brazenly deployed *alternative facts* to wage their wars on science, experts, and education.

- How during the past seventy years or so, conspiracy theories—or, as I like to call them, "distractions for when congressional conservatives can't compete in the marketplace of ideas"—almost always originate or flourish in Republican circles.

- How the GOP and conservative media have worked tirelessly to manufacture outrage, and how they've weaponized a whole set of buzzwords: socialism, cancel culture, radicalization, welfare queens, deficits, and on and on.

- How they accuse Democrats of engaging in the kinds of harmful behavior that they themselves are engaging in. If it weren't so damn harmful to our country and democracy, it would be quite pathetic.

- How screwed is American democracy and society compared to other wealthy nations? How do we stack up against, say, Germany or Japan in terms of health care, voting rights, and food safety? As you'll see, we haven't caught up to our more advanced peers—but, as I'll try to show, there's hope.

In the final section of the book, I'll provide perspective on our current situation and where we're headed. Most people like government and its policies. This is borne out in survey after survey. I discuss strategies for Americans to reclaim the rhetoric on how government is one of our strongest assets and how to combat attacks from congressional conservatives seeking to render it ineffective.

I'll leave you with this thought: The GOP has been operating in bad faith for years, striving not to improve but to sabotage our government and our society. That, above all, is what I hope to convince you of—and make you angry about—in this book. Only when enough of us recognize that the Republicans are waging a war on our democracy will we be able to rally a resistance, fight back, and reclaim our government.

SECTION 1

THE GOP'S ATTITUDE TOWARD GOVERNMENT

1

CONSERVATIVES' WAR
ON GOVERNMENT

"The nine most terrifying words in the English language are:
I'm from the Government, and I'm here to help."

**—FORMER PRESIDENT AND DISGRUNTLED EMPLOYEE,
RONALD REAGAN**

"We are radicals, working to overturn
the present power structure of this country."

**—PAUL WEYRICH,
COFOUNDER OF THE HERITAGE FOUNDATION**

WHAT?

FOR NEARLY A CENTURY, but most dramatically in the last forty years, congressional conservatives and their radical rich financial sponsors have warred with and attempted to destroy government from the inside as elected representatives, and from the outside as powerful organizations with well-funded lobbying budgets. I use the word *rad-ical*, as Mr. Weyrich uses it above, primarily to describe their view of government. And when I say *destroy*, I don't mean to literally burn the place down like Pablo Escobar tried to do to that Colombian court-house.[1] I mean render it limp and ineffective. Like overcooked fusilli.

WHY?

AS YOU WILL SEE throughout this book, there are three very simple reasons congressional conservatives and the radical rich act the way they do: money, power (of which they currently possess plenty, but their appetites are insatiable), and racism. I'm wary of the overuse of racism as a character attack, but, as you'll see, it is a highly appropri-ate labeling. By reducing the size of the federal government and its programs—which *overwhelmingly* help the poor and middle class—congressional conservatives and the radical rich effectively remove the biggest obstacle to fulfilling their dreams and desires. By reducing regulatory and tax burdens, capturing control of public resources, crushing financial assistance programs, and neutering enforcement of civil rights, they seek to eliminate all protections afforded to the poor and middle class and all obstacles to their power grab. What's worse is that they use that destructive success to implement a con-servative governing and economic agenda, tilting the benefits of government even more towards private interests and shifting fun-damentally shared responsibilities to the individual. In other words, socialism for the rich, capitalism for the rest. Yes, they are plenty happy using and expanding government to fit their needs—while rail-ing against those who seek to use government to level the playing field. In general, congressional conservatives claim they prefer private solutions to solving poverty (i.e., leaving it to churches or nonprofits), but the fact remains, conditions have gotten materially worse for the poor and middle-income under conservative stewardship of the federal government. Even more sinister is that beginning with President Reagan, Republicans realized they couldn't cut popular programs like Social Security and Medicare. So they started running up a deficit on the stuff they like—defense and war on terror—and then forced everything else to be cut.

HOW DO THEY ENACT their antigovernment agenda? A relentless multi-pronged rhetorical and legislative attack on *inefficiency, bureaucracy,* and *waste.* They'll say stuff like:

"All politicians are corrupt, you can't trust them."

"Government helps other people, not you."

"Regulation and taxes are always a burden, never helpful, and they threaten your freedom."

"Private is always better than public."

"Private enterprises are the noble, entrepreneurial beacons of hope that should wield the power, not the lazy bureaucrats."

"Government is tyranny."

If you've heard any of these or similar statements before, you've probably only scratched the surface. This is just the window dressing. The influence of powerful conservatives is far greater and more pervasive than you could imagine.

Pretend for a moment that you work for company—any company—and every four or eight years you get a new boss and executive leadership. And every two or so years, there's some standard turnover of the rank-and-file employees. Now picture that a new boss and his chosen executive team are constantly trashing the mission and function of your company and telling everyone, including customers, that this place is awful. Don't trust the products. We suck at what we do.

This is analogous to what Republican presidents and Republican congressional leadership do.

How much would you like working there? Would consumers want to purchase your products? Would they trust your company to do the right thing? Imagine if your boss, higher-ups, and colleagues said the following about your company, the government:

If government would someday quietly close the doors; if all the bureaucrats would tiptoe out of the marble halls; it would take the people of this country quite a while to miss them or even know they were gone."[2] That was your boss, Ronald Reagan, talking about the company as though it was some defunct nonentity. Once he became president, Reagan made good on his vision rhetoric and literally shut down the government—several times.

Here are a few other powerful conservative politicians in years past:

"I have little interest in streamlining government or making it
more efficient for I mean to reduce its size. My aim is not
to pass laws, but to repeal them . . ."

—BARRY GOLDWATER, 1964

"The fact is, if our primary legislative goals are to repeal
and replace the health spending bill; to end the bailouts;
cut spending; and shrink the size and scope of government,
the only way to do all these things it is to put someone in the
White House who won't veto any of these things."

—MITCH McCONNELL, 2010

"We're getting rid of Common Core. Department of Environmental
Protection. We're going take a tremendous amount out."

—PRESIDENT TRUMP, MICHIGAN DEBATE, 2016

"We are not looking to fill all of those positions. Don't need many
of them—reduce size of government."

—PRESIDENT TRUMP, TWITTER, AUGUST 29, 2017

REPUBLICAN AND CONSERVATIVE ELECTED officials weren't always this way. They used to care about good government and good governance. They were proud of the place they worked. They used their awesome power to enrich all the citizens of this country, not just big business and the wealthy.

Contrast the above quotes to those Republicans who are lionized by today's party. Teddy Roosevelt: "[T]he struggle of freemen to gain and hold the right of self-government as against the special interests, who twist the methods of free government into machinery for defeating the popular will. At every stage, and under all circumstances, the essence of the struggle is to equalize opportunity, destroy privilege, and give to the life and citizenship of every individual the highest possible value both to himself and to the commonwealth."[3]

Abe Lincoln: "Government of the people, by the people, for the people, shall not perish from the Earth."[4]

Dwight Eisenhower on his massive interstate highway program: "Existing traffic jams only faintly foreshadow those of ten years hence unless the present rate of highway improvements and development is increased. To correct these deficiencies is an obligation of Government at every level."[5]

Reagan, Speaker Newt Gingrich, Trump, McConnell—and the hundreds of others who followed in their government-bashing footsteps—not only talked about how treasonous and terrible the government was, but they pursued policy to that end. They slashed budgets of programs and gutted agencies that serve the poor, the very people the government is supposed to protect. They defunded programs within Congress to make it less functional and efficient, and when they lost majority control, they set time bombs for their Democratic colleagues that exploded in their faces once they assumed power. Like the time Republicans ceded control to the Democrats in 2007 after six remarkably terrible years of the Bush presidency, and Republicans in Congress neglected to enact appropriation bills that represented over $400 billion in spending on almost every domestic program. "They're going to leave a mess as they go out," said then-incoming Speaker Nancy Pelosi. Even Republicans were pissed. Jack Kingston of Georgia remarked, "I think it's shameful." Jo Ann Emerson of Missouri said, "There's so much to do and we're punting. It's irresponsible. There's no excuse for it."[6] Remarkable.

Worst of all, they were proud of it. Proud of *restoring* American governance to a time (circa the Great Depression) when this country was run almost completely by wealthy people, and millions were shut out of the shared prosperity that politicians talk about so much. Within the first two months of 1995, Gingrich said he had "probably the most fiscally conservative Congress since the '20s" and would consider a package of spending cuts in the 1995 budget that will be "pretty big, I think."[7] Imagine being the wealthiest country in the world and bragging about spending cuts to poor and middle-class families.

More quotes from Republicans and insiders:

"The folks who run Koch [Industries] are very clear. They would love to have government just get out of the way and allow companies to compete, whether in their particular sectors or other sectors. They are true believers in small government."

—CONGRESSIONAL CANDIDATE MIKE POMPEO IN 2011 WHEN ASKED IF HE WAS INFLUENCED BY KOCH INDUSTRIES, HIS LARGEST DONOR

"Small government is simply code for no more assistance
to poor people, particularly poor people of color."
—LEE ATWATER, REAGAN ADVISOR, 1981

"Will you resist the temptation to get a government handout for
your community? Realize that the doctor's fight against socialized
medicine is your fight. We can't socialize the doctors without
socializing the patients. Recognize that government invasion of
public power is eventually an assault upon your own business."
—RONALD REAGAN, 1964

"All the evils, abuses, and iniquities, popularly ascribed
to businessmen and to capitalism, were not caused by an
unregulated economy or by a free market, but by
government intervention into the economy."
**—AYN RAND, 1966, NOT A REGISTERED REPUBLICAN
BUT A MAJOR INFLUENCE ON MANY PROMINENT REPUBLICANS**

"The government does not add value to the economy.
It removes value from the economy by imposing taxes
on one citizen and providing cash to another."
—CONSERVATIVE TALK SHOW HOST MARK R. LEVIN

"The guiding purpose of the government regulators
is to prevent rather than create something."
—ALAN GREENSPAN, 1966

2

CHAOS AND GRIDLOCK

"I am a proud guardian of gridlock.
I think gridlock is making a big comeback in the country."

—MITCH MCCONNELL IN 1994

"They won't even be voted on.
So think of me as the Grim Reaper."

—MCCONNELL IN 2019 (SO MUCH HAS CHANGED)

WHAT?

PARTISAN GRIDLOCK: A PRIMARY reason people do not have faith in government and there is an all-time low approval of Congress. The GOP's deliberate attempts—beginning in the 1980s—to obstruct Congress and prevent it from passing bills has morphed, naturally, into total fucking chaos (as you can easily observe by picking up any newspaper today). Their mission was to create total dysfunction and ruin in their paths, and they've succeeded. What was once a great deliberative body has devolved into a muddled mess where it's all zinger one-liners and sound bites, and little of substance occurs. It's become a ratings show. Congress doesn't solve problems. It bickers, then raises money, then campaigns. In a cycle just like that. No wonder it's hard to find people who want to run for office.

This was all part of their plan.

WHY?

HERE'S AN ALL-ENCAPSULATING, one-sentence description of the GOP agenda: If Congress does not function properly, it can't pass any meaningful legislation. Why? Because dysfunction benefits private industry, particularly congressional Republican financial supporters (the radical rich), who want government to play as small and insignificant role as possible in their lives, both professionally and personally. They want to expand their share of the American pie, unchecked. The more chaos and gridlock, the less trust in the institution, the less anything gets done. I should caveat this with a crucial point. Republicans like certain legislation: cutting taxes and spending on defense.

IT'S ALL PART OF the plan. I'm no conspiracy theorist, but the connection between deliberate conservative dysfunction and non-participation in democracy is strong. Between 1960 and 2000, voter turnout in presidential elections went from 62 percent to 50 percent, and in the midterm elections, from 48 percent to 38 percent from 1962 to 1998.[1] We've experienced a slight pickup between 2000 and 2016, and in 2020, we saw record turnout. It's safe to assume it took a polarizing guy like Donald Trump to get people interested in politics again.

So how did Newt, Mitch, and their cadres of gridlockers do it? Brookings scholar Thomas Mann sums up Gingrich's toiling: "Gradually, it went from legislating, to the weaponization of legislating, to the permanent campaign, to the permanent war. It's like he took a wrecking ball to the most powerful and influential legislature in the world."[2]

As an introductory example—there are plenty of others laid out later in this book—I'll use the nomination of judges under President Obama. To assert that congressional Republicans blocked him at each turn would be an understatement. They used every trick in the book and then some (i.e., filibusters, anonymous holds) to hold up this otherwise uncontroversial process. Even the most middle-of-the-road bores waited months before they got a vote on the floor, let alone the more liberal ones. Even after some are unanimously voted out of the Senate Judiciary Committee, they are subject to long waits. It was so unprecedented and revolting.

According to the Center for American Progress, through the first twenty months of his administration, with the House and the Senate in Democratic control, fewer than 43 percent of President Obama's judicial nominees were confirmed, unlike past presidents who enjoyed a much easier time with Democrats and Republicans.[3] Observe:

% of All Judicial Nominees Confirmed in the First 14 Months

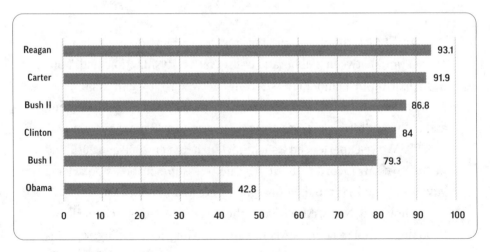

Source: Center for American Progress

Trump's success in the courts for the first two years in office was 53.5 percent.

This unprecedented obstruction extends also to the executive branch and confirming appointments to agencies. You know, the people who have to run the government. In 2015, the Senate confirmed the lowest number of civilian nominations—including judges and ambassadors—for the first session of a Congress in nearly thirty years.[4]

Not only did Obama endure unprecedented wait times for judges from nomination to confirmation, but, in his first year, he confirmed fewer judges than any president in the last forty years.

How many times did Democrats initiate a motion to end the filibuster under Obama. Clinton and Bush averaged around sixty-five times. Obama? One hundred thirty. Double![5]

It wasn't simply a matter of appointments or judges. It bled into nearly every Obama priority from financial reform to environmental protections to voting rights to curbing money in politics to immigration reform. Basically, any major legislation that was in the best interest of a vast majority of this country. Even infrastructure and small business tax cuts, which are supposedly Republican priorities—blocked. GOP Senator George Voinovich summed up their strategy with respect to Obama: "If he was for it, we had to be against it."[6] Talk about chaos and gridlock!

The author and journalist Jonathan Rauch aptly describes Republicans' philosophy as *chaos syndrome*. Basically, it's a cycle of dysfunction, anger, and distrust that continues to feed off itself. Conservatives furtively create the dysfunction, then are very vocal about it, making it their number one complaint about Washington, then proclaim they are the "only ones who can fix it." Rinse, repeat. "Like many disorders," Rauch writes, "chaos syndrome is self-reinforcing. It causes governmental dysfunction, which fuels public anger, which incites political disruption, which causes yet more governmental dysfunction."[7] In order to arrest the spiral, we must begin to understand it. The source of our political disease, as it were, is the erosion of our collective immune system. For over two hundred years, it has protected the body politic, but the slow dismantling of it in the last forty-plus years has made it susceptible to becoming really ill. New pathogens (Trump) are able to exploit vulnerabilities and fiercely attack the system. We've diagnosed the problem. We must treat it. Congressional conservatives, naturally, are standing in the way, much like how they refuse to wear masks and social distance during a pandemic.

3

GOLDWATERISM

"Extremism in the defense of liberty is no vice."

—BARRY GOLDWATER, 1964

WHAT?

IN 1964, A FIFTY-THREE-YEAR-OLD Republican senator from Arizona *absolutely burst* onto the national political scene and ran for president against Republicans like Nelson Rockefeller in the primaries and then Lyndon Johnson in the general election. I mean, this guy took every conservative with a crew-cut and a white picket fence by mega hailstorm. It wasn't so much his personality (as was the case with Trump) but his platform: antitax, antigovernment, anti-anything that smacked of *socialism*! Very original. And Goldwater benefited enormously from the backlash against the Civil Rights Movement. His famous treatise, *Conscience of a Conservative*, inspired millions of conservatives, young and old, White and Whiter. Even though he lost—he got his hat handed to him by Johnson—his words and ideas started nothing short of a revolution in the Republican Party, and particularly its elected representatives, who ever since have been pursuing the extremes of his agenda.

WHY?

GOLDWATER WAS A PERFECT vessel for conservative extremism. *Conscience of a Conservative* justified all the ways they could shrink government down to a size where they could "drown it in a bathtub," as Grover Norquist so eloquently put it. By strictly adhering to his immortal words, no amount of cutting social programs, dismantling civil rights law, or privatization was too much for a Goldwater conservative. What can also be described as a streak of anarchy (*my way or burn it all down*) played well in the segregationist and radical rich circles. The *White backlash* voter of the 1960s finally had a candidate who would reverse desegregation. And immoderate conservatives finally had an ideologue who believed that government should be gutted and destroyed from the inside.

E. J. DIONNE WRITES about how the Goldwater campaign transformed the party. Liberals and moderate Republicans were alienated and (eventually) became endangered, and as they did, the Southern realignment of the confederate states began in earnest. "The Goldwater campaign did more than create a powerful ideological legacy," Dionne writes. "It also transformed the Republican Party. Moderate and liberal Republicans were pushed out and alternative understandings of conservatism were rendered illegitimate."[1] The GOP looked nothing like it does today. Black people were once strong supporters. Eisenhower won about 40 percent of the non-White vote in 1956, and Nixon won

about a third in 1960. Since 1964, thanks to Johnson's Civil Rights passage and the Great Society, it's been all Democrats, and Republicans
are fine with that. "The Goldwater campaign and the backlash against
Johnson's support for civil rights are often cited as the twin engines
of the White Southern defection from the Democratic Party," Dionne
writes. As an aside, the transformation of the GOP wasn't complete
until the late 1980s–early 1990s. What started with Goldwater finished
with Reagan and Gingrich.

Goldwater, however, was the primary spark for the Southern
Republican Party realignment. He sped that puppy up. Dionne writes
about Goldwater's defeat and the consolation prize of public support
of bigotry. Just as his campaign predicted, Goldwater swept the Deep
South. For the first time in its history, Georgia voted Republican, and
Alabama, Mississippi, and South Carolina did so for the first time since
Reconstruction; Louisiana voted for Eisenhower and stuck with the
Republican Party, though they did vote for the party of the avowed
racist, George Wallace, in 1968. And these states effectively had an all-
White electorate, given that Blacks were still denied the right to vote.
Still! Goldwater won 54 percent of Georgia, 57 percent of Louisiana, 59
percent of South Carolina, 70 percent of Alabama and a whopping 87
percent of Mississippi.

Further, Goldwater was a bit off his rocker. Yet he had to pretend
he wasn't during the campaigns lest he alienate voters. But his later
memoirs revealed a deep belief in the lunacy. Kurt Anderson writes,
"[By] the time he wrote his memoir *With No Apologies* in the 1970s, he
felt free to rave on about the globalist conspiracy's 'pursuit of a New
World Order' and impending 'period of slavery,' the Council on Foreign
Relations' secret agenda for 'one-world rule,' and the Trilateral Commission's plan for 'seizing control of the political government of the
United States.'"[2]

Let it all hang out, Barry. We see you.

4

REAGANOMICS

"Voodoo economics."

—REPUBLICAN GEORGE BUSH (I)
DESCRIBING RONALD REAGAN'S ECONOMIC PROGRAM

WHAT?

THE ECONOMIC POLICIES OF Ronald Reagan were underpinned by his and his party's long bountiful romance with private enterprise. If one examines his approach to matters of regulation, taxes, and social welfare, one can clearly see the inner workings of the relationship. Before his highly consequential victories against labor groups (e.g., air traffic controllers), Ronald Reagan unleashed his *voodoo economics* plan in 1981. The basis of the plan, which came to be known as *Reaganomics*[1] consisted of 1) tax cuts, 2) tax cuts, 3) cutting social spending, 4) deregulation, 5) tax cuts, 6) cutting social spending, 7) more tax cuts and deregulation, and 8) ramping up military spending. Sounds familiar, doesn't it? That's because it's been the same exact platform for forty years now. We are still living with Reagan's legacy.

WHY?

REAGAN AND HIS CONSERVATIVE acolytes in the executive branch, Congress, and, most importantly, big business wanted to enrich themselves. "Show me the money!" They also wanted government "off our back!!" They also wanted to kick poor people off welfare, defund education, the arts—anything that smelled of public assistance. They also wanted to make citizens so sick of government as to reject it outright. Author Donald Cohen puts it, "Temporarily they create demand for increased regulatory oversight, but in the long run they can add to underlying discontent with government."[2] Devious.

REAGAN'S LURCH TOWARDS RADICAL conservatism first drew national attention with his thirty-minute speech on behalf of Barry Goldwater in 1964. He described "the welfare state as the path to totalitarianism."[3] Apocalyptic thinking, conspiracy theories, and bigotry haunted the movement from the start.

Reagan is worshipped as a God amongst congressional conservatives and the GOP. As I describe later, a former governor of Wisconsin was married on his birthday and celebrates with Reagan's favorite foods. Conservatives love to imagine Reagan as the knight in shining armor who rescued America from an economically disastrous Jimmy Carter administration. "It took Jimmy Carter to give us Ronald Reagan," exclaimed Ted Cruz, that lying sack of turnips. There's only one issue with this: Carter nearly outperformed or outperformed Reagan on almost every economic measure (GDP growth, unemployment rate, average job gains, new debt issued).[4] And if you consider the incessant, lofty rhetoric of Reagan and the GOP about their grand economic plans and "shared prosperity for all,"[5] Reaganomics was a disaster.

Yes, Reaganomics never worked as promised. It plainly benefited the top 1 percent and 10 percent, but that's really about it. There was little sustained economic improvement for anyone else. Lower- and middle-income wages and wealth barely budged from 1980 to 1990. And the poverty rate actually went up, too.[6]

Reagan had such a powerful effect on the trajectory of our politics. "The long cycle of growth in the role and activism of the national government in domestic affairs that began with F.D.R.'s New Deal ended with Reagan's New Federalism," Professor Richard P. Nathan has written. "The Reagan presidency has produced a fundamental redirection in the domestic policies of the US Government, both in the spending of the federal government and in the substance and purposes of its domestic programs."[7]

Reagonomics is expressly an attack on our democracy. Reagan not only waged war on the working and middle classes but he fundamentally shifted the accountability of government and our elected officials from citizens to corporations, thus beginning our long road to obscene wealth concentration not observed in our country since the Gilded Age.[8] As the late Supreme Court Justice Louis Brandeis wrote, "We can have a democratic society or we can have the concentration of great wealth in the hands of a few. We cannot have both." You'll notice a pattern in these graphs from the Economic Policy Institute, beginning in the 1980s. Around the time business lobbying began in earnest in Washington in the 1970s, hourly compensation and productivity started to diverge like a giant fork in a country road. Between 1948 and 1973, productivity (meaning how much we produce as a country) increased by 97 percent, and wages went up by nearly the same amount to 91 percent. Between 1973 and 2013, productivity increased by 74 percent. And wages? A pathetic 9.2 percent.

Workers produced much more,
but typical workers' pay lagged far behind

Disconnect between productivity and typical worker's compensation, 1948–2013

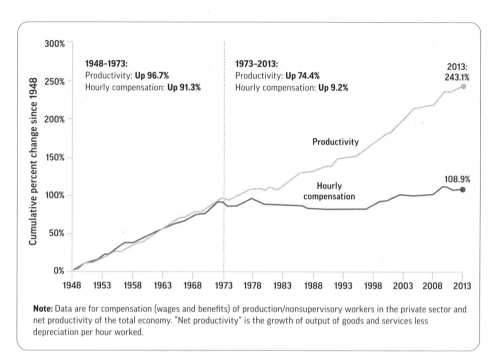

1948–1973:
Productivity: **Up 96.7%**
Hourly compensation: **Up 91.3%**

1973–2013:
Productivity: **Up 74.4%**
Hourly compensation: **Up 9.2%**

2013:
243.1%

Productivity

Hourly
compensation

108.9%

Cumulative percent change since 1948

Note: Data are for compensation (wages and benefits) of production/nonsupervisory workers in the private sector and net productivity of the total economy. "Net productivity" is the growth of output of goods and services less depreciation per hour worked.

Source: EPI and BLS

But not all wages are created equal. The top 1 percent of America saw their wages increase by 138 percent from 1980 through 2013, while the bottom 90 percent have increased their wages by only 15 percent. This is different from the last graph of hourly compensation, because wages include other benefits like stock-option grants and health care.

When it comes to the pace of annual pay increases, the top 1% grew 138% since 1979, while wages for the bottom 90% grew 15%

Cumulative change in real annual wages, by wage group 1979–2013

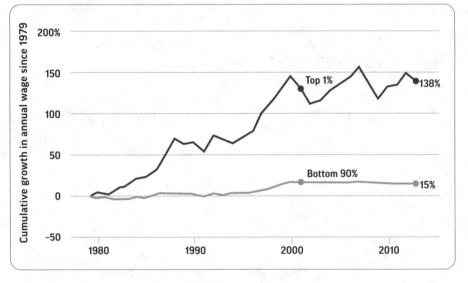

Source: EPI and Kopczuk, Saez and Song

GOVERNMENT FOR ME, NOT FOR THEE

And yet, for all the hubbub and pledges to "get government off our backs" and how "government is the problem," Reagan actually wanted *more* government, but only in spheres such as abortion, prayer in schools, birth control, and defense. He also wanted less information trickling out to the public over his failed policies and war crimes. He re-established what journalists and Washington called the *activist presidency* (Hedrick Smith, *New York Times*, Oct. 1984), which, by the way, is something conservatives chide liberals for all the time. He used the power of the executive branch to dismantle what was left of the Great Society programs. According to Lester M. Salamon and Alan J. Abramson at the Urban Institute, Reagan adopted "the approach of Wilson and Roosevelt in order to pursue the objectives of Coolidge and Harding."[9] Meaning, he used government power to enrich big business.

BIG SPENDER

Reagan spent more than any president before him besides Roosevelt, who rescued the economy from certain destruction. But he didn't spend on Americans, unless you count defense company executives. Between 1980 and 1984, Hedrick Smith in the *New York Times* writes, "Congressional estimates show military spending has risen to 26.8 percent of the budget this year from 22.6 percent in 1981, and spending on nonmilitary domestic programs has fallen to 59.5 percent of the budget from 67.5 percent. Interest on the Federal debt has risen to 13.7 percent of the budget this year from 9.9 percent in 1981."

REAGAN DID SOME OTHER funky stuff in order to make regulation slashing more palatable to the public. He created a Task Force on Regulatory Relief, managed by his new voodoo economics convert and VP, George H. W. Bush. Bush issued Order 12291, which discouraged new regulations and created the Office of Information and Regulatory Affairs (OIRA) within the Office of Management and Budget (OMB).[10] This office essentially gave political control of federal regulatory processes to the White House. Bush did this in order to "institutionalize cost-benefit analyses as the rubric to evaluate and reject proposed regulations," because he knew very well that lax regulatory enforcement led to more people being upset with government. For example, people blamed the government for the BP Gulf oil spills, although they were caused by private industry.[11]

REAGAN'S MISSION TO DEFUND PUBLIC HOUSING

Reagan slashed the budget of Housing and Urban Development by more than 60 percent (he didn't even recognize his HUD secretary at one point).[12] Reagan said, "People who are sleeping on the grates... the homeless... are homeless, you might say, by choice."[13] You might also say that by saying something like that, you come across as a heartless know-nothing who doesn't understand the plight of the average homeless person.

President Ford asked Congress to fund 506,000 new low-income housing units (including 400,000 rent vouchers for Section 8 housing). Under Reagan? The number dipped below 100,000 units, even while the population of poor people was growing. By a lot.

According to the *New York Times*, the budget of the Department of Housing and Urban Development fell by 57 percent between 1981 and 1987, and social spending, which had increased under each of the last five presidents, fell at an average annual rate of 1.5 percent during Reagan.

IN TOTAL, DISCRETIONARY SPENDING—WHICH is basically anything not related to Medicare or Social Security, and includes spending on education, the environment, or defense—dropped 14 percent in Reagan's first year. Great Society programs were cut. Programs like the Community Development Block Grant were slashed by 67 percent. There was a 33 percent cut in mass transit spending. Senator Pete Domenici called Reagan's budget "the most dramatic reduction in the ongoing programs in the history of the country."

Reagan tried his damnedest to eliminate the Department of Education, because, you know, "government is the problem." But get this, the guy Reagan put in charge of that task, Secretary Terrel Bell, over time became convinced of the department's necessity and refused to carry it out. "What he did was weave and bob," wrote John F. Jennings, the director of the Center for National Education Policy in Washington and a former longtime House Democratic aide. "He elongated the process until the momentum died."[14] According to Michael A. Resnick, the senior associate executive director of the National School Boards Association in Alexandria, Virginia, "He stood up with courage to very strong political pressures to dismantle the department."

Reagan was so infatuated with the idea of "liberty" and "small government" he compared the fight for it to what Moses did in Israel and the antifascists did in Germany. How absurd. "You and I know and do not believe that life is so dear and peace so sweet as to be purchased at the price of chains and slavery," he said. "[Should Moses] have told the children of Israel to live in slavery under the pharaohs?" he asked. "Should Christ have refused the cross? Should the patriots at Concord Bridge have thrown down their guns and refused to fire the shot heard 'round the world? The martyrs of history were not fools, and our honored dead who gave their lives to stop the advance of the Nazis didn't die in vain."[15]

Jesus Christ, Ron. Way to be overdramatic over providing health care or having a cohesive strategy for educating the youth. Much like every other industrialized nation in the world. GOP, amirite?

PROMISE OF A BALANCED BUDGET

Despite (empty) promises to balance the budget, Reagan ran the deficit up more than any other president in the last one hundred years, excluding Roosevelt, as a percentage of GDP while severely cutting taxes, particularly on the wealthy and corporations. A hundred billion dollars or more every year. The national debt went from $907 billion in 1980 to $2.8 trillion in 1989.[16] In his 1980 Republican convention speech, Reagan had pledged to "work to reduce the cost of government as a percentage of our gross national product." Reagan, building largely on the work of Howard Jarvis and Paul Gann in California, placed tax cuts at the center of GOP theology. Even worse, the reason for Reagan's boom wasn't what conservatives had been saying it was. His tax cuts did not increase personal savings—those actually fell—and didn't lead to an increase in investment in plant and equipment—those actually fell, too. What they did was provide a spending stimulus, coupled with military spending, and *that* is what boosted the economy. In other words, the antigovernment trickle downers were not only wrong but the very theory that they were so opposed to helped save the economy. Maybe he/ they knew that and just lied their way through it.

———

BETWEEN RABID ANTIGOVERNMENT SENTIMENT among government employees like the president, tax cuts, and wasted military spending, we began down a path of large structural deficits that, according to the author Donald Cohen, "...locked in an American austerity agenda: a vicious cycle of inadequate resources to meet public needs that then drove up discontent about government failure and increased calls for tax cuts." Basically, congressional conservatives charted the course to the destination of wicked inequality, crumbling infrastructure and public schools, and disastrous labor disenfranchisement. By the time Reagan was through, federal spending to states was cut by 60 percent. *Sixty!*[17]

At the end of the day, Reagan promised shared prosperity via low taxes and small government. His cronies got their IRS rebates, but he neither shrank the government nor spread the wealth. He locked us in to tremendous inequality that persists and widens each year.

As Henry Olsen, a conservative scholar, writes, "For nearly 30 years, the Republican Party has increasingly resembled a religion, with Ronald Reagan as its deity. Party leaders endlessly quote him, and every GOP presidential nominee until Donald Trump ran on a platform they thought was barely changed from Reagan's 1980 campaign. No wonder conservative talk radio icon Rush Limbaugh calls our 40th president 'Ronaldus Magnus': Ronald the Great."[18] Gross.

5

GINGRICH

"What if [Obama] is so outside our comprehension, that only if you understand Kenyan, anti-colonial behavior, can you begin to piece together [his actions]? That is the most accurate, predictive model for his behavior.[1]

The idea that a congressman would be tainted by accepting money from private industry or private sources is essentially a socialist argument.[2]

I don't object to polarization if it achieves an objective."[3]

**—FORMER REPUBLICAN SPEAKER OF THE HOUSE
NEWT GINGRICH IN THREE SEPARATE INTERVIEWS**

WHAT?

PROBABLY THE MOST CONSEQUENTIAL man in politics in the last thirty years, presidents included, is the former Republican Speaker of the House Newt Gingrich, whose anger and greed with ambitions and ego the universe cannot contain. His lust for power is unmatched by anyone—even Donald Trump. He singlehandedly managed to wreck Congress through years of assault on the governing body. I can't think of another person who's done more to harm Washington's reputation than Gingrich. He's basically the worst person in modern politics.

WHY?

WHY GINGRICH WAGED A war on Congress was simply to make it look like a dysfunctional place. That way, he could take it over with his radical conservative cronies and keep it forever dysfunctional (while making his donors rich). Remember, conservatives thrive off of Washington's chaos. Their goal is to make it so ungovernable that nothing gets done, except stuff that benefits them and their constituents. Actually, not even their constituents. Just their radical rich donors.

NEWT BURST ONTO THE scene as a newly elected member of Congress in 1978. That year, he gave an address to College Republicans (before he was elected to the House). Gingrich said, "I think one of the great problems we have in the Republican Party is that we don't encourage you to be nasty. We encourage you to be neat, obedient, and loyal and faithful and all those Boy Scout words." He continued, "Richard Nixon ... Gerald Ford ... They have done a terrible job, a pathetic job. In my lifetime, in my lifetime—I was born in 1943—we have not had a competent national Republican leader. Not ever."[4]

Fast forward to today, his phenomenal work of polarizing the two parties has reverberated through Washington and the entire country. Not since post-reconstruction have we seen that much malignancy and spitefulness in Congress, which he took on a path to new heights.

Party Polarization 1879–2013
Distance Between the Parties First Dimension

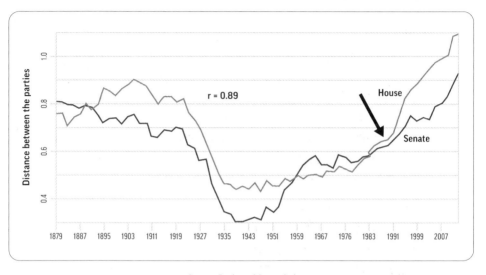

Source: Poole and Rosenthal

Gingrich's mission was clear: Make government less trustworthy than gas station sushi. He and his Republican colleagues won back Congress for the first time in forty years in 1994 (note the way in which he/they did it below). Incidentally, this coincided with the rise of Rush Limbaugh and conservative talk radio (and two years later, Fox News, whose seeds were already being planted). It's fair to argue that Rush very much enabled Newt to grab power, blaring his conspiracy theories and bigotry for every God-fearing Republican family to soak up like a sponge. After that, it was off to the races. Gingrich sought to rule as a king by fiat, completely shutting out the Democrats from legislating. I will repeat a powerful quote I've already used: "Gradually, it went from legislating, to the weaponization of legislating, to the permanent campaign, to the permanent war," the Brookings scholar Thomas Mann says. "It's like he took a wrecking ball to the most powerful and influential legislature in the world."

Let's have a look some of the things he's done and said:

- *Manufacturing outrage.* Gingrich would stand on the floor of the House with his Republican colleagues at night when everyone else went home, knowing C-SPAN cameras were still rolling, and put on fake debates with each other in order to manufacture outrage with TV viewers. He would accuse Democrats of all sorts of stuff like being communist, anti-Christian, corrupt and, ironically, McCarthyite (Joe McCarthy was a Republican Senator who trafficked in conspiracy theories and fearmongering).[5]

- *Office of Technology Assessment.* When he assumed the reins in 1995 as speaker of the House, one of the first orders of business was to do away with the Office of Technology Assessment, which had been created in a 1972 act of bipartisanship and was, as the journalist Jathan Sadowski writes, " . . . responsible for providing Congress with authoritative and unbiased reports on a wide range of present and emerging issues in science and technology."[6] This was during a time of rapid technological advancement (we had just sent a couple of dudes to space). But because it hurt President Reagan's feelings by reporting that one of his outer space programs was probably a big waste of money, OTA fell out of favor with the GOP, and Gingrich, like the extreme partisan he is, eliminated it. If you ever wonder why Congress appears to be technologically or scientifically illiterate, at least partially blame Gingrich for getting rid of the service in charge of educating them. In a 2005 article titled "Requiem for an Office" in the *Bulletin of the Atomic Scientists*, the author Chris Mooney describes how defunding the OTA was as much a political performance as it was a way of making room for new, ideology-friendly, science advisory roles. "In

OTA's absence," he writes, "the new Republican majority could freely call upon its own favorable scientific 'experts' and rely upon more questionable and self-interested analyses prepared by lobbyists, think tanks, and interest groups. A 2001 comment by Gingrich, explaining the reason OTA was killed, pretty much said it all: 'We constantly found scientists who thought what they were saying was not correct.'"[7] The former congressional staffer Lorelei Kelly referred to this as a "self-lobotomy." Democrats, of course, want to revive it.

- *"Tuesday to Thursday Club."* Gingrich shortened the workweek for Congress.[8] You heard that right. The leader of the party that champions fiscal discipline and complains about government waste limited the amount of time an employee of Washington could work in . . . Washington. This maximized the amount of time members of Congress could fundraise back home in their districts and—get this—limited the amount of time Republicans could spend with Democrats in making connections and friendships across the aisle. What kind of maniacal CEO tells a group of employees to spend as little time as possible with another group of employees to prevent fostering better communication and relationships? As a result, members stopped fraternizing with one another. The journalist and author Juliet Eilperin writes, "Members not only stopped sharing free time together over the past decade [of Republican control], they found themselves debating each other less often on the House floor . . . By limiting lawmakers to two-minute speeches, leaders stifled opportunities for real debate and encouraged pithy, partisan attacks."[9] Or as one member expressed to Eilperin, "What can you do in two minutes? Insult the other guy."

- *Consolidation.* People like Gingrich use their power to consolidate and make others in their party pay fealty, like to a king. A reminder: He is a civil servant! He made it so only the Speaker could make key appointments on committees, which allowed him to tightly control the agenda and relegate others who disagreed to the bench. "Gingrich made it clear from the outset that committee chairs answered to the leadership and, by extension, to the entire Republican Conference," Eilperin writes.

- *Partisan warfare.* His general emphasis on partisan warfare and the encouragement of an *us vs. them* mentality laid waste to the atmosphere of compromise and bipartisanship that helped get stuff done in Washington for so long. "All together, Gingrich's emphasis on partisan warfare *über alles* sped the demise of the comity that is essential to the functioning of Congress," the author Alex Seitz Wald writes.[10] Gingrich himself bragged, "The No. 1 fact about the news media is they love fights . . . When you give them confrontations, you get attention; when you get attention, you can educate. Noise became a proxy for status." McKay Coppins has a fantastic piece in the *Atlantic* on Gingrich's quest to destroy the institution of Congress. See endnote number 8.

- *Shutdowns.* Gingrich shut down the government, unlike previous speakers. And even though voters initially saw through his destructive enterprising, he charted a new course and made the threat of shutdowns a regular occurrence, particularly with a Democratic president. He actually furloughed hundreds of thousands of workers for weeks on end at Christmastime![11] He did this so the GOP could use their holiday wages as a bargaining chip in talks with the White House. That was a bust—voters blamed the GOP—but, again, it was almost guaranteed to keep occurring year after year.

- *More partisan warfare.* He created a document that he circulated to members of his party telling them what kind of language to use when denigrating Democrats. Smart, if you're a bit of a sociopath who cares only about power and not about the institution you work for, which millions of people depend on for assistance. From his GOPAC memo: "Often we search hard for words to define our opponents. Sometimes we are hesitant to use contrast. Remember that creating a difference helps you. These are powerful words that can create a clear and easily understood contrast. Apply these to the opponent, their record, proposals and their party. Decay, failure (fail) collapse(ing) deeper, crisis, urgent(cy), destructive, destroy, sick, pathetic, lie, liberal, they/them, unionized bureaucracy, *compassion* is not enough, betray, consequences, limit(s), shallow, traitors, sensationalists, endanger, coercion, hypocrisy, radical, threaten, devour, waste, corruption, incompetent, permissive attitude, destructive, impose, self-serving, greed, ideological, insecure, anti-(issue): flag, family, child, jobs; pessimistic, excuses, intolerant, stagnation, welfare, corrupt, selfish, insensitive, status quo, mandate(s), taxes, spend(ing), shame, disgrace, punish (poor...) bizarre, cynicism, cheat, steal, abuse of power, machine, bosses, obsolete, criminal rights, red tape, patronage."[12] Gingrich was the original divider and polarizer. He institutionalized the hate.

In the end, Gingrich was pushed out by his own party for being... too liberal? Yes, the party he created became even more radical than he was. Towards the end of the decade, he decided to work with President Clinton (oh, the horror!) on a few issues, most prominently to avoid shutdowns. His Republican radicals were not having any it. "Quite a few members are obviously concerned over the direction that the leadership has taken," the former-congressman-turned-MSNBC-TV host Joe Scarborough said. "We have a concern that our leadership remains shell-shocked from the government shutdown a year and a half ago. Most of us are ready for them to start leading again rather than sitting back and reading from Clinton's song sheet."[13]

No matter. By the end of Gingrich's reign, he had completely changed Washington and the Republican Party. He seeded the malice, the dysfunction, the extreme partisanship—and he left behind manuals on how to do it. We are dealing with the consequences of his actions today. Even Barry Goldwater called himself a liberal once he stood upon the wreckage of the late '90s.[14]

Final point. Gingrich's signature agenda, "Contract with America," is important because it was the first step in something Gingrich did that was very important: He nationalized all politics. Former Speaker Tip O'Neill's aphorism that all politics are local stopped being true with Gingrich. Since his ascent, every race in the country is Democrat vs. Republican rather than about the district itself.

6

TEA PARTY

"I'll tell you what, if you read our Founding Fathers, people like Benjamin Franklin and Jefferson, what we're doing in this country now, is making them roll over in their graves."

—CNBC ANCHOR, AND THE WHINING FACE OF THE TEA PARTY, RICK SANTELLI

WHAT?

AS THE SOCIOLOGIST AND author Isaac William Martin writes, "Social movements that explicitly defend the interests of the rich and the almost-rich have been a recurring feature of American politics." Conservative leaders welcomed their capital, Martin continues, to take "advantage of the structure of political opportunities established by the American constitutional order."[1] Enter the Tea Party.

The Tea Party was a fiscally conservative *AstroTurf* (masking the source of a campaign) movement *within* the Republican Party. That is, it was essentially fake, supported by radical right-wing billionaires. Let me rephrase. This was a group of people who thought the Republican

Party was not fiscally conservative *enough* and believed there needed to be an even more extreme ideological faction to drill the message of "Down with socialism!" into the American public. And boy, did they ever. The extremes the Tea Party went to while assailing the new Obama administration for trying to, you know, save the economy was nothing short of psychopathy. By the way, a very critical point to make here is this: Where were these Tea Party fanatics when Bush and Trump exploded the deficit? Answer: They weren't anywhere to be found. Because deficits matter only when a Democrat is president. Terrible way to run a company, let alone a country.

WHY?

THE TEA PARTY WAS a front created by radical rich billionaires to thwart Obama's agenda, which was actually quite moderate. The Koch brothers along with their circle of radical rich Mr. Burns (the greedy boss character from the Simpson's) types, were a major force behind the party's surge. They encircled and bought outright a small group of conservative politicians at first, then erected roadblocks to every—literally every—single move Obama made.[2]

THE UNITED STATES WAS coming off of a world-class economic disaster in 2008—thanks to incessantly low interest rates and financial chicanery of epic proportions, primarily the fault of our government and the big banks. Sure, consumers were to blame for taking out mortgages they couldn't afford, but, frankly, they were being duped with sophisticated financial schemes. The big banks were bilking people out of gobs of money, and the government was asleep at the wheel. Without rehashing details of the calamity and its causes, we should examine what happened next, because it's instructive for our education on the evolution of conservatism.

The Tea Party movement was birthed on the day Santelli made his impassioned call on the floor of the Chicago Board of Trade to conservatives and libertarians alike. That was February 19th, 2009. "Are you listening, President Obama?" he screamed at the camera.[3] Almost immediately, like it was coordinated, it launched a series of nationwide protests against Obama's agenda, which was barely even public at the time.

Those protests were led mostly by Glenn Beck. There's information on more of his work in the endnotes.[4] You have to see it to believe it.

"In an effort to simplify the complex topic of government spending for his audience," the journalist Tim Kenneally wrote, "Beck does the only rational thing—he soaks a guest in gasoline. Well, OK, it probably wasn't real gas. But the insanity was all too authentic."

The Tea Party was funded by right-wing billionaires. They created and supported highly visible campaigns and protests in parts of the country that were represented by vulnerable Democrats. The idea was that they were going to pick them off in the 2010 midterms, so that Republicans would win the House back and blockade Obama's agenda. It was wild. And it worked.

As the author Jeff Nesbit put it, "Charles and David Koch—who, if their individual fortunes were combined in one place, would quite possibly represent the wealthiest person on Earth—have almost certainly spent or raised more than a billion dollars to successfully bend one of the two national parties in America to their will. The long rise of the Tea Party movement was orchestrated, well-funded, and deliberate. Its aim was to break Washington. And it has nearly succeeded."[5]

The Tea Party has also succeeded in assuming full control of the Republican Party itself. They overtook the establishment.

E. J. Dionne writes, "In fact, the Tea Party's greatest victory was not electoral. It was to change the nature of the party and the definition of conservatism. Despite Boehner's grumbling at the end of 2013, the distinction between the Establishment and the Tea Party was now blurred."[6] The conservative writers Rich Lowry and Ramesh Ponnuru called the new takeover "Establishment Tea." The Right had caved, or joined forces, or however you would like to characterize it, with the new radicals. There was no longer any semblance of moderation or sensibility. As the political scientist Jacob Hacker wrote after the 2014 elections, "Based on voting records, the current Republican majority in the Senate is far more conservative than the last Republican majority in the 2000s."[7]

By the time Republicans and the new crop of Tea Party wing nuts took control of the House in 2010, it was ripe for chaos. That February, the House Republicans passed a budget bill that cut spending on Head Start, Pell grants for college access, teen pregnancy prevention, clean water programs, K–12 education, and a host of other programs. And this was in the middle of the second-worst financial crisis in the history of this country. They had enough money for bank bailouts and corporate welfare, but not enough for the average Joe and Jane. Incredible. The story of the last forty years.

REPUBLICANS' UNHEALTHY OBSESSION WITH PRIVATE ENTERPRISE

7

PRIVATE INDUSTRY

The "Solution to All Our Problems"

"One of the things the government can't do is run anything.
The only things our government runs are the post office
and the railroads, and both of them are bankrupt."

—LEE IACOCCA, AUTOMOBILE EXECUTIVE

"Practically no government program enacted since the
1950s in the Western world—or in the communist countries—
has been successful."

—PETER DRUCKER, FAMED MANAGEMENT CONSULTANT (1989)

WHAT?

THE PRIVATE SECTOR HAS been long touted—mostly by congressional conservatives, Republicans, and the private industry itself—as the solution to all our problems. They argue that the private sector does everything better than the public sector—by a million miles—and that, if we are *smart*, we should seek to diminish the scope of the public sector because it is bloated, inefficient, wasteful, and blah blah blah. If you haven't heard these arguments before, I suggest you simply open up any conservative publication and turn to an article on the economy. To use the parlance of our times, congressional conservatives are rabid private sector influencers. For those who need a one-sentence primer, what I mean by *private sector* is anything owned by private individuals, not by the government. Think Coca-Cola and Facebook (privately owned) vs. University of Illinois and JFK Airport (publicly owned).

WHY?

IT IS QUITE SIMPLE why congressional conservatives and the private sector demonize the government and try to weaken it: money and power (at the expense of the majority). Rules and regulations surrounding pollution, labor, executive pay, financial risk-taking, and monopolies are impediments to the desires of private industry, which generally are cloaked as the desires of a few executives and large shareholders. The fewer rules, the more power and money they accumulate. And the relationship between the private sector and politicians, particularly on the Right, is strong and deep. Corporations fund campaigns and support legislation, and when the politicians leave office, they hire them as lobbyists so they can glad-hand former colleagues in the name of private enterprise. Sounds great to me! Let me be clear, Democrats also engage in this behavior to a large extent, but there is a clear distinction, especially in today's climate. Most of the legislation on climate change, labor laws, paid family leave, education, and health care pricing was intensely fought against by private industry and the vast majority of Republicans.

I do not need to sing the praises of private enterprise and how many of its innovations have revolutionized society. You can download an app that will schedule appointments for your dog to be groomed next Tuesday without having to leave your house. If there is one advantage that entrepreneurship has given us, it is more convenience. This is not the government's bailiwick. Public enterprise is better suited to tackling the bigger, more nebulous/aspirational stuff like pollution, health care, education, and making sure the private market gives us safe products that won't harm us. Private industry does not do a universally good job at any of those, particularly the first (pollution) and the last (safety). You might say to yourself, "Well, if someone drinks a Coke and dies, we will hold Coca-Cola accountable by not buying their products, pushing the CEO to step down." Sure. In this very rare, clear-cut example, accountability works. But what about the slow-moving shifts in food safety that are making Americans extraordinarily unhealthy? Or a health care system whose prices creep up and up from years of insurance company malfeasance?

Now, you may say, "Bill, how can you judge the problems of a country and say one way or another that it's the fault of private enterprise or public?" My answer: "You know, I thought you might ask that question, so I created a comparison with other Western countries." See the chapter at the end of this section on "Where the GOP Has Gotten Us (A Comparison to Western Countries)."

LET'S RETURN FOR A moment to the distrust voters have in government and how congressional conservatives enjoy this as a cover for an unpopular agenda. The professor and author Jacob Hacker has dismantled the lame excuses they make for not wanting to make reform. He's worth quoting at length on the topic:[1]

> Consider the biggest threat facing our planet: global warming. Sowing doubt about climate change has proved a huge and hugely successful enterprise. Indeed, the fossil fuel industry deserves some special prize for chutzpah: they propagandize that the bad guys aren't carbon-emitting corporations trying to preserve trillions in dirty assets, but *instead* the climate scientists supposedly ginning up a false crisis to get research grants. The modern GOP has joined the industry in its endorsement of whatever egregious defense seems most effective at the moment. Although the first lines of resistance ("global warming isn't happening"; "it is, but for natural reasons") have more or less crumbled, and "I'm not a scientist" doesn't seem likely to work for long either, there are plenty of additional trenches to retreat to: "Reform won't work." "It will be too expensive." "It is pointless absent efforts by other countries." "We want reform, just not this one, or the next one." In the meantime, the fossil fuel industry continues to book huge profits and atmospheric carbon dioxide levels continue to rise.

Here are a few more loving soundbites from elected officials and private industry:

"When we have a lot of people in Eastern Europe trying to throw off the yoke of central government, now might be the time to ask Americans, 'How much government do you want?'"

—CLAYTON YEUTTER, GEORGE H. W. BUSH'S AGRICULTURE SECRETARY SPEAKING AGAINST REQUIRED DISCLOSURE OF FAT, CHOLESTEROL, AND SALT CONTENT ON PACKAGED FOOD (1990)

"I'm one of America's 45 million smokers.
I'm not a moaner or a whiner. But I'm getting fed up.
I'd like to get the government off my back."

—RJ REYNOLDS NEWSPAPER AD, SHOWING A MAN
STANDING IN FRONT OF A PICKUP TRUCK (1994)

"[The coalition is a] grassroots movement responding
to the belief of many Americans that our government,
at all levels, is growing out of control."

—ARNOLD HAMM OF THE TOBACCO GROWERS INFORMATION
COMMITTEE, PRESS RELEASE (NOTE: GROVER NORQUIST IS
MEDIA CONTACT FOR PRESS RELEASE) (1994)

The following chapters in this section will demonstrate how these toxic attitudes towards government and the worship of private industry have proved to be a crummy outcome for most Americans. I often allude to congressional conservative and private industry's obsession with *deregulation,* to which the average person reacts, "That sounds good; I don't like regulations." But deregulation is a way of eliminating responsibility and accountability for companies, while giving them license to exploit citizens and our planet, as you will read.

8

LIMITS OF PRIVATIZATION

"Outside of its legitimate function government does nothing
as well or economically as the private sector."

—RONALD REAGAN (1964)

"Their privatization sprees have injected needed cash into
government coffers and freed the governments to focus on
their core missions while injecting life into both markets."

—*WALL STREET JOURNAL* (2013)

WHAT?

PRIVATIZATION. IT'S WHEN AN entity that is owned or operated by the government—public schools, airports, highways, etc.—is sold or turned over to a company or organization with shareholders and investors. The process effectively removes public control (meaning we can't vote for outcomes any longer) and turns it over to the *free market* (though no market is truly free, despite what those nagging utopian-minded libertarians think). And while lots of industries run well as a private enterprise—most, in fact—there are vital businesses and industries where public ownership performs better. Well, at least for a majority of a country it does. But that's of no concern to the radical rich or congressional conservatives. They would rather turn over nearly all government function to the private market and be accountable only to those who benefit when stocks go up and down (mostly rich people).

WHY?

THE PUSH FOR PRIVATIZATION is relentless. Several articles appear each day in the press about a new effort to privatize a new service or industry—ambulance services, schools, roads, tunnels, airports, health care, etc. I'm not referring to TVs, computers, or consumer goods— the private market's natural wheelhouse—but vital societal assets that we depend on for our very survival. In other words, stuff that maybe shouldn't be governed primarily with the goal of turning profit. Maybe? More efficient? Sure. But for the sake of enhancing someone else's wealth? The United States is one of the most privatized countries in the world, and probably the most in the developed world. We never really had a strong public ownership of enterprise because, methinks, it's always been "Up with capitalism! Down with communism!" In fact, there's been such an aggressive blowback and posturing from big business that any debate on a proposal to nationalize (the opposite of privatize) is immediately shot down. Conversely, in Europe, Asia, Latin America, and even Canada you'll find state-owned enterprises in a wide variety of industries, including those shown below.

As far as I can tell, we do not observe a terribly strong push to privatize in those countries. Why? Well, because privatization takes away accountability. No longer can voters enact change at the ballot box for corporate governance and executive compensation, but rather unelected wealthy shareholders control the assets (and are less accountable, as the majority of stock is concentrated among the wealthiest 10 percent).[1] Frankly, who would you rather be in control of your health care? Or education? Or aerospace and defense? TVs and electronics, OK. Food and beverage, OK. I get it. But the big important stuff?

─────────

IF WE CONSIDER THE total value of state-owned enterprises (SOE) by country divided by the GDP of that country, according to the Organisation for Economic Co-operation and Development (OECD) in 2012, the United States had an SOE valuation of $60 billion, while our GDP totaled $16.2 trillion. Norway's SOE was valued at $288 billion with a GDP of $500 billion. Japan's valuation was $476 billion with a GDP of $5.9 trillion. The bottom line: when it comes to our share of SOE, it is the lowest and least consequential. In other words, one could argue we are the least socialist country in the world. And it's not really close.[2]

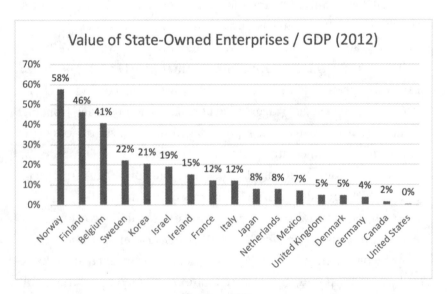

Source: OECD

Needless to say, the United States is way ahead of (or behind) its peers with respect to privatization. The privatization effort in the United States was consistently strong following WWII. Nevertheless, beginning in the 1980s, newly unrestrained congressional conservatives and radical rich—fresh off their victory killing labor reform in 1978—needed some new public enterprise target to buy out and make unaccountable to voters. You see, the picture conservatives and libertarians want to produce in your head of government is a bloated, parasitic public sector that crowds out private investment, blocking the bustle of a more harmonious shareholder-based private economy. So, they generated ideas of privatizing unnatural parts of society like infrastructure, schools, national parks, public transport, prisons, etc. Thus, a spree of new state-sanctioned privatization began, effectively legislating that those industries may be better off in the hands of a few wealthy owners rather than the American public.

PRIVATE REALLY DOES NO BETTER THAN PUBLIC

For all the commentary about how much better privatization is than public enterprise, how do we know? Where's the evidence they are doing any better? Well, there is none. In fact, there's evidence to suggest public runs better than private! I know what you're saying, "Big government bureaucracy, like the DMV, runs like Barnum & Bailey Circus." But actually, lots of research says otherwise. See a comprehensive list in the endnotes.[3,4,5,6,7]

To be clear, I am in no way saying we need to become a publicly planned economy like China. But what I *am* saying is that we need to recognize congressional conservative propaganda for what it is: an attempt by the wealthy to gaslight and shift control of resources from the people to a few wealthy citizens who are unaccountable to the American public. And the only government that will remain, in their vision, is that which protects their property rights—and the

Department of Defense. We have to recognize that there are some industries that do better as private than public and vice versa. Republicans shut down debate before it can even get off the ground, not only cutting off what could be the best solution but sabotaging the process.

The Princeton professor Paul Starr wrote about this in 1987, and it is still relevant today. The conservative goal is total privatization, and they possess lots of resources and organizational muscle to fulfill it. But since they can't enact their widely unpopular total privatization (because government programs like Medicare and Social Security are incredibly popular), they chip away at it with *partial privatizations—* you know, like baby steps. "Baby steps out of office. Baby steps down the hallway. Baby steps on to the elevator."—Bob Wiley, Bill Murray's character in *What About Bob?*

Advocates see *vouchers* and *contracting out* not as the end of privatization but as the means to the end. They seek, Starr writes, to "…gain plausibility for the more radical goal of government disengagement."[8] Milton Friedman, the closest thing to an economic God for congressional Republicans and corporate America, has said explicitly that they would very much like to end all public support of primary and secondary education, and these vouchers are a first step. (This is the same Milton Friedman who, in 1955, proposed this voucher system after the landmark *Brown v. Board of Education* case, which mandated desegregation.)[9] Stu Butler, who has an impressive list of conservative think tanks on his resumé, has argued that the real objective of these partial-privatization programs is to break up any "public spending coalition" and, according to Starr, "bring about a permanent reduction in the base of political support for government growth." In other words, shrink the heck out of it, despite its enormous support from the population at large.

Congressional conservatives have perpetuated a harmful vision of a zero-sum game between the government and private enterprise. After all, the government has made so many discoveries the private market has effectively stolen (or paid nothing for) and commercialized for trillions of dollars, like components of the iPhone, various and sundry pharmaceuticals, and the internet! Anyway, Starr makes his case very simply. If the government sector truly slowed down the private sector and the economy, then, as a result, countries with large public sectors would be struggling and bumbling along while the United States would be blasting off like a rocket ship. Sadly (for Friedmanites), this is not the case.

Anyone who watches Fox News or reads the *Wall Street Journal* on any regular basis has likely been trained to think of government spending as a waste. But the truth is, most public spending is, by design, an investment in human and intangible capital, as well as the physical infrastructure component that we touch and smell. According to Starr, the way the federal budget of the US is structured, it doesn't distinguish capital expenditures and the national accounts, which classify all government expenditures as consumption and blurs these new contributions to the country's capital stock. In other words, we can't tell the positive effects besides consumption Uncle Sam has on GDP and wage growth, for example. President Reagan understood this very well. He spent like a prince while decrying government and touting his economic record. And when it comes to public programs like job retraining, the cost appears but not the corresponding benefit to society, unless you're somehow keeping score at home.

As Starr and Yale professor Jacob Hacker note, markets usually contain bias and artificial advantages from those who create them. Markets are not creations of some natural order. They are legally and politically structured by politicians, and they favor specific property rights, who has standing in court, the rights and responsibilities of corporations and unions, etc. Hacker mocks the nonsensical libertarian utopia of naked capitalism. "The libertarian vision of a night-watchman state gently policing an unfettered free market," he points out, "is a philosophical conceit, not a description of reality."

In fact, the combination of government and markets has been a staple throughout our history. The American frontier was settled because Uncle Sam awarded land to the homesteaders and murdered and drove out the Native Americans. The government created monopolies around railroads and the industrial sector and connected the lands with a postal service the likes of which the world had never seen. Later on, in the early twentieth century, government overpowered unions that posed a threat to big business, created a reliable money supply, engaged in protectionism (to favor new manufacturers), and on and on. Then, when the Gilded Age collapsed under the weight of Jay Gatsby's giant marble pool statue, the government remade American capitalism for the benefit of everyone, not just the wealthy. The New Deal was a much-needed boon to the poor and middle class. Uncle Sam, via the tax code and public programs, created the conditions for a shared prosperity not seen in the country's history—much to the chagrin of congressional conservatives and the radical rich. Hacker continues, "But the activist state that emerged did not just involve a new layer of redistribution. It fundamentally recast the national economy through the construction of a new industrial relations system, detailed and extensive regulation of corporations and financial markets, and a vast network of subsidies to companies producing everything from oil to soybeans. It also made huge direct investments in education and research—the GI Bill, the National Science Foundation, the National Institutes of Health—promoting the development of technological innovations and a skilled workforce that continue to drive American economic productivity." The expansion and proactive role of government during the better part of the twentieth century was an enormous benefit to society.

GOVERNMENT CONTRACTING

Let me say a few words on government contracting, which allows the private market to bid on contracts for the government, and is a crowd favorite amongst congressional Republicans, particularly in the defense sector. When we contract out services or provide vouchers to private enterprise, this doesn't obviate (eliminate) the need to collect taxes. What this actually does is reduce the *accountability* of public officials for the results by creating additional layers of potential blame. As Starr notes, "Any subsidy or tax incentive is an expenditure and if we remove the locus of control from the public sphere, it removes a layer of accountability. By resorting to private contractors, we do not reduce the size of budgets. Defense, construction, and health care budgets do not get smaller but get bigger. Where's the feedback or accountability efforts?" I am no expert on contracting, but if cost and accountability are unfavorable, logic would dictate that we find a better strategy, perhaps bringing resources in-house.

CREAMING OF CLIENTELE

Private enterprise also benefits from dealing with the most capitalized client base. You know, rich people. Obviously, this creates a feedback loop for creating better products and services. The wealthy have the resources to demand more sophisticated products and services, so companies will spend a great deal in developing, for example, homes that look like castles, services like Uber Eats that are really efficient and easy to use, private jets with steam rooms and saunas, or commercial trips to the moon. Cool, right? When we say, "American ingenuity," not an insignificant portion of the time don't we really mean what next great invention can we lavish on those who can afford it? As Starr puts it, private companies benefit from the "creaming" of clientele, meaning they deal more regularly with better-educated, wealthier, less time-intensive clients. Quality of services could be better, but not necessarily. Lowering the cost to produce, which private companies primarily seek to do, also could result in deteriorating quality. Lower costs and efficiency stem from lower wages and part-time workers.

The poor usually suffer in privatization. What for-profit enterprise would want to compete for poor people's business? Privatization signals diminished access, mostly at their expense.

NEGATIVE EXTERNALITIES (THE SIDE EFFECTS OF PRODUCTION)

Think pollution. Free markets don't really care about negative externalities like pollution. What is the incentive to guarantee clean air or water when ABC private company can churn out one thousand more products a day at a lower cost and higher rate of CO_2 emissions? Then pick up and move if the area in which they produce gets too run down, dirty, or unlivable? There is no incentive unless the government steps in to create one, like a tax on turning the lake brown. Similarly, private companies might partner with colleges on engineering programs, but they won't invest adequately in education or research and development, because they invest in things that will eventually turn a profit. Some of this profit will align well with our interests, but a lot of it will not. Private companies will not guarantee high-quality infrastructure or affordable health care. Retirement programs? Not really. And they certainly don't seem to care what kind of planet we will leave our grandkids. Years and years of fossil fuel companies running amok will tell you that.

GOVERNMENT IS NOT THE ANSWER, BUT NEITHER IS PRIVATE ENTERPRISE

I am no Marxist. I am not advocating for actual socialism, but I (we) have to defend the role—the vital role—of government against conservative attacks. To have a healthy, well-functioning society, we need to strike a balance between the government and private enterprise. As it stands currently, and for the last forty-plus years, private enterprise and congressional conservatives seek to eradicate substantial parts of the government. They have manipulated the debate to equate buzz-words like "freedom from tyranny" as reason to privatize the town hospital and created entire constituencies around these harmful ideas, which ultimately benefit the small, wealthy fraction of society.

Government sweats the big stuff. Private enterprise does not. Their structural differences make it so. Donald Cohen writes, "The hard challenges that decentralized private action can't solve, the essential investments that market actors won't make, the vexing choices that individual minds don't handle well. It must be judged with an understanding of that role and with an appreciation of why it is so difficult and so vital to carry out."[10] We have to ask ourselves, under what conditions will managers be best suited to act in the best interest of the public? The debate around privatization requires us to view it within a larger context: Who do we want to be accountable? *Harvard Business Review* writes, "Privatization involves the displacement of one set of managers entrusted by the shareholders—the citizens—with another set of managers who may answer to a very different set of shareholders."[11]

9

WHAT HAPPENS WHEN GOVERNMENT HATES GOVERNMENT

"These labs are incredible national resources, and they are directly responsible for keeping us safe . . . It's because of them that we can say with absolute certainty that Iran cannot surprise us with a nuclear weapon."

—ASSOCIATE DEPUTY SECRETARY OF THE US DEPARTMENT OF ENERGY UNDER OBAMA, JOHN MACWILL IAMS

"We had tried desperately to prepare them. But that required them to show up. And bring qualified people. But they didn't. They didn't ask for even an introductory briefing."

—TARAK SHAH, CHIEF OF STAFF FOR THE DOE'S $6 BILLION BASIC-SCIENCE PROGRAM, SAID OF THE INCOMING TRUMP TRANSITION TEAM.

WHAT AND WHY?

CONGRESSIONAL CONSERVATIVE VERBAL BASHING of government has consequences. Putting unqualified people in charge of massive critical agencies has consequences. Deliberately installing political operatives in important data-driven institutions has consequences. The people Republican administrations put in charge of our nation's vital resources and institutions deliberately make us weaker from a democratic perspective and from a national security perspective.

OBSERVING THE RANK incompetence of the Trump transition team in late 2016, I began to look into the functions of each agency and how they make our country safer. I, frankly, had no idea how complex the job of each of the departments are and what it manages. Energy, Agriculture, Commerce, Education, and more—each has incredibly important missions. But you'll see here, the Trump administration had next to zero care for them and their awesome responsibilities.

Michael Lewis, in *The Fifth Risk*, tells a great story—as he usually does—about the Trump Administration's sheer lack of regard and understanding for the government's role in protecting and caring for its citizens. I refer to his sourced material often in this section.

Lewis doesn't cover all the agencies, only the Department of Energy, Department of Commerce, and Department of Agriculture. But the picture he paints from in-depth interviews is bleak. Very bleak.

DEPARTMENT OF ENERGY

The DOE is in charge of 1) managing our nuclear weapons stockpile; 2) securing our nation's energy infrastructure from cyberattacks; and 3) climate-change research. I mean, holy crap, could we have tasked a department with more critical responsibilities! Perhaps Trump gave them an errand to run on one his golf courses—the imprimatur of importance.

Rewind to the transition in late 2016. According to the DOE's chief of staff under Obama, when Trump's transition team of Koch brothers' energy lobbyists (literally) came around to get acquainted and up to speed with what the DOE does, they didn't seem all that interested. "They mainly ran around the building insulting people," says a former Obama official. "There was a mentality that everything that government does is stupid and bad and the people in it are stupid and bad," says another. "It's a thirty-billion-dollar-a-year organization with about a hundred ten thousand employees," said former Chief of Staff Kevin Knobloch. "Industrial sites across the country. Very serious stuff. If you're going to run it, why wouldn't you want to know something about it?" How comforting.

Lewis goes on to describe the funding and mission of the DOE. You'll notice a theme. Apparently, $2 billion of the $30 billion budget are earmarked for tracking down "weapons-grade plutonium and uranium at loose in the world so that it doesn't fall into the hands of terrorists." My goodness! In the years between 2010 and 2018, the DOE's National Nuclear Security Administration recovered enough material "to make 160 nuclear bombs," says Lewis. When the world needs more atomic energy inspectors, you know, the guys who make sure countries around the world aren't producing weapons-grade uranium, the department trains them. What else do they do? They supply radiation- and bomb-detection equipment and conduct an ungodly number of experiments on nuclear material to understand what happens when plutonium fissions, among other mind-bendingly sensitive and potential world-destroying missions.

Lewis writes, "The Trump people didn't seem to grasp how much more than just energy the Department of Energy was about. They weren't totally oblivious to the nuclear arsenal, but even the nuclear arsenal didn't provoke in them much curiosity. They were just looking for dirt, basically,' said one of the people who briefed the Beachhead Team on national security issues. 'What is the Obama administration not letting you do to keep the country safe?'"

Even though Obama's transition team was pleading with them to understand how crazy the world is and how the DOE does so much to protect it, the Trump team was like, "Don't care. Where are the moles?" Eerily similar to Stalin's Russia. And who was running the show at the DOE? None other than the former Texas governor Rick Perry. Who Trump once said "should be forced to take an IQ test" and that "he put glasses on so people think he's smart." Sweet, dude.

Now that Trump is out of office, we can breathe a big collective sigh of relief. His team was uniquely unfit and ignorant to manage agencies in charge of such critical concerns. But I would like to continue highlighting their sheer carelessness and stupidity, because it is likely another version of Trump et al. will come along in the GOP and for posterity. *Uniquely* unfit. With regards to research on nuclear and renewable energy, of course it was too long-term for Team Trump to care about, because it doesn't have the "How can we profit from this now?" motivation. Fracking was a product of the Energy Department. But that kind of research, even though it could lead to huge changes in energy production, doesn't pay off right away. Not even for decades. Or how about solar technology? Thanks to Obama, the DOE got the cost of solar way down, from twenty-seven cents per kilowatt-hour in 2009 to six cents today. As Franklin Orr, a Stanford professor of engineering who worked at the DOE under Obama says, "The private sector only steps in once DOE shows it can work."

What did Trump do when he saw this kind of long-range, moonshot type of research? He sought to eliminate its funding. The entire lot of it! The Trump budget totally eliminated the $70 billion wildly successful ARPA-E program, the off-shoot of DARPA, which created the internet! It also slashed funding to national labs, eliminated all research on climate change, and slashed funding for work to ensure our electrical grid did not fall prey to a foreign attack or natural disaster. With Trump, we were just asking for it! "All the risks are science-based," says John McWilliams, a risk officer at the DOE. "You can't gut the science. If you do, you are hurting the country. If you gut the core competency of the DOE, you gut the country,"

DEPARTMENT OF AGRICULTURE

Funnily enough, most of what the DOA does has little to do with agriculture. It manages *one hundred and ninety million* acres of national forest and grasslands. It also inspects almost every animal that we consume, the total of which numbers in the billions. There's a large airplane fleet for firefighting. There's a bank with $220 billion in assets. The DOA keeps track of catfish farms. The list goes on and on. In fact, as Lewis reports, "There's a drinking game played by people who have worked at the Department of Agriculture: Does the USDA do it? Someone names an odd function of government (say, shooting fireworks at Canada geese that flock too near airport runways) and someone else has to guess if the USDA does it. (In this case, it does.)"

But most importantly it pays for nearly every program in rural America. Free school lunch, housing, hospitals, fire department, water, electricity.

Who did Trump install to run the USDA? Lewis took pains to examine these, well, totally unqualified jokers, some of whom were paid $80,000 per year: "A long-haul truck driver, a clerk at AT&T, a gas company meter reader, a country club cabana attendant, a Republican National Committee intern, and the owner of a scented candle company, with skills like 'pleasant demeanor' listed on their résumés." The former transition team head had this to say about the process: "In many cases [the new appointees] demonstrated little to no experience with federal policy, let alone deep roots in agriculture. Some of those appointees appear to lack the credentials, such as a college degree, required to qualify for higher government salaries." Precisely the wrong people in place for such critical functions.

Then there's the national school lunch program. The USDA oversees it. Lewis writes, "The program that ensures that pregnant women, new mothers, and young children receive proper nutrition; and a dozen or so smaller programs designed to alleviate hunger. Together these accounted for approximately 70 percent of the USDA's budget." It takes a special kind of person to appoint people with zero experience in this field and who seem to care little about managing food supplies for the poor. But that's exactly what Trump did. The transition to managing this program never happened. Obama's team didn't report a single encounter with them. (Then Trump proposed slashing food stamps by more than 25 percent over the next ten years. But that's another story). With the Trump administration, all the gains that occurred under Obama with respect to nutrition and health were reversed. The Secretary of Agriculture—a former governor of Georgia with little experience with nutrition—decreed no more healthy food, and went back to artificially sweetened concoctions and white bread. Mind you, according to the CDC, 33 percent of kids born after 2000 are likely to end up diabetic, which poses a huge health risk and drain on our health care system. But, as expected, most decisions were made by big agriculture business, because, as Lewis writes, "... it was more profitable for them to serve pancakes and hot dogs than fruits and vegetables."

The USDA loan program is enormous. And the best/worst part is that people who were getting loans were barely aware they were from the government. You can imagine their reaction when they found out! Tom Vilsack, secretary of Agriculture under Obama and again under Biden, has a story about a Fox News–watching Minnesota businessman who was interviewed by the local newspaper after a ceremony for opening his new gig. "He's telling the reporter how proud he is to have done it on his own," said Vilsack. "The USDA person goes to introduce

herself, and he says, 'So, who are you?' She says, 'I'm the USDA person.'
He asks, 'What are you doing here?' She says, 'Well, sir, we supplied the
money you are announcing.' He was white as a sheet." Lillian Salerno,
a former deputy secretary, says, "We'd have this check. We'd blow it
up and try to have a picture taken with it. It said UNITED STATES
GOVERNMENT in great big letters. That was something that Vilsack
wanted—to be right out in front so people knew the federal government had helped them. In the red Southern states a mayor sometimes
would say, 'Can you not mention that the government gave this?'" I
can't get over this phenomenon. People hate the government but will
gladly accept their help and refuse to acknowledge the source of the
assistance. Basically they're saying, "Just give me my damn government
money and keep your government hands off my property!"

The list of agencies and Team Trump's unique incompetence goes
on and on. FEMA and the CDC, the people who are supposed to save
our butts during national crises and keep us safe from deadly viruses?
Trump didn't appoint anyone to run them.

10

LOBBYING

"As every business executive knows, few elements of
American society today have as little influence in government
as the American businessman, the corporation, or even the
millions of corporate stockholders. If one doubts this,
let him undertake the role of 'lobbyist' for the business
point of view before Congressional committees."

**—LEWIS POWELL, SUPREME COURT JUSTICE,
NOMINATED BY RICHARD NIXON (1971)**

WHAT?

IF CONGRESSIONAL DEMOCRATS PLAY footsie with corporate lobbyists, Republicans are intimate lovers. If you are reading this book, you've probably got *some* clue what lobbying is and how it functions, so I won't bore you with an explanation of the basics. What you should know is, lobbying is one of the most powerful industries on the planet. I mean, Best Buy has more employees than there are lobbyists in

America, but lobbyists have a large tangible effect on nearly every good and service sold in America, even though they don't sell anything tangible. In 2019, there were officially 12,000 registered lobbyists in America, but the real number is closer to 100,000, according the Professor James Thurber.[1] If you compare that 12,000 number to the number in 1975, when there were roughly 200, it feels kind of significant. The industry generates roughly $9 billion, which does not scream "major player" by any stretch. The porn industry brings in more than that (not that I would know). But let's get something clear: the power they wield with that $9 billion is downright ludicrous. There's only one party that is doing anything to reduce the power of these lobbyists in Washington, and it ain't the GOP. The Democrats are certainly not unified in pursuing this task (yet) but they provide the greatest hope for corrective legislative action.

WHY?

BIG BUSINESS RELIES ON lobbying to effectively write favorable legislation. In a country where laws are determined by elected representatives in Washington (and the states), if you want to impact the way they are written, you support and hassle the people who write them. You give them big financial rewards or hire a troll farm to write them millions of scathing comments telling them what an awful job they're doing on xyz legislation.[2] Americans could, in theory, benefit from this type of activism, but in reality, the rewards are highly concentrated at the top, where you find corporations and the radical rich, who have the deepest pockets and the best organizing prowess. And congressional conservatives queue up to fill their campaign coffers. Over the course of the last forty years, they have sought expressly to expand the power of corporate money in Washington. Not all lobbying furthers their interests solely. There's plenty of sensible advocacy done on climate change, labor laws, and civil rights. But the outsized affect lobbying has on behalf of a small group of wealthy citizens is very much a problem. A big problem.

***

WE'VE ESTABLISHED THAT THERE'S no such thing as a free market (chapters on Reaganomics and Private Industry), because the rules of the market are always prescribed by politicians (and rich people) with agendas. Yet another reason why markets are not free is the fact that big business molds markets into a form that is advantageous to their bottom line. While they extol the virtues of *unobstructed free markets*, they are on their way to the Capitol to push for special legislation or special measures for their own benefit. The hypocrisy is noted.

A bit of history. There was a really important bill up for a vote in 1978 called the Labor Reform Act. It would have essentially provided a much-needed updating and strengthening of American labor laws after a decade or so of being under assault from big business and its lobbyists. President Jimmy Carter and the Democrats had the votes in both chambers. Popular opinion was overwhelmingly on their side. It passed the House 257–163 and seemed destined to pass the Senate. "There didn't seem to be any way to stop it" at the time, said one opponent. However, after weeks of intense lobbying by big business, which included donations, mailers, phone calls, you name it, on conservative lawmakers, the law was eventually held up by the (undemocratic) Senate filibuster and never saw Carter's desk. According to *Congressional Quarterly*: "Six cloture votes were unable to break a five-week conservative filibuster against the bill, which had passed the House easily in October 1977. The measure was recommitted to the Human Resources Committee June 22, and never re-emerged. The legislation, organized labor's No. 1 legislative priority, would have speeded up the decision-making process of the National Labor Relations Board (NLRB) and made it easier for unions to organize workers and negotiate collective bargaining agreements ... Millions of letters and postcards for and against the bill swamped Senate offices."[3]

Consequently, congressional conservatives and corporate lobbyists felt uber-emboldened to crush any meaningful legislation that favored workers and consumers. It was, as they say, off to the races. The corporate lobbying train and their witting enablers in Congress (and a lot of key Democrats, I might add) could not be slowed down. Then Reagan got his major tax reform passed in 1981. As Lee Drutman writes in the *Atlantic*, "By the early 1980s, corporate leaders were 'purring' (as a 1982 Harris Poll described it). Corporations could have declared victory and gone home, thus saving on the costs of political engagement. Instead, they stuck around and kept at it. Many deepened their commitments to politics. After all, they now had lobbyists to help them see all that was at stake in Washington, and all the ways in which staying politically active could help their businesses."[4] As a lobbyist told Drutman in 2007, "Twenty-five years ago ... it was 'just keep the government out of our business, we want to do what we want to,' and gradually that's changed to 'how can we make the government our partners?' It's gone from 'leave us alone' to 'let's work on this together.'" Another corporate lobbyist recalled, "When they started, [management] thought government relations did something else. They thought it was to manage public relations crises, hearing inquiries ... My boss told me, you've taught us to do things we didn't know could ever be done."

Today, the environment is much worse than in the 1970s, because, today, corporations have vastly more resources to play offense and defense simultaneously on almost any critical issue. The top reason they are in Washington, according to Drutman's interviews with lobbyists, is "to protect the company against changes in government policy."

Labor unions and public-interest groups, which represent tens of millions more voters than big business, are ferociously outspent by their corporate counterparts. For every dollar spent on lobbying by labor unions and public-interest groups together, large corporations and their associations now spend thirty-four dollars. *Thirty-four to one*! Of the one hundred organizations that spend the most on lobbying, ninety-five consistently represent business. Sweet.

As union lobbying lost ground, so did union power. And unions are meant to protect workers' rights, including their ability to earn a decent wage and to collectively bargain. It's clear as day: union membership reduces the ever-growing problem of inequality. This is not to say that unions do not have their own problems, because they do: mismanagement, corruption, toxic environments. But they serve a critical purpose, and that is to ensure workers are fairly compensated, which is *the* primary motive why owners and managers wish to eliminate them. There are only a few sure things in this life. Death, taxes, and the rich hating unions.

The graph below from the Economic Policy Institute could not be clearer as to the root cause of our inequality predicament. In other Western countries, you do not see the same disparity because, strong unions. As soon as union membership begins to decline, so does the share of income belonging to the bottom 90 percent of the income-earners.

A refrain I hear from colleagues and friends is, "Well, Bill, unions are pretty unpopular." No, sorry, they are not, in fact. They are pretty *popular*, and gained popularity over the last decade. According to Gallup Research, in 1952, union popularity hit a peak of 75 percent. It fell to 55 percent in 1982, thanks to Reagan and his union-bashing blustering. It now stands at 64 percent, and even among Republicans it's at 45 percent, with Democrats at 82 percent. They are popular even after years and years of attempts to make them look like the bad guy. But actual union membership today stands at a paltry 11 percent. This is due to the severe anti-union measures private companies use to thwart employee organization. Plus, a very conservative pro-business US Supreme Court.

Unions and Shared Prosperity

Source: Economic Policy Institute

To sum up: union membership is at all-time lows, yet a vast majority of workers want to join one. How is this possible? A combination of congressional conservatives, big business and the probusiness courts effectively prevent workers from joining. Needless to say, reform is necessary. Power needs to flow back into the hands of labor. These groups perpetrate these myths to discourage union membership: that the economy won't function as well, that there will be slower growth, that the best and brightest (and the richest) will leave the country. None of that is supported *at all* in the data. As you can see, periods with strong union membership and worker protections (1937–1980) had *higher* economic growth than periods without (1980–2020).

Real Gross Domestic Product

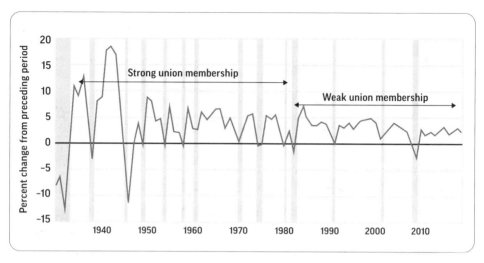

Source: US BEA and St. Louis Federal Reserve

COMPETITION

Lobbying has drastically impacted competition, which affects workers' rights, wages, and consumer power.

A bit of context: competition in the United States is down. Like, down all across the board in nearly every industry. This is not good. Competition—as any free market–touting libertarian will drone on about when defending capitalism—is vital for a healthy and vibrant economy, particularly its engine: small business (this is true). What they fail to shed a tear for is the fact that competition is rapidly decreasing. Actually, it hasn't been this bad since the 1910s, when big business effectively ran our country. It wasn't until Republican Teddy Roosevelt went on an antitrust crusade, breaking up big business, allowing for more competition from the smaller guys so they didn't feel beholden to the Henry Fords and Jay Goulds of the world.[5] This continued with his cousin Franklin Roosevelt (a Democrat) and the New Deal, all way up through the late '70s. At this time, competition started to decline. Not coincidentally, this is when Lewis Powell distributed his famous memo ("Powell Memo") and lobbying in Washington began to explode.[6] Conservative special interest groups started to take serious aim at regulation. All types of regulation (e.g., labor, consumer protection, financial). And in the process, the necessary safeguards that ensure small businesses, workers, and consumers are looked out for began to erode. Today, because of this multidecade onslaught, we face one of the most concentrated and rigged *free markets* in our history. Both Jacob Hacker and Kurt Andersen have painstakingly documented the rise of the corporatization of Washington in their books *Winner Take All Politics* and *Evil Geniuses*, respectively. They are worth the read if you ever wonder how corporate America has come to dictate our national policy discourse.

To understand the effects of government failure to protect competition in our markets, we can turn to Brookings fellow David Wessel, who lays out four measures to assess the damage done by a lack of competition: economy, profits, investment, business dynamism, and prices.[7] Three of the four categories are going in the wrong direction and the fourth has mixed evidence, at best, supporting the lack of competition.

Rising profits in an increasingly concentrated market usually signal that competition is suffering and the biggest firms are becoming more powerful. One way we can judge this is by looking at firms' markup to cost, meaning the difference between the prices firms charge and products' marginal cost. In 1980, markups were 18 percent. By 2014, they were 67 percent. Sixty-seven percent! That's a lot of margin going to the owners, as wages had barely budged in that time. Great for them (and shareholders), not so good for the consumer and the workers. What is the GOP's answer? More free markets, less government interference.

What about business investment? Another way to discern whether companies are getting too cozy is whether, while profits are going up, investment is flatlining or declining. Meaning firms are increasingly getting richer without innovating. In normally functioning markets, companies need to invest more to stay ahead of the competition. Though business investment has ticked up slightly, it is nowhere near the increase in profits. In fact, corporate after-tax profits are nearly double what they were twenty-five years ago, while business investment as a share of GDP is up only 13 percent. One hundred percent versus 13 percent. Where's all that money going? (*Whispers*: the owners). Again, how are Republicans dealing with this data? More free enterprise!

Now let's look at business dynamism. In healthy and functioning economy, companies go through life cycles. Most fail, some thrive and expand, some thrive and contract. New jobs are created while others destroyed. A slowdown in this business dynamism spells less to worry about from upstarts for big entrenched firms. Consequently, job growth suffers and so does innovation. Explain that to your rabid free-marketeer friend and see if that breaks any skull. Wessel notes, "In the U.S., the rate of birth of new firms (as a percentage of all firms) fell from above 13 percent in the late 1980s to around 8 percent in 2015, according to the most recent official data. The number of jobs created by businesses less than a year old dropped from a peak of 4.7 million in the late 1990s to 3 million in 2015." Yikes.

Thomas Philippon, an NYU economist, is the author of *The Great Reversal: How America Gave Up on Free Markets*. He asserts with plenty of evidence that the difference in growth between wages in the US and EU can be attributed to lack of competition.

Comparisons between the US and EU are totally defensible. Neither profit margins nor market concentrations have rocketed upwards in the EU like they have in the US. The proportion of wages and salaries in total profit for companies in the US has fallen by 6 percent since 2000, and hasn't really budged in the eurozone. This annihilates the hypothesis that technology is the primary cause of the downward

trend in the share of income going to workers. As we know, technology (and international trade) is just as prevalent on the other side of
the Atlantic.

The difference between the mark-up of prices over the cost of labor
has increased by more than 8 percent in the United States, meaning
companies are able to charge more for something even though they
are paying their workers less. But in the EU, the difference has shrunk
since 2000, meaning as prices rise, employers are paying their workers
more. You're making us look really bad, EU.

But don't raise Europe as a point of debate, because when you
do around mainstream conservative politicians, you get the dreaded
s-word. "I am for the Constitution; [Obama] is for European socialism," Newt Gingrich said on the campaign trail in 2012. "I think some
of the policies that he [President Obama] has adopted are very much
like the European socialist policies," Mitt Romney said in 2012. One
can't even offer a model of success without being labeled a socialist.

Wages are also impacted in a more obvious way. As competition
decreases in industries, there are fewer firms to compete for your talents. That means they do not have to compete in paying wages. Why
should they if you have only one or two other employment options?
Even better, they can collude and not have to pay you more than the
cartel price! Though this is illegal, you bet your ass it happens with little recourse to employees. Here are just a few cases of price and wage
collusion in the last decade:

- Intel, Apple, and Adobe settled a class action lawsuit for half a
  billion dollars for making secret deals with each other to not hire
  each other's engineers, which artificially holds down wages.[8]

- In 2015, the Justice Department, citing corporate documents in
  its initial objection to a subsequent Anheuser-Busch acquisition,
  said the brewer's strategic plan for pricing "reads like a how-to
  manual for successful price coordination."

- A 2010 analysis found that the typical private insurer payment for inpatient hospital stays in San Francisco (a highly concentrated market) was about 75 percent higher than in the more fragmented Los Angeles market.[9]

- University of Texas labor economist Sandra Black summarizes research that uses 2011 data from the job site CareerBuilder. She writes, "The researchers examine whether companies in cities with fewer employers offer lower wages. They find that they do. The smaller the number of companies in an industry, the lower average wages are for people who work in that field. In other words, if you are an electrician, you are better off if there are five small companies employing electricians in your city, rather than one big one, because the firms have to bid against each other for your services."[10]

- The Federal Trade Commission (under Trump, no less) issued a brief in 2019. Below is the title and summary:

THE UNITED STATES HAS A MARKET CONCENTRATION PROB-LEM: REVIEWING CONCENTRATION ESTIMATES IN ANTITRUST MARKETS, 2000-PRESENT: Since the 1970s, America's antitrust policy regime has been weakening and market power has been on the rise. High market concentration—in which few firms compete in a given market—is one indicator of market power. From 1985 to 2017, the number of mergers completed annually rose from 2,308 to 15,361 (IMAA 2017) . . . Recently, policymakers, academics, and journalists have questioned whether the ongoing merger wave, and lax antitrust enforcement more generally, is indeed contributing to rising concentration, and in turn, whether concentration really portends a market power crisis in the economy. In this issue brief, we review the estimates of market concentration that have been conducted in a number of industries since 2000 as part of merger retrospectives and other empirical investigations. The result of that survey is clear: market concentration in the U.S. economy is high, according to the thresholds adopted by the antitrust agencies themselves in the Horizontal Merger Guidelines.[11]

Here is a chart from Brookings that illustrates how concentrated a particular sector of the economy is. Any HHI score of at least 2500 is considered highly concentrated. Not one of them is below 3750.

Market Concentration with and without Adjustment for Common Ownership, by Sector

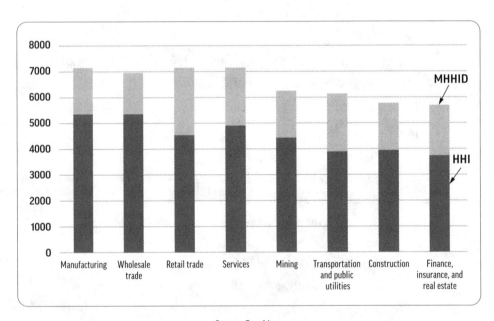

Source: Brookings

I want to make this clear: the Democrats are guilty of pandering to corporate lobbyists and weakening labor rights. President Clinton's

NAFTA was a gift to big business and a reckoning for organized labor. Senator Chuck Schumer's unyielding support for the financial services lobby paved the way for financial catastrophe in 2008. But, like all issues I cover in this book, Republicans are a thousand and one times more responsible for what has transpired.

At least the Democrats *seem* to be learning their lesson. The House recently passed the HR 1 bill and the PRO Act, which are sweeping legislation that will reduce corruption and the influence of lobbying, strengthen unions, and give some lost power back to the workers. Conservatives, predictably, call it socialism.

What did conservatives say about it?

- The Conservative Action Project released a memo calling the bill "the ultimate fantasy of the left."[12]

- From 2018 to 2020, conservative and libertarian group Freedom-Works circulated a form letter to members, calling HR 1 a "dangerous bill" and saying it would restrict free speech and open up the country to one-party rule by Democrats.[13]

- McConnell says, The bill will "grow the federal government's power over Americans' political speech and elections. It should be called the Democrat Politician Protection Act."

So, what was actually in the bills? A summary from reporters Elia Nelson and Sara Jones:

HR 1:[14]

- Require Super PACs and "dark money" political organizations to make their donors public.

- Set up a voluntary option to publicly finance campaigns, powered by small donations. The federal government would provide a voluntary six-to-one match for candidates for president and

Congress, which means for every dollar a candidate raises from small donations, the federal government would match it six times over. The maximum small donation that could be matched would be capped at $200.

- The president and vice president and presidential and vice presidential candidates would be required to disclose ten years of their tax returns.

- Put in stricter lobbying registration requirements, with more oversight of foreign agents.

- Set up nonpartisan redistricting commissions to end partisan gerrymandering, and create new national automatic voter registration asking voters to opt out, rather than opt in.

- Make Election Day a holiday for federal employees and encourage private sector businesses to do the same.[15]

PRO Act:

- Shore up workers' rights to strike, to organize, and to pursue litigation against employers who violate their rights.

- Ban employers from forcing hires to sign away their right to pursue collective or class-action litigation and from permanently replacing workers who go on strike.

- Require employers to begin bargaining a contract no later than ten days after a union has been certified.

- Ban the practice of free riding, where workers are eligible for union membership benefit from a collective bargaining agreement without paying fair-share fees to cover the costs of the union's work.

- Strengthen the right to strike by protecting intermittent strikes, when workers carry out a series of short-term walkouts to increase pressure on an employer, and by ending prohibitions on secondary strikes, known as solidarity strikes.

In contrast to the Democrats approach, I have to share a story recalled by Alan Wolfe about Republicans and lobbying. Wolfe writes that Republicans became so greedy in the 1990s that—get this—they wanted lobbying all to *themselves*. Wolfe writes about the infamous Republican K Street project, which "was designed not only to allow lobbyists to make contributions to legislators in return for laws that benefit themselves—this has always been part of the politics of democracy—but to transform lobbying, which has usually been understood as bipartisan in nature, into an arm of one political party; in return for access to government, Republicans insisted that lobbying groups fire Democrats from their leadership positions and replace them with Republicans."[16] Good Lord, man! Also, that smacks of cancel culture.

11

IT PAYS TO BE REPUBLICAN

"A new analysis by Americans for Tax Fairness estimates
that Charles Koch and David Koch and/or Koch Industries
could save between $1 billion and $1.4 billion combined
in income taxes each year from the Trump tax law—and
that doesn't even count how much the brothers might
save in taxes on offshore profits or how much their
heirs will benefit from weakening the estate tax."

—AMERICANS FOR TAX FAIRNESS (2018)

WHAT AND WHY?

AS YOU CAN SEE, it pays to be a Republican. Their platform of antitax
and antiregulation could not be *more* favorable to corporate America, so it's no mystery why corporate America supports congressional
Republicans more than Democrats. To be clear, Democrats accept
plenty of corporate money and legislate in favor of big business, but
nothing compares to earning those Republican Benjamins. Republicans' rigid economic ideology is a signal to corporations: We are
always open for business.

BEING A CONGRESSIONAL REPUBLICAN has been profitable for quite some time, but it became much more so in the 1970s and into the 1990s. As Jacob Hacker documents in *Winner Take All Politics*, big business provides significant financial support to conservatives in order to kill legislation related to labor reform, climate change, tax increases, and increased consumer protection.

Let me provide a bit of context. The floodgates of campaign contributions burst open in the midnineties. Between 1994 and 1998, Republican candidates and party committees raised over $1 billion, an amount that was previously *unheard* of.[1] No party had ever come close to raising that kind of money. Thanks were mostly due to Speaker Newt Gingrich's effort to effectively force sitting representatives to focus more on fundraising back home and less on legislating in Washington.

Since the landmark Citizens United decision of 2010, which essentially allowed unlimited anonymous spending in political campaigns, Republican groups have comprised 70 percent of *dark money* spending in every election through 2018.[2]

Between their top two priorities—legislating for the benefit of corporate America's bottom line and shrinking the public sector—congressional conservatives mounted attacks on any proposed tax increases and financial regulation. Take President Obama's proposed Dodd-Frank regulation, which sought to avoid a financial catastrophe like the one in 2008. The financial industry had long embraced support offered to them by Democrats, particularly President Clinton and Senate Majority Leader Chuck Schumer, but after Obama took office, they turned away from Democrats and embraced Republicans instead. E. J. Dionne writes,

> "It was not initially obvious that Wall Street, the hedge funds, and the venture capitalists would be a force for conservatism. Democrats raised

substantial funds from the financial world, both because many in its ranks were liberal, particularly on social issues, and because the Clinton administration was broadly sympathetic to financial deregulation. But after the 2008 crash, the performance of Wall Street came under heightened attack from the Left. Democrats proposed higher taxes on the wealthy (ironically, back to the levels under Clinton, who was nonetheless seen as more friendly to business than Obama), including increases in the low capital gains tax rates enacted under Bush."[3]

Around this time, very wealthy people began to think of themselves as victims who were under siege from intimidating groups like Occupy Wall Street (you know, that collection of two hundred potheads camping out in downtown Manhattan for a month). All the while, their share of national income continued to grow. Many a tear was shed for their plight. So they began to support those who most understood their regrettable circumstances and championed their struggles: conservatives.

For their political support, the radical rich remunerated their Republican puppets in spades. In January 2018, Americans For Tax Fairness reported,

"Last week's FEC filings show that the Kochs made a $500,000 contribution to 'Team Ryan'—a joint fundraising committee benefiting Paul Ryan, the National Republican Congressional Committee (NRCC) and a pro-Ryan PAC. On top of that, the Kochs gave an additional quarter million to the NRCC . . . The Kochs made securing big tax cuts for themselves and their corporation a key goal for their political network in 2017. The Koch groups spent over $20 million promoting the tax bill that ultimately became law, according to a fact sheet they provided to the *Wall Street Journal*. Their efforts included town halls, door-to-door canvassing, and television ads—not to mention direct lobbying—in favor of the tax cuts. Now that the bill is law, they've pledged to spend millions more promoting it to the public in an effort to protect the members of Congress who voted for it."[4]

Boy, that Trump Tax Plan has some wealthy fanboys!

The upshot of all this is that it should not *pay* to be in any party. Corporations should not have an unlimited capacity to buy congresspeople and receive untold benefits for exorbitant donations. This kind of environment benefits an increasingly smaller and smaller segment of the population, at the expense of the vast majority of voters. There should be, for example, caps on campaign spending, increased transparency, and, frankly, publicly funded elections, which is how things work in the majority of Western democracies. America is unique in that we have none of the above, and because such a small number of people can play such an outsized role in our politics.

Democrats are the only ones attempting to do anything about reducing corporate influence. The House passed HR 1 in January 2019, which stipulates, among other things, crucial restrictions on campaign finance and corporate spending in elections.

12

DICK CHENEY AND
HIS PRIVATE INTERESTS

"People like you are still living in what we call the
reality-based community. You believe that solutions emerge
from your judicious study of discernible reality. That's not
the way the world really works anymore. We're an empire
now, and when we act, we create our own reality. And while
you are studying that reality—judiciously, as you will—we'll
act again, creating other new realities, which you can study
too, and that's how things will sort out. We're history's actors,
and you, all of you, will be left to just study what we do."

**—SENIOR ADVISOR TO FORMER VICE PRESIDENT
DICK CHENEY AND PRESIDENT GEORGE BUSH (2004);
KARL ROVE HAS DISPUTED THAT HE WAS THE SOURCE.**

WHAT?

THE GOP GRADUATED FROM the Gingrich era in the '90s to an even more
chaotic authoritarian conservatism, courtesy of Dick Cheney (and Karl
Rove) with the tacit consent of George W. Bush, who was the Pinocchio

to Cheney's Geppetto. Of course, the Bush administration is famous for the worst geopolitical disaster in our history, costing trillions of dollars and killing and displacing millions of people: the war in Iraq. But what happened behind the curtains in Washington is what really eroded the trust and transparency of its institutions, giving way to more offspring from the marriage of the GOP and private enterprise.

WHY?

DYSFUNCTION AND CHAOS ARE opportune for those who seek to expand their personal power and fortune at the expense of the majority, and that seemed top-of-mind to Cheney. That, and bombing Saddam Hussein back to the Stone Age.

THE ATLANTIC **STAFF WRITER** Conor Friedersdorf concludes, "Dick Cheney was a self-aggrandizing criminal who used his knowledge as a Washington insider to subvert both informed public debate about matters of war and peace and to manipulate presidential decision making."[1] Could not agree more, Conor!

In order to properly assess the Cheney administration, one must peer through the lens of private enterprise. The primary reason for his going to war with Iraq was oil and oil field services contracts.

The war in Iraq was a disaster. The impetus for it was one big lie undergirded by private interests. This is obviously not the first time we went to war over private interests, but it stands as one of the largest, most disastrous, costly, and deadly decisions we've ever made. Cheney still considers it a success. To support this assertion, here are three notable quotes to consider:

"Oil remains fundamentally a government business. While many regions of the world offer great oil opportunities, the Middle East with two-thirds of the world's oil and the lowest cost, is still where the prize ultimately lies, even though companies are anxious for greater access there, progress continues to be slow."

—DICK CHENEY IN 1999, AS THE CEO OF HALLIBURTON, AT THE LONDON INSTITUTE OF PETROLEUM

"I am saddened that it is politically inconvenient to acknowledge what everyone knows: the Iraq war is largely about oil."

—FED CHAIRMAN ALAN GREENSPAN, IN 2007

"If we had to do it over again we would do exactly the same thing."

—CHENEY, IN 2006 (WELL, HE IS CONSISTENTLY EVIL, I'LL GIVE HIM THAT)

A report from the Watson Institute of International and Public Affairs at Brown University finds that more than 801,000 people have died as a direct result of fighting in the wars in Iraq and Afghanistan. Of those, more than 335,000 have been civilians. Another twenty-one million people have been displaced due to violence.[2] But, hey, at least we got cheap oil, right?

If you want a smart recap of the events leading up to the Iraq war and the duping of the American people, read this piece from *Mother Jones*: "Lie by Lie: A Timeline of How We Got Into Iraq," written by Jonathan Stein and Tim Dickinson.[3] Even before 9/11, President Bush told his Treasury Secretary Paul O'Neill to find him a way to remove Saddam Hussein. O'Neill recalls, "It was all about finding a way to do it. The president saying, 'Go find me a way to do this.'"[4] And yet, we were fed untold lies about Iraq's involvement in 9/11 and weapons of mass destruction.

Democrats were the only ones trying to prevent it. Or half of the party, at least, but that was not enough to save the day—and hundreds of thousands of lives. Republicans lined up like drones behind their leader (in this case, Dick Cheney). The war resolution in the House passed 297 to 133 and in the Senate 77 to 23.[5, 6] Only seven Republicans voted against it, including six House members and Senator Lincoln Chafee, who later became a Democrat.

Not to mention, the US wars in Afghanistan, Iraq, Syria, and Pakistan have cost American taxpayers $6.4 *trillion* since they began in 2001.

That's about $20,000 per person in the United States.

We could have funded health care for 325 million Americans. For two years.

To be clear, President Obama and his Secretary of State, Hillary Clinton, continued to fight the wars in Iraq and Afghanistan (and Libya and Syria), so they surely shoulder some of the blame.

The following is a selected short list of deliberately corrupt maneuvers Cheney pursued while in office:

- Cheney was the Halliburton (oil field services company) CEO in the '90s and never really gave up his association when he became vice president. He publicly promised not to do business in Iraq as VP, but then he did it anyway. He gave preferred contracts, evaded US sanctions by domiciling the company in Europe, and engaged in business with Saddam via the UN's Oil-for-Food program. Corruption was rampant.[7]

- Cheney and his consigliere David Addington have long been associated with the doctrine of the Unitary Executive: the notion that all executive functions are vested in the president of the United States of America and hence that the president has the right to direct all executive officers, who, in turn, are required to obey his orders. All except the vice president, apparently. Cheney took the position that he was not bound by an executive order requiring all entities within the executive branch to report on how they obtain and use classified information because he is not just another part of the executive branch. Yes, the vice president claimed, absurdly, that he should be treated as part of the legislative branch … when it was convenient.[8]

- He used a private email server to transact a significant amount of government business while in office. ("BUT HER EMAILS!"—a reference to cries of supporters of Donald Trump about Hillary's use of a private email server.)[9]

- While the Iraqi occupation was in full chaos mode, Cheney sabotaged the governing structure we worked so hard to establish by creating back channels to the Coalition Provisional Authority in order to replace the leaders with people who were loyal to him, so that he could expand his own power and procure those Halliburton contracts.

- The cloud of secrecy Cheney formed was unlike that of any presidential administration. He was the first VP to not provide executive branch records to the Government Accountability Office, which is akin to your boss telling the accountants and auditors, "Sorry, you can't see any of our emails or receipts before signing off on our financial reports."[10]

- Cheney employed a fellow who was wanted for bank fraud in Jordan as a primary source for his lies about Saddam's weapons of mass destruction. The CIA was highly skeptical of his credibility, and the UK authorities called him a "convicted fraudster." Of course, his intel proved erroneous. Oops, too late. He was later charged with fraud by the US for embezzling funds. Cheney continued to protect this criminal and fired key transition people like Thomas Warrick, which slowed progress in rebuilding Iraq.[11]

- Cheney radically altered the view of executive power. He held a grudge since his days in the Nixon and Ford administrations against congressional oversight—you know, separations of powers and Article 1 and all that. Charlie Savage, who penned a book on Cheney, writes: "Day upon day, the Ford White House was confronting the Church Committee's investigations of intelligence abuses and a Congress that was determined to re-impose checks and balances on the 'imperial' presidency. This seemed outrageous from Cheney's vantage point and he spent the next three decades trying, without much success at first, to roll back the changes of the 1970s and to restore presidential power to the level it had aberrantly but briefly reached before Nixon fell. As secretary of Defense to the first President Bush, he urged George H. W. Bush to launch the Gulf War without going to Congress for permission." It seems like Cheney learned a great deal from Watergate.[12]

- Between 2000 and 2006, there were next to no oversight investigations into the Bush administration courtesy of a radical hyperpartisan Republican Congress. Think about that. The worst geopolitical disaster in our history, and Republicans placated Cheney to not produce a single worthy investigation save a few exceptions. In the past, when Democrats controlled the House, they investigated Democrats and Republicans alike, because that's their job and, more importantly, it's what's best for the country. Norm Ornstein and Thomas Mann note that "vigorous oversight was the norm until the end of the twentieth century." A special committee, chaired by Lyndon Johnson, was very critical of the Truman Administration's actions during the Korean War. There were the Church committee investigations of the 1970s into intelligence failures and illegal surveillance, and in the 1980s, Congress formed joint committees to scrutinize the Iran–Contra affair. In the 1990s, military operations in Kosovo were investigated by committees in both the House and the Senate. But during the Iraq War through 2006 when Republicans held Congress, Ornstein and Mann write, "Oversight [had] all but disappeared. From homeland security to the conduct of the Iraq war, from allegations of torture at Abu Ghraib to the surveillance of domestic telephone calls by the National Security Agency (NSA), Congress [...] mostly ignored its responsibilities."[13]

GEORGE W. BUSH

Bush himself was a staunch conservative, though he often served as the empty vessel which Cheney used to live out his oil-lubed dreams of war and almighty executive authority. When Bush was actually busy being president, his first major order of business was ... drumroll ... cutting taxes! Quite the shocker. He longed to draw a distinction between him and his heathen father (who raised taxes and subsequently lost the presidency), and because he truly believed in trickle-down economics, which is one of the biggest lies in the history of modern politics. Not to mention, Bill Clinton's deficit surpluses gave him the perfect cover. But the rationale kept changing, as the author E. J. Dionne has noted. "Initially," Dionne writes, "[the tax cuts] were affordable because the economy was booming. Later, they were necessary because the economy was stalling. No matter what was happening with the economy, it was always time for a tax cut."[14] The first tax cut was part of the Economic Growth and Tax Relief Reconciliation Act of 2001, which lowered the top income tax bracket from 39.6 percent to 35 percent (and the rest of the brackets by about 3 percent). The estate tax was cut and set to be repealed entirely in 2010, which cost the government $1.35 *trillion* during that time. In 2003, it was the Jobs and Growth Tax Relief Reconciliation Act, which cut the primary capital gains tax rate from 20 percent to 15 percent, and reduced taxes on dividends, previously treated as ordinary income, to 15 percent. This was even a bigger gift to the wealthy since they owned the vast majority of stocks. The price tag for this was another $350 billion. Unsurprisingly—we now know from years of research and data—the tax cuts did not produce the growth Republicans promised, and certainly not in wages and income for ordinary Americans, as had been advertised. What then? Consumers began taking out gigantic loans to pay for houses, cars, and other big expenses, which was a result of massive deregulation. And since wages weren't rising, the average consumer got stuck with an increasingly lower expense coverage ratio. Dionne wrote, "[T]he credit markets become ever-more willing to provide credit in lieu of income for people." All the ingredients were in place for the epic financial disaster in 2008.

Bush's tax cuts also had unintended consequences for the states. Since many of them linked their tax rates to those of the federal government, Jim VandeHei wrote, the Bush-sponsored federal reductions spurred on tax cuts in these states and "drained revenue from state coffers that otherwise would have helped fund education." Given the impending crisis that Bush presided over, the states got totally screwed.

13

THE GOVERNMENT INNOVATION CONGRESSIONAL CONSERVATIVES LOVE TO FORGET ABOUT

"Indeed, nearly all the technological revolutions in the past— from the Internet to today's green tech revolution—required a massive push by the State. Silicon Valley's techno-libertarians might be surprised to find out that Uncle Sam funded many of the innovations behind the information technology revolution."

—PROFESSOR AND AUTHOR MARIANA MAZZUCATO

WHAT AND WHY?

WITHOUT A DOUBT, THE hostile actions and rhetoric of congressional conservatives towards their employer (in the name of benefiting corporations at the expense of consumers and workers) have successfully obscured the staggering contributions of government to American innovation. Our political discourse is (and has been for the last forty-plus years) dominated by talk of free markets, private enterprise, and how government is the Voldemort of capitalism. What is not well known is the fact that our government has created some pretty awesome stuff in our lifetimes. You may not be aware because 1) years of government bashing have created this image of Uncle Sam as being a slow, bloated, evil place where things go to die, and 2) the government does a *horrendous* job of marketing their successes. And why should they have to? Do you want your tax dollars going towards the government bragging about their accomplishments? Well, actually, now that I mention it, yeah, I would. Perhaps we need a government gecko with a British accent between NFL timeouts touting "the internet is our baby," or something to that effect.

LET'S EXAMINE PASSAGES FROM the book *The Entrepreneurial State* by Mazzucato.

First, here's a selected list of what the American government has created:

- The internet
- Shale gas
- Life-saving biotech compounds
- GPS
- Touchscreen technology
- SIRI
- Lots of renewable energy sources
- Lots of technologies that protect us from terrorists
- NASA technologies that benefit companies like Tesla, Space-X, Amazon, Virgin, Apple, Google, and many more

Conservative media also love to talk about what an atrocious job the government does, furthering weakening the trust from constituents. If you did not watch Fox News during President Obama's first term, you may not have heard about Solyndra, an investment in renewable energy gone bad. Conservative media *pounded* the news cycle with story after story about *fraudulent schemes* and *government waste* and the like. What they would never tell you is that the government invests in *a lot* of companies, some bad, some good. Solyndra turned out to be a bad investment. They also invested in a little company called Tesla, right about the same time. Had the government taken a stake in Tesla, it would have been able to more than make up for its losses from Solyndra. The year Tesla received its government loan, the company had an IPO (initial public offering) of $17 a share; by the time the loan was repaid, the share price was $93. In 2021, Tesla shares traded at more than $1200. As I was saying, some good, some bad.

Let's review some of Mazzucato's examples in more detail:

- The internet—you know, that thing we depend on for nearly everything? The forebearer of the internet was something called ARPANET, which was a program funded by the Defense Advanced Research Projects Agency (DARPA), part of the Defense Department, in the 1960s.

- GPS—that contraption in our phones that relieves us from having to read a map or find a destination using our internal compass. That started as a program called NAVSTAR, created in the 1970s by the US Military.

- iPhone touchscreen—was originally created by a company called FingerWorks, which was founded by a professor and one of his PhD students at the *state-funded* University of Delaware. They both received grants from the National Science Foundation and CIA.

- The government–university partnership—was expanded in the 1950s and 1960s to further innovation in national security, public health, and the economy, broadly. The federal government increased funding to research universities, which led to significant wholesale discoveries and enormous enhancements to quality of life. Lasers, radar, synthetic insulin, blood thinners, magnetic resonance imaging (MRI), computers, and rocket fuel are among the myriad of innovations in which university research has played vital role. In addition, graduates of these schools have founded loads of new businesses that have employed millions of people.

- SIRI—either you love her or hate her. But that little voice inside your iPhone that recognizes even the most asinine requests like "how many jellybeans can fit in an empty can of Monster Energy Drink?" was discovered by the government in a spin-off of DARPA (the geniuses that created the internet).

- Scores of new drugs trace their foundational compounds to the research made possible by our tax dollars at the National Institute of Health (NIH). Their budget of $30 billion, which President Trump attempted to cut each time around, has been critical in funding these new compounds. While drug companies mainly focus on developing and commercializing the drugs, they would not have made all that profit without the help of government.

- Shale gas—despite what you hear about these adventurous entrepreneurs who discover shale gas all by themselves, the government has sunk a lot of resources into the technology that spawned it. The Morgantown Energy Research Center, which was owned and operated by the Department of Energy, and the Bureau of Mines launched the Eastern Gas Shales Project, which Mazzucato writes, "demonstrated how natural gas could be recovered from shale formations . . . the federal government opened the Gas Research Institute, funded through a tax on natural-gas production, and spent billions of dollars on research into shale gas."

- The government also developed 3D geologic mapping technologies for fracking through a subsidiary of the DOE, Sandia National Laboratories.

- I'm sure you are at least somewhat familiar with Elon Musk or his companies: Tesla Motors, Solar City, and SpaceX. Would you believe they are, as Mazzucato puts it, "surfing a new wave of state technology"? Well, they did benefit from $4.9 billion as of 2016 of support from federal, state, and local governments in the form of grants, tax breaks, investments in construction of factories and underwritten loans.

- In addition, the government creates demand for Musk's products by giving tax credits and rebates to customers who purchase clean energy products like solar panels and electric cars.

- The government purchased $5.5 billion worth of procurement contracts with SpaceX and $5.5 billion (as of 2016) for the National Aeronautics and Space Administration (NASA) and the US Air Force.

- Tesla also benefited from a publicly funded loan guarantee of $465 million. *And* Tesla, SolarCity, and SpaceX have received and benefited from direct investments in game-changing technologies by the Department of Energy—battery technologies and solar panels— and by NASA with rocket technologies. SpaceX is using them in business transactions with the International Space Station.

- Beginning around World War II, the government invested significant capital in aerospace, defense, and the subsidization of suburban living. They built roads and backed mortgages that guaranteed income so workers could own homes and cars and purchase other mass-produced expensive goods.

Not only does the government assist at the supply end (like government subsidies for businesses as well as investment in business like Tesla) but also on the demand side, with the proliferation of these awesome technologies the market has adopted. In 2016, more Tesla cars were sold in Norway than in the United States, because the Norwegian government financially supports policies of buying *green*. So, by my calculation, that's supply-side support from the United States' government with demand-side support from Norwegian government.

Mazzucato isn't fazed about Republicans, media, and corporate America bashing the government. In fact, she barely bats an eye because we've come to expect this skullduggery, hypocrisy, and biting-the-hand-that-feeds attitude for some time now. Private business profits off the back of government innovation and then turns around and ghosts them like a bad date. Mazzucato puts it less colorfully: "This shouldn't come as a surprise—the State has been behind the development of many key technologies that are later integrated by the private sector into breakthrough innovations ... But all we hear in the media is the one-sided myth of the lone entrepreneur."

Even in instances where private enterprise *seemed* to be the protagonist, like the automobile revolution in America, it was, in fact, the government. The State established the facilitating conditions for putting cars on the road en masse (new street regulations, road construction works, licensing, traffic rules, etc.). When manufacturers began mass-production, for instance, the government invested in both the essential technologies and their dispersal across the economy.

Yet private business and Republicans are quite stubborn. They will not offer praise or give credit to the government but would rather bash it. "Government is the problem," said Ronald Reagan.

Imagine a country where business and government worked in a harmonious partnership. Where one did not verbally assault and try to defund the other. Where the risks and profits were more evenly distributed. Imagine how much better that country's support for *every* citizen would be.

The rest of the world emulates us, but not for reasons congressional Republicans think (high flying, unshackled private enterprise). Because the US model—what the US actually did—was based on *more*

State, not less. Apparently, we need to learn a lesson or two, as well, a critical part of which, Mazzucato writes, "should be to learn how to organize, direct and evaluate State investments, so that they can be strategic, flexible and mission-oriented. Only in this way will top minds find it an 'honor' to work for the State." Presently, this is not the case. Government-funded research, for example, continues to drop rather dramatically year after year.[1]

I want to clear up a key point: Mazzucato is *not* saying to replace private industry with the State, like libertarians want to reduce government or just flat out kill it. There's a natural division of labor that should be respected. The critical strategy for government is not to do the things that private individuals are doing already and make what amounts to minor improvements, but to do those things that are currently not done at all. But this, as Mazzucato notes, "requires the public sector to have vision and confidence—increasingly missing today." We are told over and over that governments are these lumbering evil places that kill innovation, and government should stay out of markets except to fix them when they're broken. Some conservatives don't even believe the State should do that!

The government needs to be more than just a fixer of markets. Because private industry can't take the risks that the public sector can (moonshots, we call them, in space, technology, cancer, etc.), we depend on government to be a highly functional innovating machine, and not the conservative caricature of a bloated hamster. A 2012 *Economist* article on the future of manufacturing encapsulated this common conception: "Governments have always been lousy at picking winners, and they are likely to become more so, as legions of entrepreneurs and tinkerers swap designs online, turn them into products at home and market them globally from a garage. As the revolution rages, governments should stick to the basics: better schools for a skilled workforce, clear rules and a level playing field for enterprises of all kinds. Leave the rest to the revolutionaries."[2]

Thanks, economics writers, for that lesson in producing stuff. But you left out the fact that nearly every technology that makes smart phones *smart* owes its funding or research to the government. Of course, guys like Steve Jobs were crucial to Apple's success, but simply writing off the public contribution as just some fat referee huffing and puffing down the floor calling fouls is just plain stupid. Much to the surprise of Silicon Valley's techno–libertarians, Uncle Sam created and funded innovations that are *critical* to their jobs and success. So next time you hear an engineer railing against the government, tell them not to bite the hand that feeds them.

A final point on moonshots. In 2006, John Graham, Campbell Harvey, and Shiva Rajgopal conducted a comprehensive survey that examined how senior financial executives determine which projects they undertake. Specifically, the researchers asked about "what earnings benchmarks they care about and which factors motivate executives to exercise discretion and even sacrifice economic value, to deliver earnings." A whopping 78 percent of the CFOs said they would destroy economic value (i.e., not invest in critical long-term projects) in exchange for short-term earnings that pleased Wall Street.[3] Whoa! Over three-quarters would forgo significant long-term investments in potentially transformative technologies in order to smooth quarterly earnings. In other words, it seems as though private market is setting up executives of companies to be destructively short-sighted.

14

WISCONSIN VS. MINNESOTA: A CASE STUDY

"The state of our state is strong and improving every day. The economy is dramatically better, and our finances are in great shape. Thankfully, the days of double-digit tax increases, billion-dollar deficits, and major job loss are gone."

—FORMER GOVERNOR OF WISCONSIN SCOTT WALKER

"Our new pro-growth tax policy. It will be like a shot of adrenaline into the heart of the Kansas economy."

—FORMER KANSAS GOVERNOR SAM BROWNBACK

WHAT AND WHY?

IF YOU WANT PROOF of radical conservative policy going head-to-head with sensible Democratic priorities, look no further than the Midwest. Back in 2010, Minnesota and Wisconsin took divergent economic paths. Minnesota elected a reasonable, nonideological Democrat in Mark Dayton as governor, while Wisconsin elected Trump-loving

pay-fealty-to-the-right-wing-gods Scott Walker, who several Republican pundits call "kind of a dumbass," and who once entertained the
idea of building a wall along the Canadian border, stretching from New
Hampshire.[1] As I mentioned previously, Walker was married on Ronald
Reagan's birthday so that his wedding anniversary would coincide with
it. To celebrate the occasion(s), he admittedly bought mac 'n' cheese
and red, white, and blue jellybeans (Reagan's favorite foods).

Dayton and Walker differed on how to conduct their state's economy, as you may guess. Dayton initiated a range of progressive policies,
from raising the minimum wage to strengthening social programs and
labor standards to increasing public investment in infrastructure and
education. Walker went down the predictable (failed) route of cutting
taxes, shrinking government, and weakening unions. The diverging fortunes of these two states illustrate not only the disastrous effects of
Republican policies but expose guys like Scott Walker to be frauds.

We can easily compare Minnesota and Wisconsin, because they
have similar geographies, population, climate, and workforce, and
they're right next to each other. The Economic Policy Institute analyzed the data in 2017 (seven years on) to see how they performed. And,
well, I'll just turn it over to them: "There is ample data to assess which
state's economy—and by extension, which set of policies—delivered
more for the welfare of its residents. The results could not be clearer:
by virtually every available measure, Minnesota's recovery has outperformed Wisconsin's."[2]

Their report describes how Minnesota's and Wisconsin's economies
have performed since 2010 on a host of key dimensions, and discusses
the policy decisions that influenced or drove those outcomes.

Key findings include:

• Job growth since December 2010 has been markedly stronger
  in Minnesota than Wisconsin, with Minnesota experiencing
  11.0 percent growth in total nonfarm employment, compared

with only 7.9 percent growth in Wisconsin. Minnesota's job growth was better than Wisconsin's in the overall private sector (12.5 percent versus 9.7 percent) and in higher-wage industries, such as construction (38.6 percent versus 26.0 percent), and education and health care (17.3 percent versus 11.0 percent).

- From 2010 to 2017, wages grew faster in Minnesota than in Wisconsin at every decile in the wage distribution. Low-wage workers experienced much stronger growth in Minnesota than Wisconsin, with inflation-adjusted wages at the 10th and 20th percentile rising by 8.6 percent and 9.7 percent, respectively, in Minnesota versus 6.3 percent and 6.4 percent in Wisconsin.

- Gender wage gaps also shrank more in Minnesota than in Wisconsin. From 2010 to 2017, women's median wage as a share of men's median wage rose by 3 percentage points in Minnesota and by 1.5 percentage points in Wisconsin.

- Median household income in Minnesota grew by 7.2 percent from 2010 to 2016. In Wisconsin, it grew by 5.1 percent over the same period. Median family income exhibited a similar pattern, growing 8.5 percent in Minnesota compared with 6.4 percent in Wisconsin.

- Minnesota made greater progress than Wisconsin in reducing overall poverty, including child poverty, as measured under the Census Bureau's Supplemental Poverty Measure. As of 2016, the overall poverty rate in Wisconsin, as measured in the American Community Survey (11.8 percent), was still roughly as high as the poverty rate in Minnesota at its peak in the wake of the Great Recession (11.9 percent, in 2011).

- Minnesota residents were more likely to have health insurance than Wisconsin residents, with stronger insurance take-up of both public and private health insurance since 2010.

- From 2010 to 2017, Minnesota has had stronger overall economic growth (12.8 percent versus 10.1 percent), stronger growth per worker (3.4 percent versus 2.7 percent), and stronger population growth (5.1 percent versus 1.9 percent) than Wisconsin. In fact, over the whole period—as well as in the most recent year—more people have been moving out of Wisconsin to other states than have been moving in from elsewhere in the US. The same is not true of Minnesota.

What's the moral of the story? Even though congressional Republicans scream about how trickle-down economics will (one day) be our crown and savior, and about how lifting up those not in the top 1 percent is *socialism* and holds back our economy, the reality of the situation is very different. If you take anything from this book, let it be that Republican economic policies have never worked as advertised.

15

WHERE THE GOP HAS GOTTEN US

(A Comparison to Western Countries)

"The Republican Party leans much farther right than most
traditional conservative parties in Western Europe and
Canada, according to an analysis of their election manifestos.
It is more extreme than Britain's Independence Party and
France's National Rally (formerly the National Front), which
some consider far-right populist parties. The Democratic Party,
in contrast, is positioned closer to mainstream liberal parties."

—SAHIL CHINOY, RESEARCHER FOR THE MANIFESTO PROJECT

WHAT AND WHY?

THE ABOVE FINDINGS ARE based on data from the Manifesto Project,
which reviews and analyzes each line in a party's manifesto, i.e., the documents that lay out the party's goals and policies. Then, using recurring

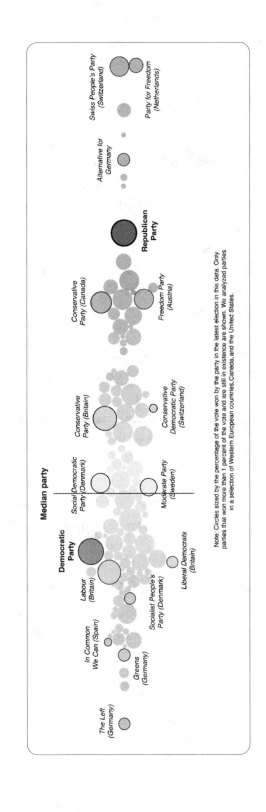

The Left
(Germany)

In Common
We Can (Spain)

Greens
(Germany)

Socialist People's
Party (Denmark)

**Democratic
Party**

Labour
(Britain)

Liberal Democrats
(Britain)

Median party

Social Democratic
Party (Denmark)

Moderate Party
(Sweden)

Conservative
Party (Britain)

Conservative
Democratic Party
(Switzerland)

Conservative
Party (Canada)

Freedom Party
(Austria)

**Republican
Party**

Alternative for
Germany

Swiss People's Party
(Switzerland)

Party for Freedom
(Netherlands)

Note: Circles sized by the percentage of the vote won by the party in the latest election in this data. Only parties that won more than 1 percent of the vote and are still in existence are shown. We analyzed parties in a selection of Western European countries, Canada, and the United States.

topics, such as market regulation and multiculturalism, the project creates a common scale for comparison. Whereas European conservatives believe in climate science, gun control, and voting rights, for example, the Republican Party believes that manmade climate change is hoax, guns should have no restrictions, and voting should be curtailed (particularly in city centers with large populations of Black people).

When I say the Republican Party is extreme, it helps to use political parties in other countries around the world as a point of comparison. For example, how conservative is the Republican Party of the United States compared with the Tories of the United Kingdom or the Alternative for Germany party (Neo-Nazis)? Or how liberal are the Democrats compared with the Labour Party or the Greens of Germany? What you'll find is that Republicans lean farther to the right of nearly every other major Conservative party in the Western world (except the Neo-Nazis). As a direct result, we, as a country at the mercy of Republican extremism, are woefully behind other wealthy nations in nearly every major socio-economic category. Now that doesn't sound very American, does it? Conservatives' disdain for government, the corporate takeover of Washington, and the massive push for privatization have all left our country in an exceedingly precarious position. Aside from consumer goods like cars, TVs, and home furnishings, we've seen, at the very least, a big increase in costs for health care, housing, and education. Congressional Republicans will say it is because those industries have more government involvement than the others. What they fail to admit is that the United States has, probably, the *most* privatized education, health care, and housing among wealthy Western democracies, and the worst outcomes per dollar spent. In other words, other countries have more *socialism* than we do, by far (see the previous chapter titled "Privatization"). Not to mention, ours is the worst regulated. Of course, these are hugely complex topics whose causes and solutions have been argued ad nauseam. But why would *more* privatization be the answer to our predicament? Why would prioritizing profit above all else be the solution to ailing industries that cannot, by nature, feasibly operate in a profit-making model?

––––––––––

FURTHERMORE, CONGRESSIONAL CONSERVATIVES ENDLESSLY blather on about "job-killing regulations."[1] When one side is so antagonistic towards, say, consumer safety or environmentalism, it becomes very difficult to write good laws. Legislation becomes so watered down and convoluted that it ends up doing more harm than good, and it generally benefits the well-established companies over the small and upstart ones.

FOOD AND SAFETY

Take laws (or the lack thereof) for food safety and quality of food. We rank poorly, to say the least, when it comes to these two categories. In 2014, for example, Oxfam, the prominent foundation that tackles global poverty, ranked the US 21st in the world for food safety. Although we have cheap food (which boosts the ranking), we score poorly in quality and population-health risks. On the latter measure alone, the US ranks in 120th place, with similar rates of obesity and diabetes as Saudi Arabia and Egypt. That's largely because of diets in poorer communities, where, as Oxfam puts it, "processed, high-fat foods are often significantly cheaper than fruit and vegetables."[2]

POPULATION HEALTH

Surprise! We have the worst rate of chronic diseases, primarily diabetes, in the industrialized world. The Commonwealth Fund ran the data on eleven countries: Canada, the US, and nine in Europe. The average rate for all eleven was 17.5 percent. Our rate? Twenty-eight percent. Nearly one third of the population![3] The next highest was Canada at 22 percent. Probably because they also eat our food. It is worth mentioning that our collective poor health has likely contributed to the worst COVID-19 pandemic outcomes in the world. People were hospitalized and died at a higher rate in America because we are so rabidly unhealthy.

The Commonwealth Fund measured the population rates of obesity, as well. The average country was 21 percent. Ours? Forty! The next highest was New Zealand, at 32 percent.

What makes Americans any more naturally susceptible to being fat and unhealthy than, say, Canadians? The answer: nothing. The only difference is that our government regulation is not only lax but goes unenforced.

The real source of our health problems is the poor quality and unhealthy food that is making us sicker long-term (think not about Coca Cola poisoning you, but rather they are slowly deteriorating your health). According to Bloomberg Health Index, our overall heath ranking is 73. Italy's is 92, Spain's is 93, Norway's is 89, Japan's is 91 (the higher the ranking, the better outcome). The US ranks 35th overall, just behind Costa Rica and ahead of Bahrain.[4]

Under President Trump, the FDA was being derelict. It was supposedly looking after the health and safety of our food, but, as *Science Magazine* has reported, when Trump was elected, the FDAs enforcement actions plummeted.[5]

Obama's FDA took official action 1,879 times per year, on average, sending out 1,532 warning letters and thirty-five injunctions between 2010 and year 2016. During Trump's time in office, there were 1,040 actions, 1,033 warning letters, and twenty-six injunctions per year. That's a huge decrease! We should be strengthening our enforcement of food violations, not loosening them.

DRUG AND ALCOHOL DISORDERS

It's hard to make a direct connection between regulation and addiction, but the fact that the United States is by far the leading distributor in the industrialized world of addictive pharmaceuticals to its citizens (and we spend the most *by far* on prescriptions) is due in no small part to very lax regulation and oversight—on the pharmaceutical companies and on doctors writing prescriptions. It's no mystery that prescribed drugs lead to abuse of illegal drugs and alcohol. We have neither the mental health counselor capacity nor the mental health care infrastructure that other countries have to handle problems like these. We are swimming against the tide of addiction. How did we get to this point? Do congressional conservatives honestly think less government is the answer to this massive public health crisis?

According to Our World in Data, the only country with similar drug and alcohol disorders by percentage of population is Russia.[6]

POLLUTION AND CLIMATE CHANGE

I do not need to make the point that manmade climate change is real. Pollution is killing our planet. The incessant attacks on scientists and government policy from private actors is a primary reason the United States continues to pollute so much. We are in the top 5 in CO_2 emissions per capita and second in absolute emissions behind China.

EDUCATION

The incessant attacks by private corporations and free marketeers have manifested in a general lack of funding and a hatred toward our public education system. As a result, according to the Programme for International Student Assessment, the US is ranked 13th for reading, 36th for math, and 16th for science. We land somewhere between Iceland and Lichtenstein, overall. To be clear, we have never been at or near the top, so these rankings are not worse than they were, say, ten years ago. However, after years of funding school choice and voucher programs, and of defunding public schools, we have not managed to move the needle. Imagine—what if we had spent all that time supporting and reforming the public sector rather than attacking it?

POVERTY

I often hear congressional Republicans say that the cure to poverty is free markets and capitalism. To reduce people's dependency on welfare and turn them into bootstrapping, hard-working young men and women, the argument goes, we need to let the market decide their fate. We have some of the least-generous welfare programs in the entire Western world. That signals to me that a lot of powerful people have decided that the market is better at helping poor people than the government. But we have one of the worst poverty rates in the world. To be clear, there are several contributing factors to this phenomenon, including but not limited to health care, schooling, and employment. But those are also parts of government that private enterprise and conservatives would like to defund and, effectively, manage themselves, unaccountable to the public.

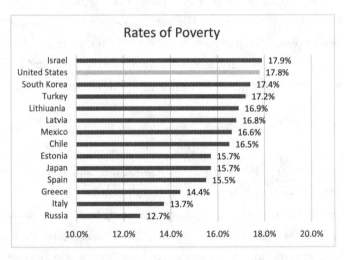

Source: Statista (2018)

HEALTH CARE

On health care spending, we are, frankly, horrendous. We spend more per citizen than any other country *by a mile*, and we have some of the worst outcomes among Western countries. In addition, we have one of the most—if not *the* most—privatized health care system in the world, based on private health care spending.

According to the Commonwealth Fund, we have one of the worst health care systems among the wealthy countries of the Western world. We rank 11 out of 11.[7]

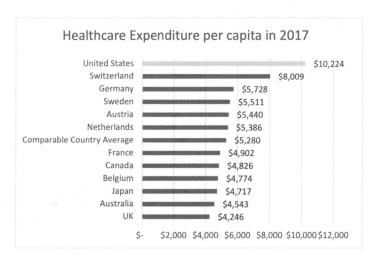

Source: Commonwealth Fund

We don't even have enough hospital beds, which became depressingly evident during the COVID-19 crisis. Compared to the rest of the world, it would appear we'd be lucky to find a hospital bed. In Finland, there are roughly four and a half beds per person, in Germany, over eight, and in Japan, over thirteen. In the US we have fewer than three beds per person.

Our average out-of-pocket monthly expenditure on diabetes, per person, is $360. The next highest is India at $112. Japan is $70. The UK is $65.[8]

On paid maternity leave . . . what paid maternity leave?

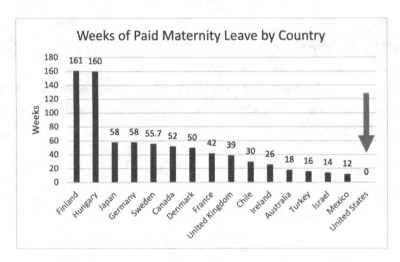

Source: Commonwealth Fund

We don't go to the doctor as much as the citizens of other wealthy countries, because we're afraid of the costs. We have the fewest doctor visits *and* the lowest number of doctors per capita. We average 4 doctor visits per person a year, while Germany averages 10. We have 2.6 doctors per 1,000 people; Norway has almost 5.

And yet, when the going gets tough, we end up in the hospital more often anyhow. We have the second highest rate of hospitalizations in the industrialized world for preventable diseases such as diabetes and hypertension. And we have the highest rate of avoidable deaths in the world, by a lot: 112 per 100,000, compared to 86 per 100,000 in Germany.

Our life expectancy is below other comparative countries: 78.6 years, compared to 83.6 in Switzerland, 82.7 in Norway, and 81.3 in the UK.

Health care procedures cost *way* more here, too. The average price of bypass surgery is nearly $100,000. In the next-highest country, Switzerland, the price is about $35,000.

An MRI? In the United States, $1200. The next highest? The UK, $800.

Appendectomy: $17,000 in the US. Next highest, UK, $8000.

Hip replacement: $30,000 in the US. Next highest, Australia, $20,000.

How about pharmaceuticals?

For nearly every popular prescription drug, the US pays through the roof compared to its peers. And we are the sickest population. How does that figure?

- Avonex, which treats multiple sclerosis? We pay $1700. Average? $270

- Dulera, which treats asthma? We pay $23.95. Average? $0.49

- Januvia, which treats diabetes We pay $15.70. Average? $1.40

- Xarelto, which is a blood thinner? We pay $13.95. Average? $2.59

- Trulicity, which treats diabetes? We pay $182.55. Average? $30.23

- Humira, which treats arthritis? We pay $2,440. Average? $494

The list goes on and on.

HOUSING

The US housing market is unaffordable for the average renter. An analysis from Harvard recently explored why. "The greater apparent cost burdens," it reported, "reflected a variety of factors, including differences in characteristics of the housing stock and differences in tax burdens, as well as measurement problems."[9] The analysis also revealed that we "exhibit more pervasive and severe rental affordability problems than the other countries considered." Not only that, "the greater cost burdens found among renters in the US, relative to most of the other countries, are largely due to greater income inequality, to more limited housing assistance programs, and perhaps to a housing supply consisting of units that are larger and better-equipped but that are consequently more expensive." To clarify, the US housing market is segmented, so aggregate data can be misleading (i.e., big cities are expensive, rural areas are not), but this is a good starting point.

I'm not suggesting that congressional conservatives and Republican presidents are the sole bearer of responsibility for these, frankly, pathetic states of affairs. These are incredibly large and complex issues with many stakeholders and decision-makers. But what I am saying is that through their efforts to wreak havoc, gridlock government, and crush efforts to reform lobbying, they advertently produce considerably worse outcomes for the vast majority of us. Other Western countries don't have a radical and powerful caucus like the GOP causing such immense damage.

ARTIFICIAL ELECTORAL ADVANTAGES

16

TRUMP'S "VOTER FRAUD"

"While it has long been understood that the Democrat
political machine engages in voter fraud from Detroit
to Philadelphia, to Milwaukee, Atlanta, so many other
places. What changed this year was the Democrat party's
relentless push to print and mail out tens of millions
of ballots sent to unknown recipients with virtually no
safeguards of any kind. This allowed fraud and abuse to
occur in a scale never seen before. Using the pandemic
as a pretext, Democrat politicians and judges drastically
changed election procedures just months, and in some
cases, weeks before the election on the 3rd of November."

—DONALD TRUMP (2020)

"Mr. President, you have not condemned these
actions or this language. Stop inspiring people
to commit potential acts of violence."

**—GABRIEL STERLING,
A VOTING SYSTEMS MANAGER IN GEORGIA (2020)**

"You're outnumbered. There's a f****** million of us
out there and we are listening to Trump—your boss."

**—ONE OF THE RIOTERS WHO
STORMED THE CAPITOL ON JANUARY 6, 2021**

WHAT?

BEFORE LEAVING OFFICE, PRESIDENT Trump disgraced our electoral processes and, consequently, our democracy. He perpetuated the Big Lie, which asserted the 2020 election was fraudulent and he was the actual winner. It was the most flagrant, undemocratic, and brazen attempt to sow mistrust in our political system. Ever. Since election day, November 3, 2020, Trump and most of the GOP have spread so many lies and so much misinformation, they were attempting to not only change the outcome of the election, but create an entirely new and alternate universe where up is down and down is up. Consequently, he inspired a violent insurrection at the Capitol building, which saw six people killed and hundreds more injured, not to mention the desecration of our distinguished institutions. We will be reeling from that day for years, if not decades, to come.

WHY?

SOWING DISTRUST IS A key Republican strategy because their interests are aligned with small, weak government. The more government looks stupid and ineffective, the more Republican officials looks like white knights riding in on their horses to tout their virtuous records and save the day. Imagine the modern-day GOP as simply a singular-minded, amoeba-like entity whose primary purpose on this planet is to ridicule their employer and muck up the job they were elected to do. This benefits, of course, the private interests of the wealthy.

SINCE ELECTION DAY 2020, there have been thousands of tweets, social media posts, and articles crafted to sow distrust in our sacred electoral process, the lifeblood of our democracy. The party of "personal responsibility" and "participation trophies are tearing at the fabric of society" has now forgone any last shred of accountability it had left—its candidate lost fair and square—to claim en masse that the election was fraudulent, led by none other than Dear Leader. (At the time of this writing, two-thirds of Republicans think Trump was cheated out of the election).[1]

Once upon a time, the Republican Party believed in fair and free elections. You did not observe guys like Thomas Dewey, Gerald Ford, George H. W. Bush, John McCain, or Mitt Romney announce the day or week after they lost the election that the Democrat cheated. Or that there were millions of fraudulent ballots cast in swing states. Or that the manufacturer of the voting machines was involved in some nefarious plot with Hugo Chavez—who's been dead for seven years, mind you—to sabotage our election and throw it for Joe Biden, of all centrists.[2] Did you?

What tickles me pink is not their incessant and dangerous cries of fraudulent elections, though it's pretty jarring. No, what gets me the most is that (as I'll detail later in this section) *they* are the ones who perpetrate all types of voter suppression and try to make it harder for people to vote. *They* engage in most of the dirty trickery. *They* admit to disenfranchising millions of voters for the good of the party. *They* love to gerrymander and draw districts that look like a "snake by the lake" (though, admittedly, Democrats love to gerrymander too). *They*

cling to this unbearably undemocratic system we have in this country, lest they become the minority party permanently. Never mind the
fact they receive less votes in nearly every presidential and congressional election nationwide since 2000 by a wide margin. The hypocrisy
is outstanding!

What is in store for the future of elections will depend entirely on
whether the GOP's effort, in what seems to be a half whining, half earnest push for authoritarianism, will dissipate, and whether President
Joe Biden will be able to govern as if he has a mandate. After all, he beat
Trump by over seven million votes and won all-important swing states
by a margin larger than Trump beat Hillary in 2016. I'd say that's a clear
victory, wouldn't you?

17

UNFAVORABLE DEMOGRAPHICS

"You cannot rebuild your civilization with somebody
else's babies. You've got to keep your birth rate up,
and that you need to teach your children your values."

—RABID TRUMP-SUPPORTING REPUBLICAN STEVE KING

WHAT?

DEMOGRAPHICS ARE A-CHANGING IN this country. In 1965, the White
population was around 85 percent. In 2015, it was about 65 percent. By
2050, White people will no longer make up more than half of the population
of this country. The combination of immigration and low birth
rates has shifted and will continue to shift the racial makeup dramatically.
That said, plenty of light-skinned Latinos and even some Asians
will self-identify as White, which will keep the number higher than
expected. To use a historical example, a demographer in 1900 would
have looked at large numbers of Italian and Jewish immigrants as evidence
the country was getting less White.

WHY?

THIS FRIGHTENS REPUBLICANS, the White, old, undereducated party who wants to build a meaningless wall at the US–Mexico border. And it should. Because they haven't adapted to changing demographics. They've continued to appeal mostly to White male voters. Hence, they are losing badly in each of the other demographics.

IN 2012, MITT ROMNEY won 59 percent of the White vote while winning independents. In 2004, he would have been elected president with the same result. In 2000, he would have won in a landslide. But in 2012 he lost.

As I mentioned, the share of White people in this country is decreasing and has been since we kept records of population statistics. Each year, the share of the pie of Hispanics, Blacks, and Asians, among other minorities, grows larger, scaring Republicans. That they will no longer be the majority dominant race is the most earth-shattering, monumentally defeating idea.

The Changing Face of America, 1965–2065

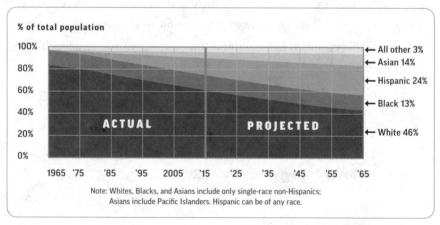

Note: Whites, Blacks, and Asians include only single-race non-Hispanics;
Asians include Pacific Islanders. Hispanic can be of any race.

Source: Pew Research

Republicans have barely appealed to anyone but straight, White Christians. That's particularly true today:

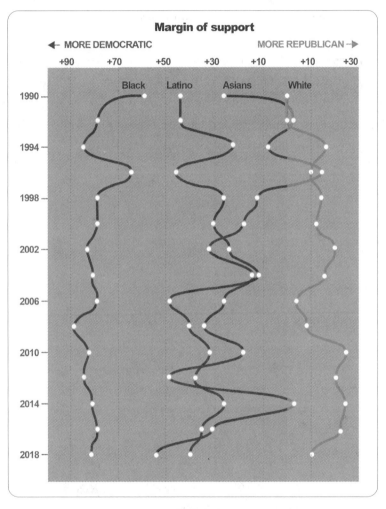

NY Times

As the country continues to get more diverse, the Republican Party is essentially alienating those minorities while becoming older, Whiter, and less educated. I don't know what that looks like to you, but to me it looks like an impending disaster. For the GOP.

Twenty-six percent of Republican voters are sixty-five and older. Over 80 percent are White, and nearly 60 percent are White without a college degree.[1] Boy, oh boy. That seems like a winning combination in a country founded and built by immigrants with rapidly changing demographics.

So rather than expand their platform to include programs that help people of color, they instead court the worst fears of White voters—with stuff like socialism! Suburban invasion! And "You won't recognize your country if Democrats are elected." These play well with bigots and places where there is a lack of diversity, ironically.

18

GERRYMANDERING

"We are in the business of rigging elections."

—FORMER REPUBLICAN STATE SENATOR MARK MCDANIEL (1998)

WHAT?

BY SYSTEMATICALLY MANIPULATING THE shape of voting districts, the GOP has concentrated power with White voters. This tactic is called *gerrymandering*, and it is a feature of life in Republican-controlled states. In other words, the party in charge gets to draw the boundaries of districts the way it sees fit. In the House and state legislative districts, this has a lot of benefits, because they can draw districts to essentially maintain majority rule for a really long time and make it difficult for the minority party to recapture power. See the diagram below. To be clear, Democrats in blue states engage in gerrymandering as well. They are guilty of producing artificially high Democratic majorities. At the same time, they are willing to do away with the undemocratic process through federal legislation.

WHY?

WHEN A PARTY KNOWS they've run out of ideas on which to campaign and no one is going to vote for their policies—when all else fails to secure victory—gerrymander! I shouldn't say no one, because they have convinced a lot of people to vote against their own economic interests, but I digress. Gerrymandering is the key for Republicans in holding power, and they will stop at little to push the boundaries of bonkers. As stated, Democrats are guilty, too (Maryland, New York, California), but they do it far less frequently and are willing to give it all up for fairly drawn districts. Meaning, no more gerrymandering. Republicans will not allow it, because frankly, that would be the end of the Republican Party.

HERE'S A GREAT VISUAL: Let's say you have a state that is 60 percent Democratic and 40 percent Republican. If you divide up the districts evenly (as in the middle graphic below) Democrats will maintain an advantage in each of the districts, for a 5-0 advantage. That's not really fair to Republicans. They should get at least one or two seats, right? However, if you draw the lines like the map on the right, Republicans get a 3-2 advantage in House seats. "Hang on one second there, chief. You mean to say representatives will really draw districts like snakes and Tetris pieces? And it's legal?" Yeah, that's what I'm saying.

While gerrymandering has been around for over 200 years and has been occasionally abused during this time, there had, until recently, been no systematic effort to feed it a dozen 24-ounce Monster Energy drinks and a prescription of Adderall. Well, that's just what Republicans did in 2010 after winning a lot of state legislative seats and governorships. They called their caffeine and amphetamine orgy experiment REDMAP. But, of course.

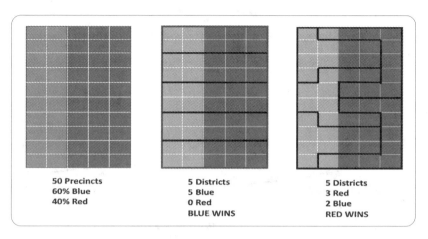

50 Precincts	5 Districts	5 Districts
60% Blue	5 Blue	3 Red
40% Red	0 Red	2 Blue
	BLUE WINS	RED WINS

Source: Washington Post

The journalist Vann Newark has reported extensively on REDMAP. "REDMAP was a spectacular success," for several reasons, he writes. First, on the bank of a massive fundraising effort in critical states with changing demographics—Wisconsin and North Carolina—Republicans overwhelmed 2010 state legislative races in rural districts, totaling nearly 700 state legislative seats, the largest increase in modern electoral history. Likewise, Republicans spent $300 million more than Democrats did in that year's gubernatorial races, which earned them six additional governorships, including the sought-after governor's mansions in Wisconsin, Ohio, Michigan, and Pennsylvania, which were all flipped from Democratic incumbents. New technology makes it much easier to gerrymander, too.[1]

To give you a sense of how bad it got, take the North Carolina election results in 2018. Democrats won 48 percent of the vote statewide, Republicans 50 percent. Yet Republicans walked away with nine of the thirteen congressional seats, or nearly 70 percent of them.

Notice how after 2010, when Republicans gerrymandered their states, they needed the same number of votes to secure more seats.

Republican Share of U.S. House Seats and Votes in North Carolina

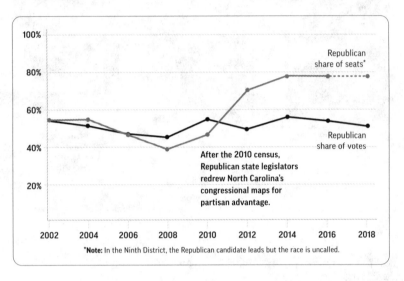

After the 2010 census, Republican state legislators redrew North Carolina's congressional maps for partisan advantage.

Republican share of seats*

Republican share of votes

*Note: In the Ninth District, the Republican candidate leads but the race is uncalled.

Source: Brennan Center

In Pennsylvania in 2016, Democrats won 46 percent of the vote and picked up only five out of eighteen seats. Less than 30 percent! Effectively, the Democrats have to win by more than 10 percent statewide in order to get a majority. What happened to one person, one vote?

America's Most Gerrymandered Districts

Most gerrymandered Congressional districts in the U.S. according to compactness index*

1. Maryland's 3rd district

2. Texas's 33rd district

3. Illinois's 4th district

4. Texas's 35th district

5. Louisiana's 2nd district

* ratio of the area of the district to the area of a circle with the same perimeter
Source: Washington Post

19

SENATE

"The Senate is an Irredeemable Institution"

—THE TITLE OF A PAPER BY THE DATA SCIENTIST
(AND MY FRIEND) COLIN MCAULIFFE (2019)

WHAT?

SENATORS REPRESENTING APPROXIMATELY 10 percent of the population of the United States (about 33 million people) can block every single piece of major legislation in Congress supported by the other 90 percent (300 million people).[1] You read that right. Wyoming, North and South Dakota, and Alaska—and any of the next sixteen smallest states—can block sweeping, meaningful bills that would provide untold benefits to a majority of the country. What a crock, huh? Needless to say, the Senate is an abomination that must be overhauled. It is the most powerful undemocratic governing body in the Western world. Even if you can find another, do you think it proves my thesis wrong about how undemocratic it is? And congressional Republicans want to keep it this way.

WHY?

THE LESS POPULOUS THE state, the Whiter and more rural it is (the exceptions are New Mexico and Hawaii). Look at California (population 40 million, with 16 million minorities) versus Wyoming (population 578,000, with 64,000 minorities). Like I said, 10 percent of the population can block every single piece of major legislation—and major legislation is usually progressive (e.g., New Deal, Great Society, Obamacare). And we need *major* legislation to fix a lot of the problems in this country (e.g., the economy, health care, inequality). So, locking in White rural voters without college degrees by making empty economic promises and fear mongering about communism works quite well for the GOP and megadonors.

I'd like to begin with a smidgen of history. In the 1790s, when the Senate was starting to find its stride, the largest state, Virginia, had a population of about 750,000, although 40 percent were Black slaves and barred from voting, and the smallest state, Delaware, had a population of about 60,000, of which 3 percent were Black and unable to vote. So, the ratio of the voting population in Virginia and Delaware was around 8 to 1. Today, the largest state, California, has a population of nearly 40 million, and the smallest state, Wyoming, has a population of 578,000, for a ratio of 68 to 1. Sixty-eight to one! And growing wider every year. Why should a state get equal representation with 1/68th the population?

The founders weren't very far-looking with respect to the Senate. The original Connecticut Compromise was not a thorough consideration of what might happen, say, 200 years from then. As the author and journalist Matt Yglesias writes, "These are enormous disparities to live with as essentially a matter of historical happenstance. Not only was the Connecticut Compromise defining Senate representation a hard-nosed plan that didn't reflect any clear larger principle, the boundaries of the states themselves were not drawn the way they are today for any particularly far-sighted reason."[2] If California had been divided up into several South Carolina-sized states, it could be easily eight or ten separate entities—each with about six times the population of Wyoming—rather than the current imbalance. Yglesias continues, "When currently big states like Texas, Illinois, Florida, and California were admitted to the Union, their populations were not particularly large, and there was no specific intention to downweight their residents." Indeed, they didn't! The founders did not account for how big these states would get. And, most likely, they would be appalled at the disparity. If a time-machine could only bring back John Adams and have him feast his eyes on this hideous mutant of a governing body, he would set his so-called fellow conservatives straight.

THE SENATE IS RACIST

I know that may sound *woke*, but it's true: The Senate discriminates based on race. How you ask? Well, first of all, as I pointed out above, the slave population of a state was not counted when it came time to vote. Racist. When Blacks eventually earned the right to vote, they immediately added to the total of the state they were in but got no additional representation. And no remedy was made on account of this. Racist. Democrats want to change this, and Republicans continue to intentionally thwart these efforts, so Black and brown folks continue to be underrepresented. Racist.

White people who have not attended college (read the GOP's base) are overrepresented in Senate. The dark bar in the following graph represents the percentage of voting eligible population in the country and gray bar represents the percentage of the group that's represented in the Senate. White noncollege people have 53 percent representation

in the Senate, while they represent 47 percent of the total voting eligible population. Hispanics, Blacks, and Asians are underrepresented.

The Senate Gives Disproportionate Power
to the Most Populous Demographics

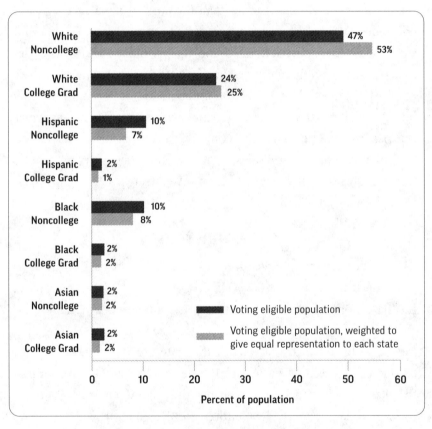

Source: US Census and Data for Progress

And the trend is getting worse. In 1960, the number of noncollege Whites who identified as Republican was no different than the
national average for Republicans. College-educated Whites, however,

voted Republican 20 points more than the national average. Today? White noncollege-educated voters make up a gigantic portion of the Republican electorate, and there is no slowing that down.[3]

Furthermore, because of these shifts in voting patterns, Republicans will increasingly need fewer votes to win a majority in the Senate, and Democrats will need more. The nightmare that keeps on trucking! For example, in 2014, Republican candidates won 52 percent of the vote and gained nine Senate seats. In 2016, Democrats won 54 percent of the vote and gained only two seats. And two years later in 2018, even if you disregard the California senate race (where both candidates were Democrats because no Republican did well enough in the first round to qualify for round two), Democrats won 54 percent of the vote and lost two seats. In other words, the Democrats collectively won senate races by more than 10 percent nationally and still *lost* seats.[4] Whoa!

It's worth repeating that senators representing only 10 percent of the population can block major legislation from passing, including overwhelmingly popular legislation like gun safety and climate change. All but one demographic thinks gun safety is more important than gun rights: noncollege-educated White people. And guess which group, to this point, has dictated the outcome of legislation?

Or immigration. Given Donald Trump's perception of immigrants from Mexico, it's no surprise noncollege-educated White people are the only group who, above the national average, believe immigrants commit more crime.[5]

20

THE ELECTORAL COLLEGE

"It's embarrassing. I think if most Americans knew what the origins of the Electoral College is, they would be disgusted."

—PROFESSOR PAUL FINKELMAN (2016)

WHAT AND WHY?

EVERY FOUR YEARS WE elect our president through an antiquated system called the *Electoral College*. Congressional Democrats would love to change this, but Republicans desperately want to keep it. For the same reason they want to preserve the undemocratic abomination that is the Senate, the GOP grip on power depends on this process that *allocates* votes to each state based on population and was created to deal with the slavery problem. In other words, the Electoral College was developed by wealthy, White land owners as a way to protect their status.

THE ONLY TIMES IN the last 110 years that the winner of the presidential election lost the popular vote were in 2000 with George W. Bush and in 2016 with Donald Trump. Before that, William Henry Harrison defeated Grover Cleveland in 1888, despite getting fewer votes. We all remember that barn burner, amirite?

'Ol Willy Will snuck it out with an eleventh-hour surge in Roanoke. No, none of us remember that. But anyone reading this book has likely been around for the last two elections, meaning that the picture is getting increasingly unfair for Democrats. The field is tilting more and more in favor of Republicans despite losing the popular vote by three million in 2016. Three million is a lot of voters. What other country in the world has a system where the winner of the popular vote by millions loses the election? I can't remember my AP Comparative Government curriculum very well, but I don't think there are many, if any.

Joe Biden won the 2020 election by more than seven million votes. In other words, Biden beat Donald Trump by the population of Wisconsin and North and South Dakota combined. He won the popular vote by nearly a 4.5 percent margin. And yet, Biden won the states that gave him the victory (Georgia, Arizona, and Wisconsin) by a total of only 50,000 votes.

BRIEF HISTORY

Like you, I learned in grade school that our country adopted a system where states are apportioned a certain number of votes—instead of deciding the president by popular vote—because small states needed to compete fairly with big states. It seemed a little unfair that the winner of Virginia (the largest state at the time) would always decide the winner of the presidency, and poor little Delaware (the smallest) was kind of shut out. That explanation never made a lot of sense to me for the simple fact that a voter in Virginia carried the same weight as one anywhere else. If Virginia was a close race for the Democrat, Republicans in Delaware could come to the rescue and push their candidate over the popular vote margin. Similar to today, a voter in Ohio should be worth the same as a voter in California. Not all people in California vote Democrat, just like not all people vote Republican in Alabama. The popular vote total would be a totally fair way to determine the presidency (i.e., first past the post, runoff, rank order, instant runoff). Why is the governor of each state chosen by the popular vote and not by electoral votes apportioned to each county?

But the more accurate explanation for the Electoral College—that congressional conservatives will deny to their graves—is slavery. During the 1800s, slaves did not have the right to vote, and slaves made up enormous portions of the populations in the South in 1860. We're talking 45 percent of Florida, 55 percent of Mississippi and 57 percent of South Carolina.[1] In a direct election, the South would lose the presidency every single time. The Electoral College was a compromise. Black people were counted as three-fifths of a person and could not vote, so votes of slave owners were magnified, sometimes by several hundred. Without the Electoral College, antislavery candidate John Adams would have beaten slave-owning Thomas Jefferson, and the South understood this well.

Even though the Electoral College is a severely antiquated system founded on the basis of human ownership, the South and congressional conservatives today will never agree to ratify the Constitution to elect our president by popular vote, despite the fact that every democracy in the world chooses its president like this, because this would mean forfeiting their minority-majority status.

Worth noting is that one of the reasons the Electoral College is a bigger problem now is because fewer states are competitive between Republicans and Democrats. In the twentieth century, a competitive election was competitive in most states. That is no longer true. Also worth noting is that inmates are counted in the congressional district and Electoral College voting just like slaves were. Even though prisoners are unable to cast votes, they are counted toward the population of a state and district, which magnifies the votes of the rest of the voters in the district. And being that Black people, particularly Black men, are incarcerated at significantly higher rates than are White men, there's a reason why the comparison between slavery and criminal justice system is justified.

21

SOUTHERN STRATEGY

"You want to know what this was really all about? The Nixon campaign in 1968, and the Nixon White House after that, had two enemies: the antiwar left and Black people. You understand what I'm saying? We knew we couldn't make it illegal to be either against the war or Black, but by getting the public to associate the hippies with marijuana and Blacks with heroin, and then criminalizing both heavily, we could disrupt those communities. We could arrest their leaders, raid their homes, break up their meetings, and vilify them night after night on the evening news. Did we know we were lying about the drugs? Of course we did."

—JOHN EHRLICHMAN, FORMER ADVISOR TO RICHARD NIXON AND CONVICTED FELON, IN AN INTERVIEW ABOUT THE DRUG WAR (1994)

"From now on, the Republicans are never going to get more than 10 to 20 percent of the Negro vote and they don't need any more than that . . . but Republicans would be shortsighted if they weakened enforcement of the Voting Rights Act. The more Negroes who register as Democrats in the South, the sooner the Negrophobe whites will quit the Democrats and become Republicans. That's where the votes are. Without that prodding from the Blacks, the whites will backslide into their old comfortable arrangement with the local Democrats."

—KEVIN PHILLIP, NIXON AIDE AND LOVER OF THE WORD NEGRO (1969)

WHAT?

ON MY FACEBOOK NEWSFEED, I have seen plenty of ahistorical, click-bait, word salad messages from prominent conservative authors that describe how the Southern strategy wasn't a *thing* (Candace Owens, ahem), but it was.[1] Congressional Republicans in the 1960s, '70s, and into the '80s and '90s needed an electoral strategy to shore up their White racists in the South by appealing to their racism! Contemporaneous with Goldwaterism, but obviously taken further than his failed presidential candidacy, the Southern strategy was highly effective in solidifying the White demographic as Republicans' core constituency and ensuring Black people vote Democratic.

WHY?

REPUBLICANS WANTED TO RETURN to a bygone era of segregation (and, for probably a decent portion, to slavery) where Whites and Blacks did not comingle by law, and the Southern strategy was the vehicle for doing so. In the wake of the passage of the Civil Rights Act and the Voting Rights Act, which effectively ended Jim Crow laws, they were desperate for a chance to preserve the heritage.

ACCORDING TO WHITE HOUSE Chief of Staff H. R. Haldeman, Richard Nixon "emphasized that you have to face the fact that the whole problem is really the Blacks. The key is to devise a system that recognized this while not appearing to."

How did they do it? Here's a verbatim excerpt from a 1981 interview with Lee Atwater, Republican strategist and senior aide to Reagan and George H. W. Bush, which includes racist language:

Atwater: As to the whole Southern strategy that Harry Dent and others put together in 1968, opposition to the Voting Rights Act would have been a central part of keeping the South. Now [Reagan] doesn't have to do that. All you have to do to keep the South is for Reagan to run in place on the issues he's campaigned on since 1964 [...] and that's fiscal conservatism, balancing the budget, cut taxes, you know, the whole cluster....

Questioner: But the fact is, isn't it, that Reagan does get to the Wallace voter and to the racist side of the Wallace voter by doing away with legal services, by cutting down on food stamps?

Atwater: Y'all don't quote me on this. You start out in 1954 by saying, "Nigger, nigger, nigger." By 1968 you can't say "nigger"—that hurts you. Backfires. So you say stuff like forced busing, states' rights and all that stuff. You're getting so abstract now [that] you're talking about cutting taxes, and all these things you're talking about are totally economic things and a byproduct of them is [that] Blacks get hurt worse than Whites. And subconsciously maybe that is part of it. I'm not saying that. But I'm saying that if it is getting that abstract, and that coded, that we are doing away with the racial problem one way or the other. You follow me—because obviously sitting around saying, "We want to cut this," is much more abstract than even the busing thing, and a hell of a lot more abstract than "Nigger, nigger."

President Nixon manifested the Southern strategy through campaigns of "Law and Order" and "States Rights." Sounds eerily familiar to President Trump's 2020 campaign, doesn't it?[3] While Goldwater was its biological father, his racism was too overt to gain widespread popularity (but not for the Deep South that voted for him in *droves*). It was Nixon's slippery coded language and appeals to law and order that softened the bigotry's edges. Like baby-proofing furniture. Let's call it racism-lite.

Goldwater's campaign, originally called Operation Dixie, did, in fact, launch the Southern strategy by directly opposing the 1964 Civil

Rights Act. Because of this, he won the Deep South in a *landslide*, including 87 percent of the vote in Mississippi. Alas, he didn't do so well in the non-Confederate states. He lost every one of them, excluding his home state of Arizona.[4]

But Goldwater laid the groundwork for Nixon. Angie Maxwell, a professor at the University of Arkansas, writes that Nixon understood the risks of such an open campaign against civil rights and "instead coded their racial appeals." Here come the dog whistles! "The 'silent majority' of White Southerners that the candidate needed to attract," she writes, "understood that Nixon's call for the restoration of 'law and order,' for example, was a dog whistle, signaling his support for an end to protests, marches and boycotts, while his 'war on drugs' played on racialized fears about crime." As for enforcement of the Civil Rights Act, she notes that Nixon "adopted a stance of 'benign neglect,'" a term coined by Nixon's urban affairs advisor, Daniel Patrick Moynihan, future Democratic Senator from New York). Separately, the avowed racist Democrat-turned-Republican of North Carolina Strom Thurmond put it this way: "If Nixon becomes president, he has promised that he won't enforce either the Civil Rights or the Voting Rights Acts. Stick with him."[5]

That marked a powerful, yet subtler turn of the Southern strategy, and it remained until 1976, when we got a respite from the dog whistles (at least from the executive branch) with Jimmy Carter. However, it came back in full force with the election of Ronald Reagan. With Atwater's help, at one of his first campaign stops at the Neshoba County Fair in Mississippi, Reagan defended "states' rights" and began anew trashing the "welfare state." The author Dan Carter writes, "Reagan showed that he could use coded language with the best of them, lambasting welfare queens, busing, and affirmative action as the need arose."[6]

Maxwell notes that the Southern strategy involved much more than just racism. It involved the religious community and women in the household—and it continued on for *decades* in Republican politics.

"The GOP successfully fused ideas about the role of government in the economy, women's place in society, White evangelical Christianity and White racial grievance," Maxwell wrote, "in what became a 'long Southern strategy' that extended well past the days of Goldwater and Nixon." In four decades, Republicans fine-tuned their song and dance and won the devotion of Southern Whites (and their sympathizers nationwide) by reorganizing their party in the Southern White mold.

The strategy worked remarkably well. Just take a look at the percentage of committee chairs from the South in 2005 and 2006 (the last time Republicans held Congress): twenty. By 2018 it was seventy!! Holy cow! That's a Southern takeover by the party if y'all have ever seen one![7]

22

DIRTY TRICKS

"If we don't win this election, you'll
never see another Republican."

—DONALD TRUMP (2016)

"In an illegal late-night coup, Nevada's clubhouse Governor
made it impossible for Republicans to win the state. Post
Office could never handle the Traffic of Mail-In Votes without
preparation. Using COVID to steal the state. See you in Court!"

—DONALD TRUMP (TWITTER, AUGUST 3, 2020)

"Traditionally it's always been Republicans
suppressing votes in places."

**—JUSTIN CLARK, TRUMP CAMPAIGN ADVISOR IN WISCONSIN, WITH AN
"OOPS, I JUST SAID THE QUIET PART OUT LOUD" MOMENT (2019)**

WHAT AND WHY?

IT HELPS TO IDENTIFY the difference between negative campaigning
and dirty tricks. Not that you are champing at the bit to learn the distinction, but the difference is that negative campaigning, while lots of

times laughable and gross, is sourced from at least a kernel of reality. Like, "Don't vote for Hillary Clinton, she's as crooked as they get."
Clinton is certainly not the most crooked politician, but the embel-
lished claim is based on her being at least a little crooked. Dirty tricks,
on the other much greasier hand, are deliberate, dishonest attempts
to sabotage a candidate or a group of voters, as when Trump says,
"rampant fraud in mail-in ballots." They are sometimes conspiratorial
in nature and have little to no bearing on the quality of the candidate
or election. And a lot of the time they are illegal.

———————

TO FURTHER ILLUSTRATE THE difference, let's examine one of the
more rancid ads from Vice President George H. W. Bush when running
against Governor Mike Dukakis in the 1988 presidential campaign:
the Willie Horton ad. It was so off-putting and racially offensive that
at the time it was something of a revolution in political campaigning.
Willie Horton, a Black prisoner convicted of murder, was released on
a prison furlough program in Massachusetts. While out on furlough,
Horton kidnapped a young couple, stabbed the man, and raped the
woman. Bush featured a menacing photo of Horton and under a photo
of Dukakis, which read "Allowed Murderers to have Weekend Passes."
Never mind that the weekend furlough program was created under a
Republican governor in 1972 in Massachusetts—Dukakis had to defend
himself against the charges.[1]

Nevertheless, both the program and Horton were real, and the
details surrounding the crime were accurately relayed. The images,
while racist dog-whistle-y and grotesque, were true to form, though
obviously dramatized.

Contrast this with Pizzagate, a wild conspiracy theory in 2016 in
which absolutely nothing was true. The story about how hacked
emails of John Podesta, Hillary Clinton's campaign manager, somehow

contained secret incriminating messages about a human trafficking and child sex ring run by high-ranking officials in the Democratic Party, spread like wildfire on social media. Apparently, this sex ring was being run out of the basement of Comet Ping Pong, a popular Washington, DC, pizzeria. Funny, right? It wasn't so funny when a North Carolina man drove 500 miles and shot up the place in order to *rescue* the children.[2] A side note: conspiracy theories are well-worn as a strategy Republicans have employed for seventy-plus years, usually when they fail to compete in the marketplace of ideas.

See the difference between Willie Horton and Pizzagate?

To comprehend the universe of dirty tricks, it helps to comprehend their utility in the context of election season. Because elections are conducted over a relatively short period, their impact, if well-timed, can be devastating. As long as the dirty trick isn't debunked by the time voters cast ballots, they are highly effective, because elections cannot be rerun. Brookings Fellow Elaine Kamarck notes the primary objectives of dirty tricks:

- create doubt around a candidate's character, and negative campaigning does this too;
- confuse the voters about the election;
- break into the opponent's sphere and get information on them;
- affect the actual outcome by interfering with the counting process.

Dirty tricks are mostly a Republican affair. I've compiled a list of some of the most notable by candidate and description:

- George W. Bush, during his primary campaign against John McCain in 2000. "Would you be more or less likely to vote for John McCain... if you knew he had fathered an illegitimate Black child?" McCain and his wife Cindy had adopted a dark-skinned girl from Bangladesh in 1991, and that child, Bridget, was campaigning with them in South Carolina. This dirty trick is known as a "push poll" and was a deliberate attempt to play the racism and adultery card.[3]

- Richard Nixon. The term "Canuck," a derogatory term for French Canadians, was falsely used to describe how the Democratic presidential candidate, Edmund Muskie, had referred to New Hampshire residents during the primary.

- George Walsh (R), the swift boat campaign against John Kerry. Kerry had served in Vietnam and was awarded a purple heart, a bronze star, and a silver star. In 2004, his service and his heroism in war stood in contrast to President Bush, who had not gone to Vietnam and who got into the Air National Guard through his political connections. Sowing doubt about Kerry's war record was important to the Bush campaign. In the spring of 2004, a group called Swift Boat Veterans for Truth, composed of Vietnam veterans who claimed to have been with Kerry during the incidents he was awarded medals for, began to hold press conferences and buy television ads questioning each of his medals. A long-time critic of John Kerry (for his later public opposition to the Vietnam War) wrote a book about Kerry called *Unfit for Command*.[4]

- Steve May, Republican trickster in Arizona. He populated the ballot in 2010 with a third-party candidate with the express purpose of siphoning votes from the Democratic candidate (similar to Republicans and Kayne West in 2020). He recruited a bunch of homeless people to run on the Green Party ticket. Among them, Kamarck notes, were "a tarot card reader with less than a dollar to his name who was signed up to run for State Treasurer, a homeless man who went by 'Grandpa' on the streets who was recruited to run for the State Senate, and a young street musician who was recruited to run for a seat on the Arizona Corporation

Commission." Democrats and the Green Party were incensed and filed a lawsuit, to no avail.[5]

- Scott Walker (R). In 2012, Wisconsin Democrats mounted a recall effort against Walker because he was such a corrupt, mindless governor. His recall election was scheduled for June 5th. As the date approached, voters reported getting robocalls that told voters that if they had signed recall petitions, they were not required to vote in the recall election, which was a lie. Walker ended up winning the race with 53 percent of the vote.[6]

- Lee Zeldin (R). Another well-worn dirty trick is to confuse the voters about when they're supposed vote. In 2018, Zeldin sent out flyers informing his constituents that they had to send in their absentee ballots by November 6. There was only one problem. The deadline was actually November 5. Any ballots received after that were not counted. Zeldin's campaign said, "Oops, it was a printer mistake," and denied any wrongdoing. The only problem with that excuse was that the Zeldin campaign made the same "mistake" in 2016 as well.[7]

- Roger Stone (R). What *hasn't* this guy done? His entire career has been one enormous dirty trick, scheming on behalf of Republicans up and down the ticket, from Nixon to Trump, to candidates in local races. Stone: "Attack, attack, attack—never defend" and "Admit nothing, deny everything, launch counterattack."[8]

Those who care about governments doing the most good should be concerned about dirty tricks. They are incredibly deceitful, toxic, and, often times, illegal. More importantly, they likely alter thousands of votes unfairly. With the advent of internet politics, it's gotten a lot worse. Kamarck continues, "Every dirty trick that was possible before the internet is possible today. The biggest difference is that they are cheaper, faster and easier to hide."

Under President Trump, these tricks became even dirtier and more, shall we say, Sovietesque. As you probably are aware, Special Counsel Robert Mueller indicted a busload of Russian nationals for the crime of interfering in our elections. In fact, the director of National Intelligence warned that Russians continued to meddle in our elections in 2020, and Republicans did less than zero to stop it. They encouraged it![9] But this type of interference is nothing new, only the source wasn't a foreign adversary: It was the White House. The Cold War historian Michael Koncewicz explains that the tactics currently employed by the Russians began with Nixon and have only been gaining steam since. "Russian meddling is the culmination of a style of politics launched during President Richard M. Nixon's 1972 reelection campaign," Koncewicz writes. "Nixon's administration ushered in a Watergate culture in which winning, not governance, was the end goal of politics."[10]

Watergate didn't end the divisiveness. Nixon and his minions, Roger Stone and Paul Manafort, both senior Trump campaign officials, fomented it. The technology has improved, but the strategies are the same. Nixon was the shepherd of the dirty tricks campaign. He developed explicit plots to attack his enemies, establishing a climate of corruption that led to Watergate. The fraudulent mailers were just the tip of the iceberg; the administration utilized the power of the federal government to do its bidding. Throughout 1971 and 1972, Nixon and his inner circle of advisors progressively pressured the Internal Revenue Service to target people on their enemies list, including suspiciously auditing scores of antiwar activists and Democratic Party officials. Koncewicz: "Administration officials who were morally opposed to Nixon's plan ultimately blocked its implementation, but the attempt exposed Nixon's desire to win by any means necessary."

Nixon may have resigned from the presidency, but his legacy thrives. Lee Atwater, Republican campaign strategist for Bush and Reagan, made a career out of dirty tricks and disseminating fake news. During the 1988 campaign, he circulated a story about Michael Dukakis being treated for depression (not true).[11] Karl Rove, Bush's senior political advisor, was allegedly the source of a rumor during the 1994 gubernatorial campaign that Texas governor Ann Richards, a Democrat, was a lesbian.[12] Trump and the GOP sabotaged the postal service, engaging in massive voter suppression in swing states and pushing conspiracies about mail-in ballot fraud and Democrats drinking the blood of infants.[13, 14] I'd say Nixon's legacy is *booming*.

What can we do about putting a stop to this practice? Well, Democrats want to secure elections against fraud and dirty tricks, particularly from Russia and other foreign adversaries. But the GOP has zero interest, because having insecure elections helps them. Senate Republicans recently blocked an effort by Democrats to pass three election security-related bills and an effort to require campaigns to alert the FBI and FEC about foreign offers of assistance—legislation to provide more election funding and ban voting machines from being connected to the internet. One particularly appalling example is Senator Marsha Blackburn of Tennessee, who blocked every single one of these requests. Because of the Senate's arcane rules, any one senator can ask for unanimous consent to pass a bill, but any one senator can also object and block their requests.[15]

23

CORPORATE MONEY

"We now know that government by organized money
is as dangerous as government by organized mob."

—FDR (1936)

I AGREE WITH A lot of well-informed political scientists and observers that *money in politics* is one of the most destructive issues of our time. Probably in no other Western democracy is so much of government bought and sold—and by such a small group of very powerful rich people. They exert an outsized influence on everything concerning our political system, from who gets elected to how the rules of the game are played to laws that are written. In a so-called democracy, it's a tragedy so few people have that much power. Call me an idealist, but 96 percent of Americans agree![1] They also believe money is the cause of dysfunction in our politics. You can't get 96 percent of people to agree on the color of the sky! The other 4 percent are just trolling or very rich. And there is currently only one party interested in doing anything about it: the Democrats.

WHY?

CORPORATIONS AND RICH PEOPLE love to buy politicians, so those politicians write laws that effectively increase their wealth and power.

TO ROUND OUT THE stats for you:

- Again, 96 percent of all Americans—including Republicans—believe money in politics is to blame for the dysfunction of the US political system.

- Eighty-four percent of Americans—including 80 percent of Republicans—believe money has too much influence in politics.[2]

- Seventy-eight percent of Americans say we need sweeping new laws to reduce the influence of money in politics.[3]

- Seventy-three percent of registered voters have an unfavorable opinion of the Supreme Court's *Citizens United* decision (the infamous SCOTUS case that opened the last line of defense against money in politics).[4]

Though there are plenty of wealthy people who donate to Democrats—and who are, sadly, fiscally conservative and support the same terrible policies as their compatriots on the other side of the aisle—it's mostly a Republican affair. Hacker and Lowentheil write, "Rich conservative voters make for well-funded Republican campaigns. Right-wing super PACs have flourished, not just because conservatives were the first to embrace them, but also because the superrich are mostly Republicans." In the 2012 election cycle, Karl Rove's Crossroads GPS disclosed that nearly 90 percent of its financial support came from about twenty donors, with two donors making up $20 million. In a joint report, Democrats and US Public Interest Research Group revealed that more than 50 percent of the $230 million in Super PAC donations from individuals came from only

forty-seven people, who gave at least $1 million. Hacker and Lowen-
theil write, "This is one of the reasons why the GOP has moved so far to
the right over the past generation: The rising sway of lobbying and big
donors has generally reinforced their policy leanings."[5]

For Democrats, this poses a serious dilemma. They have to match
Republican heft by appealing to wealthier donors, who on economic
issues don't see eye-to-eye with the middle class and the poor.

And for big business, especially the financial sector, campaign contributions are just one arrow in the quiver. Another ginormous one is
direct spending to influence policy. Hacker and Lowentheil: "Indeed,
for most organized interests, spending on elections is just the training season; the real games begin once elected officials start governing."
David Koch, from the Kochtopus, puts it bluntly: "Our main interest is
not participating in campaigns.... Our main interest is in policy." Now,
consider this: Koch and his brother, Charles, spent more in the 2012
election cycle than the John McCain for President campaign did in all
of 2008. No person should have that much power.

Being Republican pays. Democrats just can't match the special-
interest and financial-heft power that Republicans wield per donor.
The need for money filters out a lot of the strong progressive candidates and shifts a candidate's position to the right.

Money is a primary determinant in candidates winning office, but
it's probably less a cause than a correlate. A better explanation is that
when wealthy donors see candidates who are winning, they will give to
their campaigns in order to garner favors from them down the road.
According to FiveThirtyEight, a well-known polling website, since 2000,
nearly all of the House candidates that have raised the most money
win their election. For the Senate, it's nearly 85 percent.[6]

FUNDRAISING SUCKS

The job is perpetual and nonstop, and it's a drain for both the candidates and our politics. The never-ending quest for campaign dollars

absolutely destroys the legislative function of the House, in particular. Because elections are every two years, candidates and incumbents are compelled to fundraise, even as soon as members are elected. This obviously constrains the time they can spend in Washington doing the job they were elected to do (to legislate). For Democrats, the job is even harder because they, on average, don't rely on one or two big fish donors, as Republicans do. They depend more on small donors, from whom raising money takes more time. A couple of caveats: 1. Most members of the House do not have competitive general elections (though the primaries are more so) and 2. All members of Congress have to raise money according to FEC regulations, so small donors are still important in that sense (super PACs are different, obviously).

If you want to get a sense of how crummy it is for members, here's an interview by CBS's Norah O'Donnell with former Congressman David Jolly on fundraising:

Rep. David Jolly: We sat behind closed doors at one of the party-headquarter back rooms in front of a white board where the equation was drawn out. You have six months until the election. Break that down to having to raise $2 million in the next six months. And your job, new member of Congress, is to raise $18,000 a day. Your first responsibility is to make sure you hit $18,000 a day.

Norah O'Donnell: Your first responsibility—

Rep. David Jolly: My first responsibility—

Norah O'Donnell:—as a congressman?

Rep. David Jolly:—as a sitting member of Congress.

Norah O'Donnell: How were you supposed to raise $18,000 a day?

Rep. David Jolly: Simply by calling people, cold calling a list that fundraisers put in front of you. You're presented with their biography. So please call John. He's married to Sally. His daughter, Emma, just graduated from high school. They gave $18,000 last year to different candidates. They can give you $1,000 too if you ask them to. And they put you on the phone. And it's a script."

So glad we elect our representatives to do this, aren't you?

What are the Democrats doing about it?

Since at least 2009, when Senator Dick Durbin (D) introduced the Fair Elections Now Act to publicly fund campaigns, they have been trying to scrub politics of corporate money. A whole roster of Democratic candidates supported this bill—and one Republican, John McCain. The legislation provided for eligible Senate candidates to earn grants, matching funds, and television vouchers to run competitive campaigns sourced from small-dollar contributions, rather than depend on funding from wealthy donors and big corporations.[7]

Congresswoman Pramila Jayapal has called for a constitutional amendment for the regulation of campaign finance. It has seventy-two co-sponsors, all Democrats. Another amendment proposed by Congressman Ted Deutch has garnered 220 co-sponsors, including one Republican (whoa, we're making progress).[8]

Sounds great to me—and to 96 percent of the country who agree—so what's stopping it? The GOP!

How does the US stack up against other Western countries on elections and campaign financing?

For one, the United States has no limits on campaign spending. Though there are a few other Western democracies that have no-limits as well (because there's no need), they are still constrained by a variety of factors such as restrictions against advertising on TV (good or bad). From a European perspective, as Paul Waldman of the *Washington Post* writes, "The idea of someone spending two or three million dollars to get a seat in the national legislature, the way American House candidates routinely do, would seem absurd."[9]

Here's a sample of what politics is like in Germany. Olga Khazan in the *Atlantic* writes, "The scale of the campaign is just the start. There are no attack ads, because, in post-reunification in German culture," a German politician explained to Khazan, "the attacker would always turn out to be the loser. It is completely different from the States. And I'm happy about it."[10]

Khazan goes on:

Each party creates just one ninety-second ad for the entire election, and the number of times it airs on TV is proportional to the number of votes the party garnered in the last election. For smaller parties like Die Linke, that means about four times on each of the two major channels. Total. In the last US election, Barack Obama and Mitt Romney spent more than $400 million each on TV ads, the vast majority of them negative.

Unlike in the US, where elected officials start campaigning almost as soon as they set foot in office, German campaigns last only six weeks. Because there are small parties to soak up hardline voters and a lack of primaries—candidates are put on a party list—there's no need for candidates to swing wildly toward a radical base for one part of the election, then gradually ease toward the center as it wears on.

Die Linke's total campaign cost just four million euros (about $5.4 million)—for all of its candidates across the entire country. The German government and party-membership dues pay for the bulk of the country's political campaigns, while corporate and individual donations make up just one-third of the cost.

Imagine the vast sums of money saved, all the acrimony and division avoided, and the focus on real policy. An American kid can only dream.

REPUBLICANS AND DEMOCRATS AGREE ON A LOT

Surprisingly, rank-and-file Republicans and Democrats agree on a wide variety of issues, but you wouldn't know it from listening to and watching congressional conservatives or conservative media.

As I mentioned, Peter Dreier aggregated surveys from 2017 in his piece "Most Americans Are Liberal, Even If They Don't Know It."[11] When it comes to the economy, 82 percent of Americans think wealthy people have too much power and influence in Washington, and 78 percent of likely voters support stronger rules and enforcement on the financial industry. On inequality, 82 percent of Americans think economic inequality is a "very big" (48 percent) or "moderately big" (34 percent) problem. Even 69 percent of Republicans share this view. On taxes, seventy-six percent believe the wealthiest Americans should pay higher taxes, and 87 percent of Americans say it is critical to preserve Social Security, even if it means increasing Social Security taxes paid by wealthy Americans. Don't tell Mitch McConnell that! On fair wages, 74 percent of registered voters—including 71 percent of Republicans—support requiring employers to offer paid parental and medical leave, and 78 percent of likely voters favor establishing a national fund that offers all workers twelve weeks of paid family and medical leave. This is the *opposite* of the Republican platform of the last forty years.

On health care, 60 percent of Americans believe "it is the federal government's responsibility to make sure all Americans have health care coverage" while 64 percent of registered voters favor their state accepting the Obamacare plan for expanding Medicaid in their state. On education, 63 percent of registered voters—including 47 percent of Republicans—favor making four-year public colleges and universities tuition-free, and 59 percent of Americans favor free early-childhood education. Concerning the environment, 76 percent of voters are "very concerned" or "somewhat concerned" about climate change, and 72 percent of voters think it is a "bad idea" to cut funding for scientific research on the environment and climate change.

The list goes on and on. I cover immigration, abortion, and gun safety in their own chapters later on. As you can observe, even though Democrats and Republicans overwhelmingly agree on major policy legislation, Congressional Republicans stand united in opposition.

24

VOTER SUPPRESSION

"The things they had in there were crazy. They had things, levels of voting that if you'd ever agreed to it, you'd never have a Republican elected in this country again."

—DONALD TRUMP (2020)

"I just want to find 11,780 votes."

—TRUMP THREATENING THE SECRETARY OF STATE OF GEORGIA AFTER HE LOST THE STATE BY 11,779 VOTES (2020)

"We are focused on making sure that we meet our obligations that we've talked about for years. Voter ID, which is gonna allow Governor Romney to win the state of Pennsylvania, done."

—MIKE TURZAI WITH A BIG "OOPS, DID HE JUST SAY THE QUIET PART OUT LOUD?" MOMENT (2012)

WHAT?

WHY IS ACCESS TO voting even a discussion? Every citizen over eighteen years old should have the right to vote (and they do, except in some cases like former felons in states with those restrictions). But legally possessing this constitutional right is not the issue here. The issue is why are there *barriers* and *obstacles* to voting? And why are they purposely enacted to prevent certain people from voting? Do we have restrictions on free speech, free assembly, freedom of religion, or freedom to petition government for redress of grievances? Hundreds of thousands of voters have been disenfranchised over the last decade through Republican voter-suppression efforts.

WHY?

IT'S QUITE SIMPLE. The tighter the voting restrictions, the fewer people vote. Specifically, the restrictions are targeted at poor inner-city Blacks, who tend to vote overwhelmingly for Democrats, and Latinos, particularly in the West and Southwest. So, Republicans purge them from the voter rolls and enact voter ID laws to prevent them from voting. As Trump said, if everyone voted, there wouldn't be any more Republicans. It's an exaggeration, but not by much.

————

LET'S BEGIN WITH THE most egregious perpetrator of them all in recent memory (at least since Black people in the South won the right to vote in 1965): Governor Brian Kemp of Georgia. When he was secretary of state, he stood on stage at a campaign event in 2018, when he was running for governor, and said voter turnout "continues to concern us, especially if everybody uses and exercises their right to vote."[1] He's the damn secretary of state! The guy responsible for counting the votes. During the election for governor in 2018, calls for him to recuse himself from the election process fell on deaf ears, though *he* was in charge of vote counting.

What did Kemp do to disenfranchise Black voters in Georgia? He tossed their applications in the garbage by claiming mistakes were made, like the signature wasn't a perfect match, or they didn't vote in the prior election, or the person didn't write the four-digit zip-code extension (you know, the ones no one uses except the post office or credit-card companies). As the journalist Jamil Smith reported,

"Kemp's recent decision to suspend more than 53,000 voter applications, 70 percent of which were filed by Black residents, for violating the state's 'exact match' verification standard has drawn attention to his penchant for restrictive voter laws and purging of voter rolls. American Public Media reported last week that Kemp purged an estimated 107,000 voters last year simply because they didn't vote in the prior election. He is also being sued for leaving more than 6 million Georgia voting records open to hacking. . . . Kemp, a staunch Trump supporter who has echoed the president's language concerning Russia's election interference, was also the only secretary of state in the nation to refuse Homeland Security's help prior to the 2016 election."[2]

Nothing gets my blood boiling more than a politician from the Deep South who hasn't learned anything from the Civil Rights Era. Or I should say, he has learned a lot; now that the violations of voting rights from that era are illegal, politicians like Kemp have adapted and adopted new strategies, officially racially neutral, to prevent Blacks from voting.

In March 2021, Kemp and the Georgia House of Representatives wasted no time in passing a 100-page omnibus bill to restrict voting.[3]

After the 2020 election and the 2021 Senate runoffs in Georgia where the state voted for a Democratic president in Joe Biden and not one but two! Democratic senators, Republicans are absolutely petrified. But rather than update and improve their platform to attract more voters, they target the process by which people cast their ballots, all the while justifying these restrictive measures with Trump's outrageous claims of voter fraud. It is deeply pathetic and dangerous.

Even though there is next to zero evidence of rampant voter fraud, that's what a majority of the GOP uses to rationalize their voter suppression. Particularly regarding mail-in ballots, given the COVID-19 pandemic, and in-person voting posing health risks.

"Get an ID!" they say. Yet there are other ways to identify a person. Do you know who doesn't have government-issued ID? About 8 percent of voting-age White people and 25 percent of voting-age Black people, according to the Brennan Center, one of the leading think tanks that researches voting rights.[4]

The Brennan Center has reported in great detail on the subject throughout the country. They found that 11 percent of all eligible voters who lack the required photo ID must travel to a designated government office to obtain one. Though lots of people have trouble making this trip. In the ten states with restrictive voter ID laws:

- Nearly 500,000 eligible voters do not have access to a vehicle and live more than ten miles from the nearest state ID-issuing office that's open more than two days a week. Many of them live in rural areas with dwindling public-transportation options.

- More than ten million eligible voters live more than ten miles from a state ID-issuing office that's open more than two days a week.

- Regarding eligible Black voters, 1.2 million live more than ten miles from an ID-issuing office that's open more than two days a week, as do 500,000 eligible Hispanic voters. People of color are more likely to be disenfranchised by these laws since they are less likely to have photo ID than the general population.

- Many ID-issuing offices maintain limited business hours. For example, the office in Sauk City, Wisconsin, is open only on the *fifth Wednesday* of every month. But only four months—February, May, August, and October—have five Wednesdays. In other states—Alabama, Georgia, Mississippi, and Texas—many part-time, ID-issuing offices are in the rural regions with the highest concentrations of people of color and people in poverty.

- More than one million eligible voters in these states fall below the federal poverty line and live more than ten miles from an ID-issuing office that's open more than two days a week. These voters may be particularly affected by the significant costs of the documentation required to obtain a photo ID. Birth certificates can cost between $8 and $25. Marriage licenses, required for married women whose birth certificates include a maiden name, can cost between $8 and $20. By comparison, the notorious poll tax—outlawed during the civil rights era—cost $10.64 in current dollars.

The result is plain: Voter ID laws will make it harder for hundreds of thousands of poor Americans to vote, probably more. They place a burden on a core constitutional right that should be universally available to every American citizen. More from the Brennan Center on voter suppression in individual states:

- Observe North Dakota: a federal district court found that when the state enacted its current ID law in 2017, 19 percent of Native Americans lacked qualifying ID compared to less than 12 percent of other potential voters.

- Likewise, Texas permits voters to use a handgun license to vote, but not a student ID from a state university. More than 80 percent of handgun licenses issued to Texans in 2018 went to White

Texans, while more than half of the students in the University of Texas system are racial or ethnic minorities.

- Strict voter ID law is just one of a number of racially charged voting restrictions that states have adopted this decade. For example, following the election and reelection of President Obama—and the concomitant surge in turnout by Black voters—states like North Carolina imposed new restrictions on early voting, which was disproportionately used by people of color. Sixty-four percent of Black people vote early, but only 49 percent of White people do.

- Other states imposed new restrictions on the voter-registration process. In 2019, for example, Tennessee imposed new hurdles for third-party voter registration drives in response to what the Brennan Center called a "large-scale effort to register Black voters" ahead of the 2018 election.

- In 2017, Georgia enacted an "exact match" law mandating that voters' names on registration records must perfectly match their names on approved forms of identification. In the leadup to the 2018 election, approximately 80 percent of Georgia voters whose registrations were blocked by this law were people of color, even though only 32 percent of Georgia is Black. (A lawsuit forced the state to largely end the policy in 2019.)

The voter purge rates pre- and postgutting of the Voting Rights Act by the SCOTUS are downright criminal. Republican governors pursued it with the intent to disenfranchise poor Blacks. Now, somebody might suggest to those people that they *do something* about their situation and *stop complaining.* One way they might do that, conceivably, is by voting for people who will help provide them with opportunity (jobs, education, social programs). But that avenue is cut off, of course, because they've been disenfranchised. What a terrible cycle of poverty.

Particularly in states where Republicans held both the governorship and the state legislative majority, harsh voter suppression laws were enacted.

Returning to the above "Oops, I said the quiet part out loud" moment by Mike Turzai, in red states (like Wisconsin, North Carolina, Kansas, Ohio, and Pennsylvania) where Republicans held both chambers and the governorships in the mid-2000s through 2020, budgets and taxes were slashed across the board. New restrictions on abortions cropped up, and voter protection laws were passed in the name of preventing voter fraud, even though there was virtually no evidence of fraud to begin with. What these measures did was make access to a ballot box more difficult for specific groups of Americans: minorities and younger people, the very people who came out in droves for Obama in 2008. Some new laws involved voter ID, while others shortened early voting periods and made voter registration exceedingly complicated. ("Voter ID, which is going to allow Governor Romney to win the state of Pennsylvania, done.") E. J. Dionne writes, "[Voting restrictions] were one of many marks of a conservative movement not only on the move, but also determined to use the power it had to lock in its advantages for the future."[5]

One would think, from seeing all these voter-suppression laws enacted, that voting rights and accessibility are pretty unpopular, right? I mean, voters must really hate increased access to vote freely and fairly, right? Well, not exactly. But what do you expect from congressional Republicans who carry on without regard for democracy?

According to Pew in 2018, every one of these measures below have been blocked by congressional Republicans:[6]

- Eighty-seven percent of people favored automatically updating voter registrations when people move (that's a no from congressional Republicans).

- Eighty-five percent favor requiring electronic voting machines to print a paper backup of the ballot (another no from congressional Republicans).

- Sixty-five percent support making election day a national holiday (another no from congressional Republicans).

- Sixty-five percent want automatic registration of all eligible citizens to vote (big no from congressional Republicans).

- Sixty-two percent are against removing people from voter lists if they haven't voted recently (no, because Republicans do this all the time).

It'll be a cold day in hell before Republicans agree to an election holiday. That seems pretty unpatriotic to me ... from the party who wraps itself in the American flag and sails down the intercoastal in boats with MAGA flags.

You might be saying to yourself, "Showing an ID to vote doesn't seem that bad. Democrats are making a fuss out of nothing." It sure seems that way on the surface. We show our ID for a lot of things. Buying alcohol, getting on a plane, entering a big office building. What's wrong with showing it for voting?

OK, let's perform a little experiment. Let's say you're a Republican residing in a state where my friends and I—all Democrats—occupy most of the elected positions in the local government.

We think voter fraud is a big problem because our Dear Leader said so. We would like a voter ID law to ensure there's no chance of fraud ever again. Fact-check: In April 2020, MIT performed a voter fraud study going back twenty years and found instances of fraud to be "exceedingly rare" since it occurs "0.00006 percent" of the time—about five times less likely than getting hit by lightning in the United States.[7]

So, after we pass the voter ID law—this is where a political observer may begin to question our fraud motivation—which requires you to show your driver's license to vote—my buddies and I on the oversight committee pass *another*, seemingly unrelated law, that stipulates you can only obtain your license, or renew your license, at the *local* DMV office where you live. Nowhere else. Oh, and you can no longer renew your ID by mail; you must come in person. Because . . . fraud, or the like. You have to make an appointment beforehand, to the tune of six weeks ahead of time. Lo and behold, a week before your appointment, my buddies and I begin shutting DMV offices—for *legitimate* budgetary reasons, of course—mostly in neighborhoods where Republicans tend to reside, which is, naturally, a coincidence. The nearest office now is an hour away, and since you don't have a car, you have to take two buses to get there. But that office operates on a weird schedule, like 10:30 a.m. to 2:00 p.m. every other Tuesday. Even when they are open, there is often an excuse for emergency closings (e.g., a pipe burst or there's another issue with the plumbing or HVAC). Or, we may have laid off 80 percent of the staff. Apologies, but the state coffer just doesn't have sufficient funds to perform the requisite repairs right at the moment or hire enough clerks to work the stations. All the while, my friends and I open several new, state-of-the-art DMV offices in Democratic-leaning areas, replete with refreshments, co-working stations, and extended hours. It's a shame you can't utilize those, because you don't live in those neighborhoods.

I foresee that, come time to vote, a lot more Democrats are going to make it to the polls in our imaginary state, and a lot of Republicans will be deterred, either voluntarily or will be turned away by poll workers. And when you protest, we tell you sorry, voting demands sacrifice; if it really mattered, you'd find a way to get a proper ID.

(Incidentally, in my story, you are a married woman who took her husband's last name, thus you cannot prove you are who you say you are because the name on your birth certificate does not match the name on your photo ID; regardless of which ID you show the poll workers, you'll likely be turned away from casting your vote.)

The above example is a bit of hyperbole, but requiring strict voter ID laws is, in fact, part of Republicans' scheme to deny the right to vote to people who are not voting for them. Republicans have closed down DMV offices in predominantly Black neighborhoods after enacting voter ID laws. They have created elaborate rules that result in the rejection of people who likely vote Democrat. And, they have passed laws that excessively favor certain IDs that Republicans tend to own in higher numbers while discrediting those that Democrats typically own in higher numbers. For example, in Tennessee, polling locations accept expired gun permits but reject student IDs.[8]

The DMV-office-closing strategy is particularly noxious because, while laws limiting the actual voting are subjected to strict oversight by the courts, regulatory activity to close state offices or change hours of operations are considered low-level activities subjected only to the rational-basis standard. Saying it a different way, if there is a lawsuit, the state can get away with the slimmest justification for restricting people's access to the DMV, even if we *all* know the real reason why [insert majority Republican state] did this.[9]

Ultimately, the reason why most Democrats are leery of voter ID laws is because we know they are passed in bad faith. They are meant to be an obstacle that would allow Republicans to keep Democrats away from the polls.

SECTION 4

WAR
ON FACTS

OVER THE LAST SEVENTY-PLUS years, but in earnest for the last forty years, congressional conservatives have waged war not only on proper functioning government but on our relationship with reality. They have succeeded in doing this through a variety of strategies; most notable are the creation and/or dissemination of conspiracy theories about government being an evil institution hell-bent on destroying humanity. What began as the John Birch Society in the 1950s morphed into today's QAnon. Worse, the entire party has transformed into this antiscience blob whose top priority, it seems, is to discredit scientists and industry experts. Herein is a breakdown of the conservative war on facts.

25

WAR ON SCIENCE

"Science should not stand in the way [of opening schools]."

**—FORMER WHITE HOUSE PRESS SECRETARY
KAYLEIGH MCENANY (2020)**

"Mask-wearing has become a totem, a secular religious
symbol. Christians wear crosses, Muslims wear a hijab,
and members of the Church of Secular Science bow to
the Gods of Data by wearing a mask as their symbol,
demonstrating that they are the elite; smarter, more
rational, and morally superior to everyone else."

**—ALEX CASTELLANOS, A REPUBLICAN STRATEGIST FOR
BOB DOLE, GEORGE W. BUSH, JEB BUSH, AND MITT ROMNEY**

THAT SECOND QUOTE REALLY does sum it up, doesn't it? "Members of
the Church of Secular Science." "Bow to the Gods of Data." Sure Alex,
we are simply attempting to survive a public-health crisis, that is all.
Just get vaccinated and wear a fucking mask. It's not political.

WHAT?

OVER THE LAST FORTY years, the GOP has waged a war on science, in the process weakening our institutions and our belief in the critical data they produce. Look no further than the recent COVID-19 pandemic as proof of Republican masochism. Science is fascinating and indispensable, but it can be annoying and frustrating for us emotional and agenda-driven humanoids to accept at times. It may contradict our biases or get in the way of our utopian ideals. Most of us learn to accept how science has the final say in, for example, whether to wear masks during a global airborne pandemic. The others tend to disregard science completely and create their own set of facts. Let's call them *alternative facts*, to use Kellyanne Conway's phrasing of President Trump's reality.[1] To be clear, all human beings are susceptible to doing this, but there's a clear winner. This group earns a living out from making a mockery of and *debunking* the scientific community. For the last forty-plus years, the GOP has not only ignored and discarded prevailing science but has gone one step further: They invent their own science and create elaborate conspiracy theories to prove their alternative facts. (For example, did you know that Dr. Fauci created COVID-19 in a lab beneath Comet Pizza in Washington? Or was that Hillary Clinton? Hard to keep track.) During the last forty years, the GOP has engaged in, to put it simply, a *war* on science. While the Left has had its issues accepting scientific consensus, the Republican Party has made denialism part of their platform. Quite literally.

WHY?

PRIVATE ENTERPRISE, CONGRESSIONAL REPUBLICANS, and the wealthy ideologues deny science for the simple reason that doing so allows them to generate higher profits and accrue more power. They accomplish this through massive, coordinated, and well-funded campaigns that attack and thwart scientific research that would have the effect of reducing their income and limiting their control in an industry. Science is often squarely in their sights. From evolution to climate change to endangered species to health risks to health care to voting rights, the aforementioned have really sophisticated methods for denying science. And in the process, they degrade our most critical institutions.

IF YOU THINK THE recent COVID-19 science-denying debacle is the lone example of Republican ignorance, think again. And *again*. While it is the pinnacle of their destructive efforts, they began on this crusade well before Trump was elected. The GOP had, in fact, planted seeds forty-plus years ago for this catastrophic failure in governance. I'll begin with a brief intro on COVID-19 and work backwards to the '80s.

There's really not much I can write that hasn't already been written in the papers and said on TV about the Trump administration's utterly disastrous response to COVID-19. It was the worst in the world, in terms of cases and deaths during the initial outbreak, all the while Trump played down the severity so his supporters could run around without masks, screaming at Fauci on Fox News. As of this writing in December of 2021, 780,000-plus people have died, which represents about 15 percent of the deaths worldwide (the United States has 4 percent of the total world population).

2016 AND 2020 REPUBLICAN PARTY PLATFORM

The website LiveScience did a fact-check of the 2016 Republican Party platform (and, by default, the 2020 platform since they failed to update the 2016 one), which included sections on abortion, women's health, climate change, stem-cell research, cloning, Keystone Pipeline, fetal-tissue research, endangered species, coal, nuclear energy, electromagnetic pulse attacks (think the conspiracy theorist Alex Jones and his 5G loon-iness), pornography, married mothers and fathers, and abstinence and sex ed. Check it out.[2] Nearly every single issue has a glaring or multiple glaring alternative facts. In other words, it's a joke and should be studied in schools nationwide for how not to develop party platforms.

New York Magazine writer Jonathan Chait believes the well-funded, organized efforts of business to undermine science were seeded in 1977. That was the year the neo-conservative godfather and intellec-tual, Irving Kristol implored the leaders of corporate America to direct their donations to probusiness foundations rather than those that ser-viced, you know, people who actually needed the money. "Corporate philanthropy," he wrote, "should not be, cannot be, disinterested." It was then that the conservative think tank marketplace, according to Chait, "*exploded* with reports questioning whether pollution, smok-ing, driving, and other profitable aspects of American capitalism were really as dangerous as the scientists said."[3]

Chait's descriptions read like they're describing a horror movie from Soviet Russia. Of course, the irony is that conservatives accuse liberals of being communists.

"With the collapse of the Soviet Union," the historians of science Naomi Oreskes and Erik Conway have written, "Cold Warriors looked for another great threat. They found it in environmentalism." The idea was that climate change was a pretext the Left could use to exert government control over the economy. Since the 1990s was also the decade in which scientific consensus solidified that greenhouse gas emissions were permanently increasing temperatures, the political stakes of environmentalism soared.[4]

Needless to say, the Right pushed back. The number of books criticiz-ing environmentalism increased several-fold from the previous decade. Oreskes and Conway report that "more than 90 percent cited evidence produced by right-wing foundations." So much of this new critique was filled with the same sensational paranoia as their McCarthy-era brethren. The seeds were planted of the current incarnation of the con-spiracy theory—that scientists across the world conspired to embellish or falsify global warming data to increase their own power.

In the 1980s, President Reagan's political appointees at the EPA kept a *hit list* of scientists. As the reporter Scott Waldman writes, "Menace. Horrible. A real activist. Bleeding-heart liberal. Clean air extremist. Those were the descriptions leveled at scientists serving on EPA's advisory boards and written on an infamous document known as the 'hit list.'"[5] This resembles Soviet-style academic purges, doesn't it? Dozens of researchers and scientists were expelled from the EPA who were deemed a threat to industries like oil, tobacco, and food. And they were replaced by those whose commitment to science was, let's say, a little less honest. Anne Gorsuch Burford, the head of the EPA, whose political appointees kept the hit list, ended up resigning in 1983. Even more shameful, the hit list turned out to have been written on Heritage Foundation stationery, the powerful conservative think tank! The Reagan administration didn't even bother to make its purges look somewhat respectable. We owe the Democratic senator Gary Hart a debt of gratitude for publishing the list, which was written by Louis Cordia, a guy who had been appointed to a senior position in the EPA from, you guessed it, the Heritage Foundation.

There are few extremes to which Republicans won't go in their attacks on science. Climate and science reporter Chris Mooney con-veys as much in his brilliant (and depressing) book on the topic, *The Republican War on Science*. Here are a few select examples:[6]

- *The war on science began in earnest under Speaker Newt Gingrich.* (That ball of greed and destruction is a shoe-in for science denier of the millennium). His very first act as speaker was to eliminate the Office of Technology Assessment (OTA), which was absolutely critical and upon which Congress relied to interpret research and write laws. Mooney writes, "This dubious approach helps explain the science politicizing bonanza of the Gingrich Congress. The dismantling of the Office of Technology Assessment contributed to a 'free market' for scientific expertise all right—with alarming consequences." With the OTA eliminated, Gingrich's soldiers did not hesitate to send forth their own favored experts to undermine the scientific mainstream on ozone depletion and global warming. The attacks were fierce while the new Republican majority desired to free up the market in another way: by jamming through a major *regulatory reform* bill that, according to Mooney, "would have prescribed rigid and inflexible rules governing the use of science to protect public health and the environment."

- *The destruction of the ozone layer.* Apparently, it's just another liberal conspiracy to hold back America's greatness. Republicans held a hearing on its depletion and it, according to Mooney, "put the new Congress's poor understanding of science—and simultaneous willingness to politicize it—on full display." The most memorable moment was when John Doolittle, a California Republican, when asked which scientific studies he could cite that promoted his position about the ozone layer *not* depleting, said "I'm not going to get involved in a mumbo-jumbo of peer-reviewed documents." Oh, for sure, all that mumbo-jumbo, peer-reviewed stuff. Who needs it? Give me the quackiest paid-for researcher to write a half-page opinion about our nonexistent environmental problems, and call it a day!

- *Gun safety measures.* The best available science determines that gun safety measures reduce homicides. But, according to congressional Republicans, we shouldn't pursue them. Why? Well, when you boil it down, we're all just apes and mud. As the House Majority Leader Tom Delay (a Republican) put it during a hearing on gun safety held after the thousandth mass shooting that year: "Our school systems teach the children that they are nothing but glorified apes who are evolutionized out of some primordial soup of mud." Thanks for the brilliant insight, Tom.

- *Food quality.* Congressional Republicans, or should I say, big companies selling stuff like trans fat-laden foods or tobacco, frustrated by regulations to protect the consumer and determine health risks when consuming the product, came up with a *sound science* approach (catchy ain't it?). The goal was to essentially regulate the agencies and the science itself. Huh? Not the noxious products that are killing Americans, but the ones trying to stop them? I'm lost. It's like a judge being told how to rule on a case by the defendant. In support of their case, the GOP cited highly problematic anecdotal research, which basically concluded, "Government is the problem!" And in order to address this injustice, Republicans like Bob Dole and his acolytes sponsored bills that required the government agencies that actually deal in science research to apply the same one-size-fits-all standards for whether smoking, unhealthy foods, weed killers, and more should be regulated. This may seem harmless, as Mooney notes, but it's "perfectly tailored for tobacco and other industries aiming to tilt the rules under which regulations are scientifically adjudicated." Agencies would have been mandated to undergo "risk assessments" before doing anything of a regulatory nature. *And*, they would have to adhere to a strict set of rules laid out by Republicans in Congress who were effectively working for the industries that are making us sicker, masquerading under the guise of *sound science.* The Georgetown University law professor David Vladeck wrote at the time that the Republicans' attempt to hamstring science was just "paralysis by analysis."[7] It would have been a whole lot easier if they just said, "We don't give a damn about your health concerns, just buy our crap."

- *Slashing budgets.* If the Soviet-style obstruction wasn't enough, congressional Republicans slashed budgets for research and attempted to kill an entire agency that administers life-saving scientific data! Gingrich and his minions tried to literally get rid of the US Geological Survey, which tracks earthquakes and volcano eruptions and was hugely critical in analyzing the fall out of the Asian tsunami in 2004. Sweet. Great use of resources.

- *Fossil fuels.* Sure, Oklahoma's tax base is dependent on oil revenues (which provide 11 percent of total tax revenue), and climate change is just the greatest threat facing our planet today, but the lengths to which Republicans from Southern and Midwestern states go to scapegoat science is really impressive. Jim Inhofe, the Oklahoma senator and good 'ol boy of good 'ol boys, was long the de facto commander in chief of the GOP's war on climate science. In 2003, he singlehandedly defeated John McCain's and Joe Lieberman's Climate Stewardship Act, the first bill that would have created caps on greenhouse gas emissions. Ever. He deviously stacked a Senate panel with climate-change deniers and took to the floor to read a 12,000-word essay, written by the energy lobby, on "The Science of Climate Change," which could be summed up in its authors' own words: climate change may be "the greatest hoax ever perpetrated on the American people." In 2015, Inhofe brought a snowball into Congress to prove that climate change was a hoax.

- *The Data Quality Act (DQA).* Yet another major Republican effort to slow Congress from adopting twenty-first century scientific standards, this act was a way for Congress to hip check the science agencies by subjecting them to even more onerous oversight— again, not the products causing unnecessary health risks, but those regulations trying to protect the consumer. More formally, the Act "provides policy and procedural guidance to federal agencies for ensuring and maximizing the quality, objectivity, utility, and integrity of information (including statistical information) disseminated by Federal agencies." As soon as the DQA was ratified in late 2002, "corporate interests took it for a test drive," Mooney writes. A very powerful lobbyist named Jim Tozzi and his Center for Regulatory Effectiveness teamed up with the Kansas Corn Growers Association

and a group called the Triazine Network to render limp an EPA
risk assessment that had found that atrazine, a common herbicide
sprayed on our food, causes gonadal abnormalities in male frogs.
"There are no validated test methods," they wrote, "for determining
whether atrazine causes endocrine effects." Jesus Christ!

- *The Cheeseburger Bill.* In March 2004, congressional Republicans
  passed a bill that effectively sought to protect the food industry from lawsuits against health risks. In essence, the bill that
  stipulated that cheeseburgers don't cause obesity. Utah Congressman Chris Cannon pronounced, "It is not junk food that
  is making teenagers overweight, but rather a lack of activity."
  There's. So. Much. Research. To. The. Contrary. Mooney continues, "When it comes to the relationship between various
  unhealthy foods and the global rise of obesity, conservatives
  and food industry interests have led an all-out attack on a 2003
  World Health Organization report that dared to suggest a connection between consuming sugar-sweetened foods and poor
  health. On the issue of mercury contamination of fish, meanwhile, conservatives similarly hype uncertainty and cherry-pick
  their science." Considering that the rate of childhood obesity
  in the United States has nearly quadrupled in the last 40 years
  and one in three kids born after 2000 are at risk for developing
  diabetes, I'd say Mooney is on to something.[8, 9]

- *The Endangered Species Act.* Congressional Republicans, under
  the guise of *sound science,* would like to annihilate this act, even
  though research shows that such a move would have tremendous
  negative effects on the environment in and around protected
  areas like Oregon's Klamath River Basin. Republicans' defense?
  They compare the environmental movement to communism and
  assert that without humans killing off animals (for sport) there
  will be a decline in biodiversity because "some species tend to
  dominate others." What a crock!

- *Intelligent Design (ID)*. The belief that humans were created and sculpted by a supreme being (not factual) rather than natural selection (factual). In 2001, Senator and former CNN talking head Rick Santorum attempted to enshrine ID into law, joining forces with other religious ideologues to insert language into a major education bill titled "No Child Left Behind." It stated that "good science education should prepare students to distinguish the data or testable theories of science from philosophical or religious claims that are made in the name of science." Sounds harmless, until you understand that this precise language was sourced from one of the ID movement's founders, Phillip Johnson, who believes that "Darwinism is based on an a priori commitment to materialism, not on a philosophically neutral assessment of the evidence." Nonneutral is a new one! The Discovery Institute, another wing-nut conservative organization, celebrated Santorum's amendment, proclaiming, "The Darwinian monopoly on public science education . . . is ending." Ugh. Facts and scientific theories don't have a monopoly on settled science? Lordy, this is so dumb. Santorum called ID a "legitimate scientific theory that should be taught in science classes," and said, "Students studying controversial issues in science, such as biological evolution, should be allowed to learn about competing interpretations." Legitimate scientific theory, huh? Because a bunch of radical Christians haven't gotten over the Scopes Monkey Trials?

- *Abortion*. What chapter on Republicans' science proclivities would be complete without discussing abortion? Still steaming mad over *Roe v. Wade*, Joe Pitts, a conservative congressman from Pennsylvania, in 2011, sponsored a bill that provided for $15 million in funding for research into "postabortion depression" (no such diagnosis exists), even though the APA says abortion is "a safe medical procedure that carries relatively few physical or psychological risks." Plenty of experts sponsored by the American

Psychiatric Association say that this nonsense does nothing to overturn established researched.

- *Sex ed.* Dr. Joe McIlhaney, of the Austin-based Medical Institute for Sexual Health, was the de facto leader of the Republican prudence movement. He preaches that abstaining from sex is the only way to not contract an STD. Condoms, he says, are "ineffective." Mooney reported in 2005 that Douglas Kirby, a teen sexuality expert at the California-based research organization ETR Associates, explained that "strong data show that some comprehensive sex-ed programs work to change behavior by increasing contraceptive use or delaying or reducing the frequency of sex among teens. McIlhaney knows that, but he counters that 'just because you've increased condom use by maybe five or ten or twenty percent for kids in a program, does not mean you're actually going to impact the STD rate for them.'" Good Lord, this guy is a doctor? Sadly, yes! And he served under the Bush administration on the advisory committee to the director of the Centers for Disease Control and Prevention and the President's Advisory Council on HIV and AIDS. Perfect assignment for a guy who claims that the only effective protection from STDs is not having sex.

- *Lamar Smith.* Emily Atkin in the *New Republic* reports on Lamar Smith, a former Republican chairman of the Science, Space, and Technology Committee, which has jurisdiction over NASA, the Department of Energy, the Environmental Protection Agency, the National Science Foundation, the Federal Aviation Administration and the National Institute of Standards and Technology. Smith has a knack for making science effectively disappear. In 2017, the House Science Committee passed two of Smith's colossally foolish bills: The Honest and Open New EPA Science Treatment Act (HONEST Act) and the Science Advisory Board (SAB) Reform Act. Together they would substantially alter how the Environmental Protection Agency uses science to make rules

that protect our health. Atkin: "The HONEST Act is essentially a
re-brand of Smith's notorious Secret Science Reform Act, a bill
that would have required the EPA to only use scientific studies
for which all data is publicly available and the results are easily reproducible. The SAB Reform Act would change the makeup
of the board that reviews the 'quality and relevance' of the science that EPA uses. Scientists who receive EPA grants would
be forbidden from serving, while allowing the appointment of
industry-sponsored experts who have a direct interest in being
regulated—so long as they disclose that interest."[10] I just can't.
Scientists and former EPA officials have lined up in opposition
to argue these bills will add major expense and time to the scientific process and just embolden the polluters and discourage
competent people from working in government.

- *Scott Pruitt.* Atkin writes about the influence that Lamar Smith
  had on Trump's former EPA administrator and full-time earth
  annihilator, Scott Pruitt. During an interview with Tucker Carlson's *Daily Caller,* Pruitt announced "significant changes to the
  way the agency uses science." The change? They aren't going to
  use research that includes "confidential data" to develop regulation that seeks to protect the environment. Huh? "We need to
  make sure their data and methodology are published as part of
  the record," Pruitt said. "Otherwise, it's not transparent. It's not
  objectively measured, and that's important." Huh? Turns out, the
  new Pruitt policy was almost an exact match to Smith's Honest
  and Open New EPA Science Treatment Act, which was a sham and
  opposed by the vast majority of the scientific community. Both,
  according to Atkin, intended to "force the EPA to ignore most of
  the research showing air pollution can cause premature deaths
  (including a landmark MIT study in 2013 that found air pollution
  causes about 200,000 early deaths each year). That's because the
  bulk of the peer-reviewed literature on effects of fine particulate

matter and other pollutants is based on confidential data: human medical records, which are protected by federal law." Ah! Makes sense now. Never mind the fact that *hundreds* of scientists have seen and approved the data in the studies and have gone through an *extensive* peer-review process.

- *Anti-vax movement.* Despite cropping up on both sides of the aisle, the movement quickly caught fire among Republican elected officials, particularly at the local level, where officials cited "freedom from tyranny" or some hogwash like that. From *Politico*: "The anti-vaccine movement, which swelled with discredited theories that blamed vaccines for autism and other ills, has morphed and grown into a libertarian political rebellion that is drawing in state Republican officials who distrust government medical mandates." Picture the Boston Tea Party, except instead of tea, these *patriots* throw into the harbor medicine that scientists and researchers have perfected over decades. Though the anti-vax movement is as old as this country, the current measles-vax scare has resulted in 990 reported cases in 2019 alone. Yet we eradicated measles *nineteen years ago*! And, I won't even get into the COVID-19 anti-vax catastrophe.

- *Snake-oil vitamins.* It's natural when people who don't believe in science ascend to the higher echelons of the government that we see an increase in whackadoo, pseudohealth cures from various licensed quacks and ordinary civilians. That's because these people let regulation in those industries collapse. The author Rick Perlstein has written about receiving emails for products such as the "23-Cent Heart Miracle," which "Washington, the medical industry, and drug companies refuse to tell you about."[11] The former Republican presidential candidate Herman Cain—you know, the guy who died because he didn't follow COVID-19 guidelines—used his platform to promote "The 4 Sneaky Hormones That Are Making You Fat and How to Stop Them Now." Conservatives like the former governor Mike Huckabee, the former HUD secretary Ben Carson, and the lunatic radio host Alex Jones have all hawked ludicrous health treatments while claiming "the deep state doesn't want you to know about this." Jonathan Chait writes, "The subculture that subsisted on secret knowledge suppressed by the authorities, which once existed only in crank pamphlets, had become a mass culture and was now claiming the minds of nearly half the country." Millions of Americans no longer trust mainstream sources of knowledge—scientists apparently conspire with snobbish academics and scheming bureaucrats under the guise of so-called experts to be discounted and defied.

- *The Trump administration used scientists who are not honest and credible.* Among them is climate-change denier Steven Milloy of the Heartland Institute, a science-skeptic conservative think tank funded by big tobacco and oil. Naturally, Milloy served on Trump's environmental transition team. Then there's libertarian stan-boy idol Richard Epstein, of the conservative Hoover Institution, who once said, "The evidence in favor of the close linkage between carbon dioxide and global warming has not been clearly established." He also predicted just 500 people will die of COVID-19 in the United States.[12] Total. And Dr. Scott Atlas, Trump's resident *expert* on the Pandemic Response Team, who recently had a tweet taken down from Twitter for spreading false information about the effectiveness of facemasks. How did we get here!

I'll just finish with a couple of Mike Pence quotes:

"Frankly, condoms are a very, very poor protection against sexually transmitted diseases."

And how about this?

"Smoking doesn't kill."[13]

I must be living on another planet.

26

WAR ON EXPERTS

"The greatest danger to liberty today comes from the men who
are most needed and most powerful in modern government,
namely, the efficient expert administrators exclusively
concerned with what they regard as the public good."

**—FRIEDRICH HAYEK, THE AUSTRIAN-BRITISH
ECONOMIST AND LIBERTARIAN IDOL (1960)**

WHAT?

ANALOGOUS TO THE WAR on science, the war on experts has been
transpiring in GOP politics all across the country, in nearly every field,
for the last forty years.

WHY?

FOR THE SAME REASON children don't like their parents telling them
not to eat candy before dinner. Even though it's the smart, prudent
thing to do and prevents stomachaches, they're kids with a sweet

tooth. The radical rich and congressional conservatives are like children, and the experts are parents who stand in the way of their sickeningly sweet fantasies.

━━━━━━━

LET'S START WITH COLLEGES. As I explain in the chapter "War on Education," conservatives launched attacks on education and universities long ago, and they continue apace. Don't get me wrong, there are legitimate reasons to not care for our education system, but the one-sided attempts to thrash and bankrupt it are a far cry from constructive. It's propaganda to indoctrinate. The idea is to crush universities—which, by the way, house most of the experts—and bend the truth to their will. By definition, through progress in science and research, the expert community advances towards greater truth and discovery, and each year, the expert-hating, science-denying groups run in the opposite direction. As George Wallace, the racist former governor of Alabama in the '60s used to say, all professors are just "pointy-headed intellectuals."[1] He and his ilk (then Southern Democrats, now Republicans) showed complete disdain for intellectual types. And the venomous movement today has never been fuller in the Republican Party.

Matt Motta, of the *Washington Post*'s Wonk Blog, has been studying this phenomenon for years. Motta writes that it wasn't until the 1990s (Gingrich!) that Republicans started to doubt those "pointy-headed intellectuals." "During the 1990s, conservatives started to distrust experts," he reports. "From the early 1970s through early 1990s, I found little ideological divide on this question. In 1991, for example, 47 percent of liberals and 46 percent of conservatives expressed high levels of trust in the scientific community. By the mid-1990s, however, views began to diverge. In 2014, 53 percent of liberals and only 36 percent of conservatives held high levels of trust in the scientific community."[2]

Tom Nichols is a conservative author and professor who finds himself disgusted by the Republican Party's know-nothingness. He wrote a book on this topic, aptly titled *The Death of Expertise*, in which he argues that populism (read the Trump Republican Party) is responsible for this preponderance of sheer ignorance and hatred towards experts. And populism and ignorance haven't made any ground-breaking discoveries. Nichols writes, "Populism actually reinforces this elitism, because the celebration of ignorance cannot launch communications satellites, negotiate the rights of US citizens overseas, or provide for effective medications, all of which are daunting tasks even the dimmest citizens now demand and take for granted. Faced with a public that has no idea how most things work, experts likewise disengage, choosing to speak mostly to each other rather than to lay people."[3]

And who personifies anti-expert, anti-intellectualism more than Donald "I know more than the experts" Trump? Trump:

- Drones: "I know more about drones than anybody. I know about every form of safety that you can have."

- Campaign finance: "I think nobody knows more about campaign finance than I do, because I'm the biggest contributor." (1999)

- TV ratings: "I know more about people who get ratings than anyone." (2012)

- ISIS: "I know more about ISIS than the generals do." (2015)

- Trump has similarly pronounced himself the world's greatest authority on social media, the courts, lawsuits (well, that one may be true), the visa system, trade, the US government, renewable energy, taxes, debt, money, infrastructure, borders, Democrats, construction, the economy, technology, and Senator Cory Booker.[4]

27

THE ENTWINING OF CHURCH AND STATE

"[Trump] is literally splitting the kingdom of darkness right open. The Lord has put His favor upon him."

—CONSERVATIVE RADIO HOST MARK TAYLOR

▬▬▬ **WHAT?** ▬▬▬

I DON'T KNOW HOW else to say this, but there is no such thing as separation of church and state in America. The Religious Right has invaded much of society, not the least of which is Washington, DC. Beginning in the 1970s (and even prior to that, but in earnest during the '70s) religious conservatives began to feel like they were losing *their* country to the "immoral Left" and "heretical liberal college campuses." (Sound familiar?) "Our universities are the training grounds for the barbarians of the future," exclaimed the conservative religious publication *Freeman*.1 Ooooo! Those scary, pot-smoking, messy-haired freshmen! And they figured the best means to return America to the path of glory and free us of Satanic liberalism was through the political system. "What's happened to America," argued Jerry Falwell, Sr., "is that the wicked are bearing rule. We have to lead the nation back to the moral stance that made America great...we need to wield influence on those who govern us."[2] So evangelical leaders like Jerry Falwell, Ralph Reed, James Dobson, and Pat Robertson formed what was dubbed the "Moral Majority" (if you don't know, ask someone over 50). And, promptly, they began jumping into bed—not literally, because homosexuality is a sin!—with the Republican Party who, at the time, were a natural fit for their bigotry, racism, and homophobia, to advocate their agenda in Washington. They opposed anything that supposedly broke up the family, like pornography and lack of prayer in schools, and, most importantly, made clear their desire to return to the good ol' days of segregation. You know, *keep the Blacks out!* As the author John Newsinger writes, "[Falwell] condemned integration as something that the 'true negro does not want,' claiming that he could 'see the hand of Moscow (socialism reference) in the background' and that it was all the work of the 'Devil himself.' Indeed, the 'Hamites were,' he insisted, 'cursed to be servants of the Jews and Gentiles' and if segregation were ended 'God will punish us for it.'"[3] In my best Church Lady voice, "Well, isn't that speeecial?"

WHY?

AS I ADDRESSED ABOVE, evangelical leaders needed a way to turn back the clock on integration, equal rights, and the lack of religion in schools. So they latched onto a party that would accept their bigotry and in return provided Republicans with a massive voting bloc. The result is Republican policy based not on facts, science, need, or human dignity, but on the religious beliefs of evangelical leaders.

WRITING ABOUT THIS MOVEMENT, Brad Christerson, a professor of sociology at Biola University, together with USC's Richard Flory, explain how this movement regarded Donald Trump as all part of that plan. They call this type of Christianity: Independent Network Charismatic (INC). Christerson and Flory believe this to be the fastest-growing Christian group in America, and possibly in the world. Between 1970 and 2010, mainline Protestant churches shrank by an average of .05 percent per year, but INC grew by an average of 3.24 percent per year. This number, they say, was "striking," when considering the fact that US population grew an average of 1 percent per year during this time period.[4]

Let's see what the Religious Right has to say today:

"I believe the 45th president is meant to be an Isaiah 45 Cyrus [who will] restore the crumbling walls that separate us from cultural collapse."

—LANCE WALLNAU, EVANGELICAL AUTHOR AND SPEAKER

"When you're in a war, you don't worry about style . . . Nobody would have criticized General Patton because of his language. We're in a war here between good and evil. And to me, the president's tone, his demeanor, just aren't issues I choose to get involved with."

—PASTOR ROBERT JEFFRESS, WHO CALLED JEWS EVIL AND YET OPENED ISRAEL'S NEW EMBASSY IN JERUSALEM, COURTESY OF TRUMP

"God called King David a man after God's own heart even though he was an adulterer and a murderer. You have to choose the leader that would make the best king or president and not necessarily someone who would be a good pastor."

—PRESIDENT OF LIBERTY UNIVERSITY JERRY FALWELL JR.,
WHOSE MOTTO MIGHT BE *PRACTICE-WHAT-YOU-PREACH IS FOR EVERYBODY ELSE.*

"[American evangelicals] have a moral obligation to enthusiastically back [the president]."

—RALPH REED, FIRST EXECUTIVE DIRECTOR OF THE CHRISTIAN COALITION

Now that Trump lost the 2020 election, I wonder if anyone has checked in on them.

THE 1970S

Beginning in the '70s, Falwell talked about elevating "kingdom-minded people" in "powerful positions at the top of all sectors of society."[5] (He'd likely decide today other kingdom-minded people include former Secretary of Energy Rick Perry, Secretary of Education Betsy DeVos, and Secretary of Housing and Urban Development Ben Carson.) And Falwell, if you could believe it, was further to the right of the original radical conservative Barry Goldwater. "If you would like to know where I am politically," Falwell said, "I am to the right of wherever you are. I thought Goldwater was too liberal." Whoa!

This was *the* de facto leader of Religious Right for a long, long time.

For posterity, the other bigots and their organizations who made up this Moral Majority included James Dobson's Family Research Council and Focus on the Family; Pat Robertson's Christian Coalition and American Center for Law and Justice; the Alliance Defense Fund (now Alliance Defending Freedom); Donald Wildmon's American

Family Association; Michael Farris's Home School Legal Defense Association; Ralph Reed's Christian Coalition; and Charles Colson's BreakPoint.

The links between the Republican Party and Religious Right are lengthy and undeniable. Predictably, for forty years they have used the cudgel of religion to drive wedges through the fault lines of society and create the very polarization we are dealing with today. Paul Weyrich, a cofounder of the Heritage Foundation, declared in the mid-70s, "The new political philosophy must be defined by us [conservatives] in moral terms, packaged in non-religious language, and propagated throughout the country by our new coalition. When political power is achieved, the moral majority will have the opportunity to re-create this great nation."[6] Weyrich believed that the political potential of this synergy between conservatives and religion was endless. "The leadership, moral philosophy, and workable vehicle are at hand just waiting to be blended and activated," he wrote. "If the moral majority acts, results could well exceed our wildest dreams."

While these opportunistic faux-Jesus devotees were plotting a government takeover, religion's popularity was struggling. Partisan religion, as I like to call it, kills American Christianity. The American church has been declining by nearly every data point since the Moral Majority's formation. As the authors Robert Putnam and David Campbell argue in an article in *Foreign Affairs*, "In effect, Americans (especially young Americans) who might otherwise attend religious services 're saying, 'Well, if religion is just about conservative politics, then I'm outta here.'"[7] Between 1976 and 2016, the share of the population claiming they are "religiously unaffiliated" went from 7 percent to 25 percent, according the General Social Survey and PRRI American Values Atlas. That is a disturbing statistic for what's left of the Moral Majority.

Not to mention, according to Pew Research, there is a really large generational gap in American religion. Among the oldest and largest generation, the Silent Generation, 84 percent identify as Christian. They're followed by Boomers at 76 percent, Gen X at 67 percent, and, Millennials at 49 percent, with 40 percent unaffiliated. In addition, 50 percent of the Silent Generation and 35 percent of Boomers say they attend religious services at least weekly or more. Millennials? Only 22 percent.[8] Side note: This phenomenon also has to do with how Christianity is defined. Younger Americans see Christianity as meaning the Christian Right, so they do not identify with it, but they are still, in many respects, Christian. The data here is not so simple.

Back to the '70s. Falwell was *elated* about his new-found love for politics and how politicians on the Right seemed ready to do their damnedest to turn back the clock on civil rights. The religious author and scholar Jonathan Merritt remembers a conversation Falwell had with his pastor father. "James," he said, "we've got the numbers. We've got the resources. We've got the leadership. I've spoken to conservative Christians in churches all across this country, and they know what is at stake. We've got to get serious about Jesus, and we need to call this nation back to its roots. It's time to stand for what is right. We've got to get our folks to the polls next year, and we need to do a better job telling people what will happen if liberal Democrats remain in control of the White House. We must save this nation!"[9]

As you can see, establishing your alliance with Jesus and hating liberal Democrats is not a new reality for the Right. Using religion as a tool for political gain has been quite a popular strategy for the Right for decades now.

JOHN NEWSINGER PAINSTAKINGLY DETAILS the ascendance of the Religious Right and their influence on politics in "The Christian right, the Republican Party and Donald Trump." The following demonstrates how the Religious Right has infiltrated our democracy—like the

Ayatollah's Islamic Republican henchmen in Iran—and have effectively controlled how we prescribe policy. Here are a few clips:

- *The Civil Rights Act.* Falwell first attacked the 1964 Civil Rights Act as "a terrible violation of human and private property rights" and said it "should be considered civil wrongs rather than civil rights." This effectively began the Southern strategy (see the chapter "Southern Strategy"). Republicans were entirely influenced by the reaction of the Religious Right to desegregation.

- *Welfare.* They went after welfare because it benefited poor Black people, though the majority of people on welfare were/are White. "Our giveaway programs, our welfarism at home and abroad," the elder Falwell once sermonized, "is developing a breed of bums and derelicts who wouldn't work in a pie shop eating the holes out of doughnuts." You didn't hear them talk about poor White Christians like that before the '60s. During Ronald Reagan's administration, the Religious Right had an outsized influence in setting the agenda for poverty, which was cruel, as described in the chapter on Reaganomics. Ken Blackwell of the Family Research Council, a major Christian-right activist group, even went as far as to say food stamps and other government assistance did not fit the "biblical model." Only small government is "godly government." Sure, Ken.

- *Equal Rights Amendment* (to enshrine the same rights and opportunities for women as men). Oh, the horror! I'll quote Falwell again because it's so pitiful: the ERA "strikes at the foundation of our entire social structure" and was a "satanic attack on the home." And wouldn't you know it, the ERA was defeated over and over by congressional Republicans. Note: Gloria Steinem, the civil rights icon, contends, probably correctly, that it was really big business that killed the ERA: "Because the Equal Rights Amendment was defeated by the insurance industry and other people who were profiting off women's cheap labor." But Falwell certainly helped.

- *Climate change.* Katherine Stewart of the *New York Times* writes, "Today, the hard core of climate deniers is concentrated among people who identify as religiously conservative Republicans. And some leaders of the Christian nationalist movement, like those allied with the Cornwall Alliance for the Stewardship of Creation, which has denounced environmental science as a 'Cult of the Green Dragon,' cast environmentalism as an alternative—and false—theology." The irony is the Earth is heating up courtesy of fossil fuels and the "Green Dragon" is a primary strategy to cool it down. Conservative groups, fueled by rich fossil fuel execs, spend north of $1 billion every year throwing sand in the gears of climate-change research and our understanding of how it affects our planet. One billion clams![10]

- *Antitax, limited government.* Without a doubt antitax, because their places of worship are tax-exempt and they fight like mad to preserve this. Although nonprofits are not supposed to engage in political activity, have you heard evangelical leaders fawn over Donald Trump on Sundays? They were practically political rallies.[11] But their primary antitax, limited government stance has just as much if not more to do with segregation and racism. Let's take a short trip down memory lane. In June 1971, the US DC District Court issued its ruling in *Green v. Connally*. The decision effectively upheld the new policy from Richard Nixon's IRS: "Under the Internal Revenue Code, properly construed, racially discriminatory private schools are not entitled to the Federal tax exemption provided for charitable, educational institutions, and persons making gifts to such schools are not entitled to the deductions provided in case of gifts to charitable, educational institutions."[12] Meaning, the all-White schools who said, "Sorry, Black people, your money is no good around here" couldn't legally do that any longer. Correction, they could but they had to give up receiving money from the federal government. Well, this *enraged* evangelicals. The Dartmouth professor Randall Balmer writes that the Green decision "captured the attention of evangelical leaders, especially as the IRS began sending questionnaires to church-related 'segregation academies,' including Falwell's own Lynchburg Christian School, inquiring about their racial policies. Falwell was furious. 'In some states,' he famously complained, 'It's easier to open a massage parlor than a Christian school.'" Bob Jones University, a fundamentalist Christian college in Greenville South Carolina, did not admit African Americans, nor was it going to be bullied into doing so. The school's founder argued that "racial segregation was mandated by the Bible." So this way they could frame the debate in terms of religious freedom rather than simply "Keep the Blacks out." Civil Rights Act? Doesn't apply, they imagined, because it doesn't mention anything about religion. The lengths these people go to keep segregation legal. Up through today, the Religious Right is very much on the side from whence they started. They are one of the strongest advocates and loudest voices in support of economic policies that benefit the radical rich, *and* they even trade congregation votes for it, though these policies do not help their constituents. They even say the quiet part out loud. Ralph Reed, in an interview with the *New York Times* in 2015, warned business leaders flat out, "You're not going to get your tax cut if this vote doesn't turn out. If evangelicals don't pour out of the pews and into the voting precincts, there isn't going to be any successful business agenda."[13] In other words, pray to God and get your tax breaks, like good God-fearing Christians.

- The Southern Poverty Law Center has documented actual biblical scriptures that members of the Religious Right use to justify their antitax argument. "They most often cite Old Testament scriptures, which reference paying usury and taking money from the poor, such as Ezekiel 22:12-13, Proverbs 28:8, Deuteronomy

23:19, and Leviticus 25:36-37. Sovereign citizen extremists further cite Nehemiah 9:32-37 to bolster the belief that oppressive taxation results from sin. Also, 1 Kings 12:13-19 is used to justify rebellion against the government for oppressive taxation."[14] Ah, yes, 1 Kings. Famously supporting not funding programs for the poor because... socialism!

There's so much more. They are against gay marriage. And abortion (in any circumstances). And any gun safety. And immigration. And, basically, progress of any sort. On the other hand, they're for bigotry and obscene corporate money in politics. So, in short, they're against what the vast majority of Americans believe in. Sweet. And, if you haven't noticed, this was the Trump Republicans party platform to a T.

A slight digression, but you need to understand how depraved and hypocritical these people are who have such an outsized influence in Washington. Let's compare what these religious bigots said about Clinton's transgression with Monica Lewinski and what they said about Trump's with Stormy Daniels (not to mention the twenty-five other women he's assaulted and/or raped):

About Clinton:

Gary Bauer, who is president of an organization called American Values, which often promotes Trump's policies, was president of the conservative Family Research Council during the Clinton impeachment. He chided Clinton for lying about the Lewinsky scandal. "Day after day," he said, "children hear adults saying that it doesn't matter if the President lied." Character, he preached, "is destiny."

Franklin Graham, the son of Billy, and the CEO of Samaritan's Purse: "Much of America seems to have succumbed to the notion that what a person does in private has little bearing on his public actions or job performance, even if he is the president of the United States. Last week Mr. Clinton told 70 million Americans that his adulterous actions with Ms.

Lewinsky were a 'private' matter 'between me, the two people I love the most—my wife and our daughter—and our God.' But the God of the Bible says that what one does in private does matter. Mr. Clinton's months-long, extramarital sexual behavior in the Oval Office now concerns him and the rest of the world, not just his immediate family."

James Dobson, one of the architects of the modern Christian right, told his followers that he was "alarmed" at "the willingness of my fellow citizens to rationalize the President's behavior even after they suspected, and later knew, that he was lying." Dobson, who was part of Trump's evangelical advisory council during his campaign, claimed in 1998 that "you can't run a family, let alone a country, without [character]. How foolish to believe that a person who lacks honesty and moral integrity is qualified to lead a nation and the world!"

Pat Robertson, another architect of the Moral Majority, called Clinton a "debauched, debased, and defamed" politician who turned the Oval Office into a "playpen for the sexual freedom of the poster child of the 1960s."

Falwell wrote a "nonpartisan" paper with one article titled "Why Congress Must Impeach Bill Clinton." And it came out before anyone ever heard of Monica Lewinsky. Falwell really hated Clinton, but yeah, totally nonpartisan.

In 1998, many mainline Protestants, Catholics, and progressive evangelicals agreed with above.

On Trump:

Paying off a porn star to hide an extramarital affair? Eh, no biggie. Tony Perkins, the president of the Family Research Council: "We kind of gave him—'All right, you get a mulligan. You get a do-over here.'"

Graham: "I believe that Donald Trump believes—he believes in God. He believes in Jesus Christ. His depth—he doesn't, you know, he went to churches here in New York; he didn't get a whole lot of teaching."

Dobson: "First, Trump appears to be tender to things of the Spirit. I also hear that Paula White has known Trump for years and that she personally led him to Christ."

Robertson, addressing Trump: "I'm so proud of everything you're doing. I appreciate so much what you're doing. By the way, the evangelicals of America voted 83 percent in the last election for you. And I want you to know there are thousands and thousands of people praying for you all the time."

Falwell Junior: "I don't think he needs to come forward. I think everyone knows his past. I'm one of the 85 percent or so of evangelicals who supported him. We knew about his past as a real estate mogul, as sort of a playboy, as the owner of a beauty pageant, and we supported him for one reason: because of his position on the issues."

Robert Jeffress: "What is immoral is for Democrats to continue to try to block this president from performing his God-given task of protecting this nation."

I'm so happy our nation's spiritual leaders have learned to forgive and forget and focus on what's really important: moralizing a thrice-married, porn-star sexing conman because he is the empty vessel that congressional conservatives use to push through their wildly unpopular economic agenda.

28

CONSERVATIVE MEDIA

"Some may believe we're on the road to the Hitler youth."

**—FOX NEWS HOST GLENN BECK ON TEACHING
KIDS ABOUT CLIMATE CHANGE (2009)**

"The President and the people around him are convinced that God has anointed him to fix everything in one fell swoop."

—FOX NEWS HOST TUCKER CARLSON DISCUSSING OBAMA (2010)

WHAT?

IF THERE IS ONE facet of politics and conservatism that's become a model for how to ruin a country, it is conservative media in the last thirty years. Holy hell. What a fear-breeding, conspiracy-laden catastrophe it has grown into and how it perpetrates and potentiates the toxicity and awfulness of the radical Republican platform (to the detriment of its constituents). The primary goal of right-wing media is to gaslight people, manufacture outrage, and distract consumers with misinformation, disinformation, and conspiracy theories about *leftists* in order for congressional Republicans to push through a wildly unpopular agenda and cast doubt on the very idea of government as a functional entity. This is not to say the mainstream media is guiltless. They have played in the sandbox of faux outrage and done the bidding of corporations for a long time now, particularly cable news. And during the Trump era, their tardiness in understanding the threat represented by Trump and deep commitment to both-side-ism was pretty egregious. But just like any other noxious idea in this book, the Right is a thousand times worse and more harmful. It's. Not. Even. Close.

WHY?

CONSERVATIVE MEDIA HAS THE blessing and financing from conservative backers (the radical rich) because they benefit directly from said gaslighting. While Fox News et al. distract the electorate, the looting in Washington carries on in full force, while they criticize looting in the streets (oh, the irony). For example, take a look at conservative economic plans. The primary ones seek to rob the poor and middle class to pay the rich. They utilize the massive burgeoning conservative media apparatus as a cover for their malfeasance, and it's worked out quite well for them. Wealthy liberals, mainstream media, and Democrats are at fault here too, but there is no comparison.

THE EFFORT BEGAN, IN earnest, in the 1990s with Fox News and Rush Limbaugh on radio. What started as a somewhat legitimate counterbalance to liberal print media like the *New York Times* and *Washington Post* (note: CNN was not really considered liberal media until the Trump era, and MSNBC began in 1996) morphed slowly and deceptively into likely the largest propaganda arm of any party in our history (and probably in any Western democracy). Make no mistake, it is *instrumental* in getting Republicans reelected and covering up their criminality (just look at Trump). If Nixon had Fox News, he would not have been impeached.

RUSH LIMBAUGH

Rush was a provocative conservative political commentator and full-time bigot who began his career in the early '70s and became prominent in the late '80s. He used radio, TV, and books to project his loathsome views to world. In 2019, he attracted around 15.5 million listeners to his radio show, which made him one of the largest consumed shows in the United States.[1] I do not intend to speak ill of the deceased, but he was a terrible human being. Though not to many. Trump gave him the Presidential Medal of Freedom, and his supporters loved it. Let's run through some of his highlights (er, lowlights?), shall we?[2]

- "The NFL all too often looks like a game between the Bloods and the Crips without any weapons. There, I said it."

- "I think it's time to get rid of this whole National Basketball Association. Call it the TBA, the Thug Basketball Association, and stop calling them teams. Call 'em gangs … "

- "Have you ever noticed how all composite pictures of wanted criminals resemble [former Democratic presidential aspirant and prominent Black reverend] Jesse Jackson?"

- "The NAACP should have riot rehearsal. They should get a liquor store and practice robberies."

- "Everything in Africa's called AIDS. The reason is they get aid money for it. AIDS is the biggest pile of, the biggest pot they throw money into … "

- Responding to a caller who said Black people should have a greater voice on issues: "They are 12 percent of the population. Who the hell cares?"

- "If any race of people should not have guilt about slavery, it's Caucasians. The White race has probably had fewer slaves and for a briefer period of time than any other in the history of the world."

- "Women should not be allowed on juries where the accused is a stud..."

- "Women still live longer than men because their lives are easier."

- "When a gay person turns his back on you, it is anything but an insult; it's an invitation."

- On Beyoncé: "She's married to a rich guy. She now understands it's worth it to bow down..."

- On LGBT politicians getting elected: "I guarantee there'd be some people in the Republican establishment who will now think, 'Yeah, we need to do this. We need to provide a home, we need to provide a comforting atmosphere for the tranny community and the gay community.' But those people are voting Democrat anyway..."

- On the dangers of secondhand smoke, and smoking in general: "That is a myth. That has been disproven at the World Health Organization and the report was suppressed. There is no fatality whatsoever. There's not even major sickness component associated with secondhand smoke. It may irritate you, and you may not like it, but it will not make you sick, and it will not kill you... Firsthand smoke takes 50 years to kill people, if it does. Not everybody that smokes gets cancer. Now, it's true that everybody who smokes dies, but so does everyone who eats carrots..."

- On Clinton's health care plan: "I don't have time to beat around the bush. The health-care plan as proposed by Mrs. Clinton is socialism. There's no soft way to peddle it. There is no other way to describe it."

To say Rush Limbaugh has poisoned the airwaves with racism, bigotry, conspiracy theories and disinformation is an understatement.

FOX NEWS

David Frum, George W. Bush advisor and speechwriter, properly called out Fox and conservative radio: "Republicans have been fleeced and exploited and lied to by a conservative entertainment complex." Former Republican Congressman and MSNBC host Joe Scarborough joined in, arguing the Right's radio/television/website complex profited by offering a distorted view of reality. "That's not an electoral strategy," Scarborough said. "That's a business strategy for them."

A compilation of how Fox News and conservative media treated Obama from the *Daily Show* for your enjoyment:

- "Fox News on Deploying Federal Agents 2020 vs. 2014," The Daily Show
- "Fox News Is Very Concerned About This Presidential Candidate's Brain," The Daily Show
- "Fox News's Law & Order Experts," The Daily Show
- "Fox News Doesn't Think This Man Is Fit to Be President," The Daily Show
- "Fox News: Fair and Balanced Misogyny," The Daily Show
- "The Daily Show Foxsplains Coronavirus," The Daily Show
- "Fox News is Suddenly Anti-Protest," The Daily Show

ROGER AILES—THE CREATOR OF FOX NEWS

To understand Fox News, you have to understand the person who started it: Roger Ailes. I never met the guy personally, but I have watched his network quite a bit. If you're reading this book, you probably have some idea about the relationship Fox News has to this country.

For more information on Roger and the malignant monstrosity of a network he created, or just an initiation into it, read Gabe Sherman's book, *The Loudest Voice in the Room: How the Brilliant, Bombastic Roger Ailes Built Fox News—and Divided a Country.* And watch the series with Russell Crowe on Showtime, too. Excellent and scary. In the meantime, what follows are the highlights.[3]

It all started in 1968, when Ailes was on *The Mike Douglas Show.* He got to talking with Richard Nixon who was a guest on the show, and then went to work for his campaign. Sherman writes, "In the crucible of the '68 campaign, Ailes adopted a new view: journalists were the enemy." (By the way, Ailes hated the "fake news media" well before Trump). He wanted to merge conservative news media with the Republican campaigns he was running. It was fairly remarkable that a news executive was doing both at the same time, but Ailes was motivated and predicted it would eventually be that way. After the 1968 election, Ailes fantasized of a time when news and cable shows would replace the political party, the most popular mass organizer of the twentieth century. With Fox News, Sherman notes, "that reality was arguably established." Just to be clear, Republicans and conservatives complain about the "Clinton News Network (CNN) and MS-DNC," but it was Fox who seemed to start this "trend" of networks essentially being media arms of parties. Fascinating, isn't it?

A *Boston Globe* profile noted that Ailes was aggressively signing up Republican clients and was involved in a half dozen races that year. In the interview, Ailes boasted that one day television could supplant the party itself: "The skeletons of political parties will remain. But television will accelerate the breaking down of mass registration by party. The figures show this already. Youth are independent." He worked on over twenty successful campaigns for GOP senators and congressmen between 1980 and 1986. He worked on Nixon's campaign. Bush's. Reagan's. Janine Pirro's (a.k.a. Judge Janine, that inebriate who rails about culture wars on Fox every night).

Fast forward to Fox News, which was up and running by 1996. It

found its niche by giving spectacular cover to Speaker Newt Gingrich's abhorrent shenanigans. To get a sense of how Ailes ran things
at Fox, check out segments of the internal memos that flew around
management inboxes. Hilarious and frightening. Sort of like reading
Mussolini's correspondence to Hitler regarding setting up a pan-Euro
state TV. "Internal memos when Fox started," Sherman writes, "were
discussing ways to 'manipulate' audiences (terms like Pretense Balancing, the goal of which is showing 'all sides' of a particular story when, in
fact the balance is tilted." The Hold Frame holds a subject "in a flatter-
ing or unflattering position" (depending on the agenda) and gives "the
impression of 'catching an event,' or 'catching a person.'" Catch Phrases
are easily remembered words "which seem to be factual though they
are, in fact, editorializations." Repetition, the last concept on the list,
creates a news event through repeated assertion. "The creation of
the most important story today" becomes "the truly most important
story a week from today." ("We can send a newsman and a camera crew
over to the Capitol and talk to a congressman or senator about 'the
story,'" he wrote. "If the congressman or senator is willing, we can create news in an instant. Most are willing.") Repetition, the senior Fox
executive Bruce Herschensohn wrote, is "the oldest and most effective propaganda technique. With a nightly news package, we can create
ongoing stories of importance," (Fox would do the same with sagas
such as the "War on Christmas," "Obama's Czars," "Fast and Furious,"
and "Benghazi.") Herschensohn encouraged conservatives to identify
whipping boys that played to their audience's resentments. "Whereas
others selected the CIA and the FBI, we can take HEW and HUD," he
wrote, referring to the Department of Health, Education, and Welfare,
and the Department of Housing and Urban Development. You know,
those agencies that help poor and middle-class people survive.

Bobby Kennedy once had this to say about Ailes, who was a long-time
friend: "His views are sincere. He thinks he's preserving the American
way of life. In his heart, he thinks America is probably better off being a
White Christian nation. He's driven by his own paranoia and he knows

how to get in touch with his own paranoia. He makes Americans comfortable with their bigotry, their paranoia and their xenophobia."

As for Ailes's personal beliefs, well, he's further to the right than his network. "I am more conservative than the network. I could never be elected … We have no obligation to tell the viewer anything not to our advantage." Good Lord!

Examples of Fox News propaganda abound. From giving cover to Dick Cheney and the War in Iraq to McConnell's unprecedented obstructionism to Trump's epic failures and corruption. But let's examine how Fox News dealt with the coronavirus.

"Fox News pushed coronavirus misinformation 253 times in just five days"—Media Matters.[4] Wow! That's impressive. I don't think Trump lied that much in one week.

Here's a breakdown of what happened during those five days (July 6–10, 2020):

- Nearly half of Fox's coronavirus misinformation was about the science of coronavirus and health recommendations from experts (115 instances).

- Fox politicized recommended public health measures, such as face masks usage and business closures, 63 times.

- Fox emphasized the economy and reopening schools 46 times despite public health concerns.

- Fox's "The Ingraham Angle" was responsible for a quarter of all coronavirus misinformation on the network.

- Fox's "straight news" shows accounted for more than one-third of all coronavirus misinformation.

COMPARISON BETWEEN EXPECTATIONS OF MAINSTREAM AND CONSERVATIVE MEDIA

The journalist Matthew Yglesias of *Vox* has come up with an interesting concept called the "hack gap."[5] It's basically the highly visible difference between what conservatives expect from the mainstream media and what they expect from conservative media (hint: something *completely* lopsided). In other words, they nitpick at the smallest error on mainstream media but allow gigantic lies to perpetrate on conservative media.

Yglesias writes, "The hack gap explains why Clinton's email server received more television news coverage than all policy issues combined in the 2016 election. It explains why Republicans can hope to get away with dishonest spin about preexisting conditions. It is why Democrats are terrified that Elizabeth Warren's past statements about Native American heritage could be general election poison in 2020, and it's why an internecine debate about civility has been roiling progressive circles for nearly two years even while the president of the United States openly praises assaulting journalists."

A classic example was when Hillary called a portion of Trump supporters "deplorables." Attending a fundraiser in the fall of 2016, she was asked how to explain the appeal of Trump: "To just be grossly generalistic, you could put half of Trump's supporters into what I call the basket of deplorables. Right? The racist, sexist, homophobic, xenophobic, Islamophobic—you name it."

Yglesias notes that mocking rank-and-file Republicans (even if it was only about half of them) was dubbed an enormous national scandal. Congressional Republicans and conservative pundits dwelled on the line, which proved to be a point of party unity at a moment when many establishment officials were reluctant to praise Trump. Mainstream media covered the controversy like it was going out of style, and center-left talking heads weighed in with a range of takes, including one from Yglesias himself, which determined that Clinton really had screwed the pooch by violating "the norm against attacking the other party's constituents" and not its politicians.

Meanwhile, simultaneously, President Trump said that 100 percent of people planning to vote Democratic in the 2020 election were "crazy evil socialists." Nobody lifted an eyebrow, let alone conservatives who were pissed off about a candidate insulting the other side.[6]

29

WAR ON EDUCATION

"They're government schools, not public schools. They're owned by the government, located on government property, started by government employees, and funded with money the government seizes from taxpayers. And, like most things government, they are complete disasters."

—NEIL BOORTZ, CONSERVATIVE PUNDIT (2009)

"School choice reaches right into the heart of the Democratic coalition and takes people out of it."

—GROVER NORQUIST, DURING AN 1998 INTERVIEW WITH THE *WASHINGTON TIMES*

WHAT?

SINCE THE 1930S (but in earnest since the 1970s) conservatives have attacked education in America. From public schools to public universities, academia became a target for the Right not only in rhetoric—which was fierce by the most extreme definition—but in their actions.

WHY?

JUST LIKE THEIR WAR on science and government, education represents an evil socialist institution the Right must vanquish in order
to sustain their power. School choice, the seemingly innocuous movement that gives families vouchers so they can choose where they
want to school their kids, actually started in opposition to desegregation in 1954. School choice, no surprise, benefits the affluent more
than the low-income people it purportedly helps. Most of the attacks
on education have centered around a common culture-war thread
that congressional conservatives consistently pull on when they've
run out of ideas. You can find seemingly limitless written and video
works on this with their primary thesis: "The Marxists are coming!" If
you read the attacks on education in the 1970s and compare them to
today's, nothing has changed. Irving Kristol, the godfather of neocon-
servatism in the '70s, called the educational system "a radical mood
in search of a radical program . . . the last, convulsive twitches of a
slowly expiring American individualism."[1] And Donald Trump Jr., that
character right out of a Bret Easton Ellis novel on steroids who also
happens to be a son of the former president, has proclaimed: "You
don't have to be indoctrinated by these loser teachers that are trying
to sell you on socialism from birth, you don't have to do it."[2] The
only thing that's changed is the critiques have become cruder and
less articulate. Perhaps it's a lack of education?

LET'S GO BACK FURTHER. David Austin Walsh, of the Urban Institute,
takes us through a bit of history on the assault on education by conservatives beginning in the 1930s at the hands of . . . the Walgreens. He
writes, "As early as the 1930s, conservative philanthropists attempted
to finance their preferred vision for American higher education."[3] In

1935, Charles Walgreen demanded that either the University of Chicago stop indoctrinating students with "communism" or he would pull his niece from the school and cease donations. Well, that threat spurred on a statewide malaise. The Illinois Senate took up the charge and commenced hearings that prominently and primarily focused on Walgreen trashing the university. He eventually relented and donated $550,000 to the university, but not without strings. "[Foster] greater appreciation of American life and values among University of Chicago students," he demanded, or no more money.

As I detail in the chapter "UnKoch Your Campus," the attacks on education became better funded and organized courtesy of right-wing radical billionaires.

Fast forward to where I began this chapter: the 1970s, a time when conservatives began to feel threatened by the emerging liberal majority in academia. Their argument was simple, if not idiotic: Infiltration of "Marxists!" was a "clear and present danger to American way of life." It was *immediately* evident that the white knights of the conservative roundtable had to swoop in and save the day. As Jason Blakely has written in the *Atlantic*, "The trope of portraying American universities as a threat to society emerged with particular intensity in the 1970s and '80s. Neoconservatives including the journalist Irving Kristol and the philosopher Allan Bloom developed a discourse around what they saw as the moral laxity and corrosiveness of the 1960s counterculture. As one neoconservative intellectual put it, thinkers like Kristol and Bloom saw themselves as being born out of a 'reaction against the Left's nihilistic revolt against conventional morality and religion.'"[4] In fact, we saw this self-proclaimed superhero role assumed by Ronald Reagan in his 1966 campaign for governor of California.

Sounds like the plot of a bad horror movie. In the Spring of 1973, Kristol penned his famous essay "Capitalism, Socialism, and Nihilism" and spoke about this topic wherever anyone would listen. In the essay,

Kristol argued that libertarians were unable to defeat the counterculture political agenda. Ha! You know what that sounds like? It sounds
like they couldn't compete in the marketplace of ideas, so they had to
resort to favoritism. Doesn't seem very capitalistic to me. The reason
they couldn't compete, Blakely notes, is because "libertarians reduced
political life to economics." While Karl Marx had been concerned with
economics, the new hippies were less economic-thinking and appealed
more to the moral and virtuous aspects of human nature. "The enemy
of liberal capitalism today," Kristol wrote in his 1972 lecture, "is not so
much socialism as nihilism." Thank the good Lord that Bloom and Kristol were able to identify these horrific forces infecting young American
minds, otherwise they surely would have succumbed in no time to the
evil powers of Ginsberg and Kerouac.

What Kristol and Bloom mistook for nihilism and socialism was
simply a debate over American values, not a rejection of capitalism,
morals, or religion. The Right, of course, used it as evidence of moral
atrophy (as if they have any standing whatsoever: ahem, Jim Crow!) and
browbeat White suburbia into believing colleges were hellscapes for
conservatives. It was simply a way to demonize the institutions that
were challenging the status quo.

Presently, Republicans and conservatives have reached the pinnacle
of their dislike for academic institutions. They've even started websites targeting liberal academics, like Professor Watchlist and Campus
Reform. Pretty gross. Several professors have been doxed by right-
wing nuts and have received death threats.[5]

You'll find endless drivel about how academic institutions are
indoctrinating our kids, including language parroted by GOP congressmen and, of course, Trump. And while the field of academia is
dominated by left-leaning professors and has its issues, don't get me
wrong, this, like most gripes from the Right, is manufactured and
overblown. But it's having a huge effect on how people (Republicans)
perceive colleges.

Bashing education for 50 years will do that. As recently as 2012, Republicans had a 53 percent positive view of universities. Now? Just 33 percent, and going lower by the tweet.[6]

How about that scary liberal indoctrinating? A study by the Cooperative Congressional Election Study Panel shows that not only are students *not* being indoctrinated, but they are putting a slight dent in Democratic party identification (top left chart). How about all that scary liberal indoctrinating?

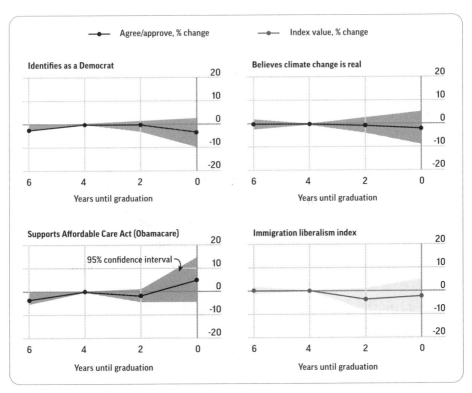

Source: Cooperative Congressional Election Study Panel

Let's dive a little further into the research. Scott Jaschik of *Inside Higher Ed* summarizes the most well-known and comprehensive studies about liberal bias on campus. And guess what? Though the majority of faculty are on the left end of the spectrum, this is (shocker) not the Marxist horror show that congressional conservatives make it out to be. He writes, "Yes, professors lean left (although with some caveats). But much of the research says conservative students and faculty members are not only surviving but thriving in academe—free of indoctrination if not the periodic frustrations. Further, the research casts doubt on the idea that the ideological tilt of faculty members is because of discrimination. Notably, some of this research has been produced by conservative scholars."[7]

REAGAN

To truly understand the Republican war on education, we must return to the 1960s, '70s and '80s and examine the record of a guy who arguably had the biggest impact on education in the last forty years: Ronald Reagan, the idol of every conservative White boomer with a second-mortgaged vacation home.

In *The Educational Legacy of Ronald Reagan: The Cutting Edge*, Professor Gary Clabaugh details Reagan's legacy on education, and it's something to behold. Like a composting bin in hundred-degree weather.

It is safe to assert Reagan is lionized because he is the face of capitalism. The free-market cowboy who took on the evil communists and won. The guy who unleashed the "animal spirits" of big business so the prosperity would trickledown to everyone. "Some enthusiasts have even proposed carving the former president's countenance into Mount Rushmore," Clabaugh writes. However, much like his management of economic policy, Reagan's management of our education system did lots of damage to the middle and lower-income strata of the population.

In order to gauge Reagan's legacy on education, we must first peer into his record as the governor of California. According to Clabaugh, Reagan royally screwed the network of University of California schools. For example, he demanded that the legislature launch an investigation into "Communist activities" and sexual misconduct at Berkeley, which he turned into a spectacle by claiming "a small minority of hippies, radicals and filthy speech advocates" had meddled in university affairs and should "be taken by the scruff of the neck and thrown off campus permanently." He called protesting students "brats," "freaks," and "cowardly fascists." And when it came to "restoring order" on unruly campuses, he observed, "If it takes a bloodbath, let's get it over with. No more appeasement!" Then there was Max Rafferty, Reagan's superintendent of education in California who referred to UC Berkeley as a "four year course in drugs, sex and treason." Note that the job of superintendent was an elected, not appointed, position, but the quote reflects Reagan's views of the UC system. Rafferty was a Republican.

Once elected, Reagan set the tone for his administration by calling for an end to free tuition for state college and university students, demanding, on an annual basis, a sweeping 20 percent cut in higher education funding, repeatedly cutting construction funds for state campuses, arranging the firing of Clark Kerr, the highly respected president of the University of California, professing that the state "should not subsidize intellectual curiosity." Ha!

To recap: Get rid of free tuition. Cut education funding. Intellectual curiosity? Bad.

Reagan slashed spending not just on higher education, Clabaugh writes, "but consistently opposed additional funding for basic education." As a result, taxes increased and public schools deteriorated, because the persistent underfunding resulted in "overcrowded classrooms, ancient, worn-out textbooks, crumbling buildings, and badly demoralized teachers. Ultimately half the Los Angeles Unified School

District's teachers walked off the job to protest conditions in their schools. Mr. Reagan was unmoved." What an unapologetically anti-education jerk. Needless to say, he left the California public education system much worse off than he inherited it.

Let's discuss his presidency. In campaigning, Reagan called for the elimination of the Department of Education, severe cuts to bilingual education, and enormous cuts to the role of the federal government in education. When he was elected, he tried to do even more! However, like a typical congressional Republican, he wasn't into federalism for local school districts. He sought to increase state power over localities by redirecting federal funds to states from local districts, which meant to "seriously erode [their] power." When he was elected, the federal share of education spending was 12 percent. By the time he left it was 6 percent—while costs for education were increasing.

His demagogic Secretary of Education Bill Bennett called the teacher's union the "Blob" and justified massive cuts in public education saying that education is not going to be fixed "by throwing money at it." He also mocked the idea that being poor limited educational possibilities, and called the kind of social-science research that led to such a conclusion "sociological flimflammery." Never mind the fact that 11 million children (and growing) were living in poverty.

Attacking teachers and students and slashing budgets—that just about sums up Reagan's record on education. As governor and president, he subversively whipped up discontent with public education, then exploited it for political gain. As governor and president, he crucified educators and cut education spending while feigning understanding of how valuable it is. And as governor and president, he crushed the spirit of the nation's educators and left them demoralized. Clabaugh asks, "Does this sound like a man whose countenance should grace Mount Rushmore? We'll leave that up to you."

To say Reagan left the United States worse off as a country in educational competitiveness is an understatement. This was the president of the United States, the leader of the free world. For eight years he walked the halls of Washington making grand pronouncements about the evils of public education, and the people he hired shared his worldview. This destructive idea that public education—and its teachers—are nefarious forces we should be scared of is so amazingly arrogant and obnoxious.

Here's further rhetorical proof of Republicans' war on education, courtesy of a whole set of ideologues:

"I've used the word public schools a fair bit [but] I am beginning to change my own terminology. I would encourage you to either improve on mine or adopt it. 'Public schools' is such a misnomer today that I really hate to use that. I've begun to use the word 'government schools' or 'government-run-schools' to describe what we used to call public schools because it's a better descriptor of in fact what they are. Because the public school creates this aura that if anyone walks in off the street into a 'public school' they would be welcome."
—DICK DEVOS, BILLIONAIRE AND HUSBAND OF
FORMER SECRETARY OF EDUCATION BETSY DEVOS (2002)

"There is no failed policy more in need of urgent change than our government-run education monopoly."
—DONALD TRUMP (2016)

"Until we can get government entirely out of education, we'll have to keep fighting to preserve and expand our ability to choose what's right for our kids."
—THE REASON FOUNDATION (2018)

"It's school choice week! What's that? It's a week about
giving parents and kids a choice of schools, so they aren't
stuck in failing, government-run schools."

—JOHN STOSSEL (2018)

The war on education has backfired, to a degree. According to Pew
Research, Republicans used to appeal to college-educated voters, but
not so much anymore. In 1996, college-educated graduates preferred
the Republican Bob Dole, by 2 points over Bill Clinton. And noncollege educated graduates preferred Clinton by a whopping 16 points. By
2016, wowzers! College-educated voters supported Democrats by 23
points! Noncollege educated supported Trump by 5 points. Including
a 25-point margin for White noncollege grads.[8] Boy, the Republican
Party has found its sweet spot, hasn't it?

30

UNKOCH YOUR CAMPUS

"The [Koch] network is fully integrated, so it's not just
work at the universities with the students, but it's also
building state-based capabilities and election capabilities
and integrating this talent pipeline. So you can see how
this is useful to each other over time. No one else has this
infrastructure. We're very excited about doing it."

—KEVIN GENTRY, A TOP AIDE TO CHARLES AND DAVID KOCH,
OTHERWISE KNOWN AS THE KOCHTOPUS (2014)

WHAT?

FOR NEARLY A CENTURY, right-wing billionaires and industrialists
have bristled at the thought of students being "indoctrinated by liberal
academic elite" and have approached this "threat" with the same intensity as the Mongols conquering China's Song Dynasty, though with less
bloodshed and pillaging. They have funded everything from think tanks
to buildings on college campuses to hospitals to entire universities in
an effort to impede this purported brainwashing. I know what you're

saying: "Who cares, plenty of filthy rich people donate tons of money to universities." Yeah, sure, but it's commonly for leverage in getting their undeserving lackey sons admitted (*cough*, Kushner; *cough*, Don Jr.). But these particular radical-rich donations are not your typical nepotistic back-scratching ones, because they have had a profound influence on what the colleges actually teach and, by extension, have shaped debate, policy, and research in the views and, more importantly, the financial interests of these God-playing rich folk.

WHY?

THE KOCH BROTHERS AND other radical billionaire ideologues require their own brand of academia to counter what essentially is consensus opinion on everything from climate change to economics to health care and food safety. If research from a nonpartisan research institution like Harvard or an independent think tank like the Kaiser Family Foundation says one thing, the Kochs' Heritage Foundation or American Enterprise Institute counters with another, despite their sole reason for existence being to "pursue conservative policies to help Americans build a better life."[1] It says that on the damn website! So any research on the negative effects of fossil fuels on climate change could be refuted by seemingly equally accurate research from conservative organizations. And the sophistication with which these institutions carry out such endeavors is really impressive. With money and smart people who will play along, anything is possible.

SINCE 2005, THE Kochs had spent over $450 million funding academic programs at no fewer than 550 higher education institutions.[2]

In fact, they dedicated $50 million to a single flagship campus in the Koch system: George Mason University, which Bill Koch (their brother) described as a "lobbying group disguised as a disinterested academic program."

David Austin Walsh of the Urban Institute in history at Princeton University, where he has studied the evolution of conservative philanthropy in great detail. In the conservative crusade to fundamentally alter higher education, Walsh contends, there are a few key figures: John Olin (whose Winchester Repeating Arms Company made a fortune during World War II manufacturing arms and ammunition for the US Army); Richard Mellon Scaife (heir to the Mellon banking fortune); John D. Rockefeller and Henry Ford (no introduction needed); and, of course, David and Charles Koch.[3]

These guys *really* disliked liberals. Especially those in academia. Take John Olin. His philanthropy focused on the Ivy Leagues, an academic community whose influence is deep and global. Walsh notes that Olin, who died in 1982 but whose foundation continued operations until 2005, handed out nearly $300 million to conservative causes. Olin's devotion to conservative politics in charitable giving dated to the late 1960s. Walsh writes, "Long an archconservative, he was horrified by that era's campus uprisings, especially the armed takeover of the Cornell student union building by Black student protestors in 1969."

Outraged by these protests, he decided to support conservative causes to right this desegregated ship. In the 1980s, the Olin Foundation adopted what was called a "beachhead strategy," which meant installing smaller conservative programs within top universities and was premised on the notion that these schools were "emulated by other colleges and universities of lesser stature." The idea was to "slowly burrow" conservative ideas and figures into top institutions. He funded law programs, economic programs, and research grants to those who "fit the mold." He had deans and faculty appointed who were ideologically similar to him. Walsh writes, "Olin's legal scholarship was influenced by law and economics and he was a reliable ally in the foundation's efforts to expand law and economics at Harvard." The intellectual climate Olin fostered at Harvard paved the way for critical hires with conservative bents.

And of course, there's the Federalist Society, a bleached white orgy of the brightest and fiercest conservative ideologues that spawns some of the most radical judges in our nation's history. Walsh writes, "The Federalist Society has given educational and social support to a generation of right-wing judges, attorneys, and legal scholars." The monumental cases settled by a conservative-leaning Supreme Court in the past decade—*Citizens United v. FEC*, *Shelby County v. Holder*, *Janus v. AFSCME*, and *Trump v. Hawaii*—would have been significantly more difficult for conservatives to be victorious without the Federalist Society's supremacy. When you realize that Chief Justice John Roberts and Associate Justices Samuel Alito, Neil Gorsuch, Brett Kavanaugh, Amy Coney Barrett, the late Antonin Scalia, and Clarence Thomas are all Federalist Society alumni, you sort of go "holy shit!" Known as the "farm system for the judiciary," it all but ensures ideological reliability and guards against mishaps like Bush's appointment of David Souter, and Nixon's of Warren Burger and Harry Blackmun, who wrote the majority opinion for *Roe v. Wade*.

Many of the Federalist Society's early members procured jobs in the Reagan Administration.

Last but certainly not least, the Kochtopus. The sheer number of Koch-funded ideologues in positions of power within government in the Trump administration is impressive:

- Andrew Wheeler, the former head of the Environmental Protection Agency, who opposes environmental regulations, received his MBA from George Mason University in 1998.

- Brian Blasé, a special assistant to President Trump on health care policy, is a former senior research fellow at the Mercatus Center.

- Neomi Rao, the chief administrator of the Office of Information and Regulatory Affairs, who was nominated by the president to the Court of Appeals for the DC Circuit in late 2018, is a former law professor at the Antonin Scalia Law School.

- Daniel Simmons, an assistant secretary in the Office of Energy Efficiency and Renewable Energy, was also a research fellow at Mercatus.

The above all have connections to Koch and played active and prominent roles in pushing Trump's deregulatory agenda. The Kochs' Mercatus Center on their campus at George Mason has been a training ground for these antiregulation free marketeers.

The Kochs' vision of society was laid out to a reporter by the men themselves. Charles Koch once told a reporter that he views the future as "vertically and horizontally integrated."[4] Purchase universities, own the means of knowledge production while funding student scholarships, granting professors endowments, and having those students work at jobs Koch provides when they leave college. Christ, they want to own society!

31

RISE OF CONSERVATIVE
THINK TANKS

"The mission of The Heritage Foundation is to formulate and
promote conservative public policies based on the principles
of free enterprise, limited government, individual freedom,
traditional American values, and a strong national defense."

—MISSION STATEMENT, THE HERITAGE FOUNDATION

"We are different from previous generations of
conservatives. . . . We are no longer working to preserve
the status quo. We are radicals, working to overturn
the present power structure of this country."

—PAUL WEYRICH, FOUNDER OF THE HERITAGE FOUNDATION (1984)

WHAT?

IN THE 1960S AND 1970S there was a sharp increase in the amount of
conservative research pumped out in academic and policy-making circles. This was the result of the founding of a few critical institutions called
think tanks, namely the Heritage Foundation, the Cato Institute, and the

American Enterprise Institute (AEI), which churned out reports about everything from defense to the economy to health care to the effectiveness of government. These expressly conservative institutions served an important purpose for the radical rich and congressional Republicans.

WHY?

AS THEY WERE GETTING their sea legs back in Washington after the *abhorrent* passage of the Civil Rights and Voting Rights Acts in '60s, conservatives needed name-brand, reputable, data-driven institutions that rivaled those in the center and left such as Harvard University and the Brookings Institute. They wanted arguments showing that the Great Society and Civil Rights Act weren't actually helping Black or poor people (they were). Corporate America needed a win too. Those poor little industry titans feared the government was butting in too much into business affairs. With reputable institutions at their sides, they could hold up what appeared to be academically sound data-driven research supporting the corporatization of society.

BILL BAROODY, THE PRESIDENT of AEI in the '70s, argued there had been an "abdication of the corporate class" when promoting probusiness policies in Washington and "a monopoly hostile to business." As he put it, "To break this monopoly requires a calculated, positive, major commitment—one which will ensure that the views of other competent [business-friendly] intellectuals are given the opportunity to contend effectively in the mainstream of our country's intellectual activity. There are such people. They can be encouraged and mobilized. Their numbers can increase. But that can hardly happen without reordering priorities in the support patterns of corporations and foundations—at

least by those corporations and foundations concerned with preserving the basic values of this free society and its free institutions."[1]
Baroody was effectively sounding the alarm to CEOs far and wide to
get involved in politics, like it or not.

So began the emerging dominance of conservative think tanks in
public-policy discussion.

A reminder as to what end these conservative think tanks operate:
to erode public trust of government and write policy that benefits the
wealthy and business elite. Conservatives have used public distrust of
government (see Conservative War on Government) to remake society
the way they see it. When it comes to taxes, regulation, and corporate
socialism such as subsidies and special financial incentives unavailable
to the general public, they've been hammering home a "winner take all"
strategy for decades now.

Think tanks like AEI, and later the Heritage Foundation—one of the
cofounders of which, Paul Weyrich, was instrumental in turning out
the Moral Majority to prevent Black people from gaining equal rights—
inundated the public with their data-disguised partisan research
through the 1990s and into the 2000s. Today, they've effectively abandoned all conservative principles in their defense of Donald Trump
and cadres of wannabe authoritarians.

THE KOCHTOPUS

The Koch machine, known as the Kochtopus, the right-wing billionaire
brothers and their network of wealthy conservative peers, knew what
it would take to consume one of the political parties. As Rich Fink,
their political advisor duly outlined, they needed the following:[2]

- an extensive academic network to support it intellectually;
- policy networks in every state to draw on that intellectual under-
  pinning from hundreds of American universities;

- a true political grassroots alliance that extended to all of those state capitals and worked closely with the academic and policy network;

- a propaganda arm that could bring tightly controlled messaging and narratives to the fore in the state networks in a way that looked like independent journalism;

- and a national coordinating group that could enforce discipline in what would otherwise be a chaotic, unruly, wildly disconnected political network that ran the gamut from the patriot movement to American exceptionalism.

Smart, if not so sociopathic and ruinous for the country.

Another critical development in the conservative corporate takeover of public policy was a memo written by the future Supreme Court Justice Lewis Powell. "As the experience of the socialist and totalitarian states demonstrates, the contraction and denial of economic freedom is followed inevitably by governmental restrictions on other cherished rights," Powell wrote. "It is this message, above all others, that must be carried home to the American people."[3] Yet more "socialism" nonsense, from a SCOTUS justice, no less.

THE POWELL MEMO

The Powell Memo is regarded by many to be *the* singular most important document related to the economy in the last half century. Not a law or executive order or a ruling. Just an outline of how business should interact with and gain favor with Washington. Businesses, Powell professed, needed to operate as a coordinated group of stakeholders rather than independent entities, because ... there's no I in team.

Lewis Powell (a Nixon appointee) wrote a blueprint in 1971 for businesses to "get organized" in order to overcome the true "enemy of corporate America:" the liberal establishment. It gained widespread popularity and biblical adherence amongst conservatives and big business. According to Jane Mayer, *New Yorker* columnist and author of *Dark Money*, it "electrified the Right, prompting a new breed of wealthy ultraconservatives to weaponize their philanthropic giving in order to fight a multi-front war of influence over American political thought."[4] To an audience of business executives in Dallas in 1974, Charles Koch concluded a speech by saying "As the Powell Memorandum points out, business and the enterprise system are in trouble, and the hour is late." He needed no further explanation.

THINK TANKS STARTED PRODUCING policy papers about "job-killing and economy-crushing regulations." For example, in 1978, the economist Murray Weidenbaum wrote a highly circulated treatise for AEI in which he pointed to federal regulation as the primary source for the high inflation that was killing the economy. He also surmised it cost the economy over $100 billion per year. This was a load of nonsense. As you can read from the chapter Climate Change, "job-killing," like most other conservative propaganda, is extreme embellishment *at best*. Any legislation that proposed raising taxes, even on a bipartisan basis, was blindly dismissed by conservative think tanks. In 1997, President Clinton proposed a bill that was, by all accounts, either a compromise or tilted rightward. The centerpieces were a $500 per-child tax credit (good for middle-income families) and a cut in capital gains taxes (good for rich people). What did the Heritage Foundation say about it? That it hid "substantial growth in the size and scope of the federal government." Republicans were "selling out," they wrote. "While the President's agenda is revealed explicitly in the documents accompanying the agreement, the congressional agenda is left largely up to the imagination . . . Taxpayers are being asked to accept bigger government in exchange for the promise of a 'balanced budget' and a small cut in their taxes."[5] Blah blah blah. Same old pathetic excuses for policy critique. Any bill that seeks to use government for good is socialism! So tiring, isn't it?

CONSPIRACY THEORIES

32

CONSPIRACY THEORIES: THE WHOLE LOT OF THEM

"I have people that have been studying [Obama's birth
certificate] and they cannot believe what they're finding . . .
I would like to have him show his birth certificate, and can I
be honest with you, I hope he can. Because if he can't,
if he can't, if he wasn't born in this country, which is a
real possibility . . . then he has pulled one of the
great cons in the history of politics."

—RACIST OLD MAN DONALD TRUMP YELLING AT THE TV (2011)

WHAT AND WHY?

CONSPIRACY THEORIES ARE A thing. They've always been a thing. As
long as there have been *evil secretive institutions* to pin blame on some
societal phenomena, there have been conspiracy theories. In fact, they
flourished at the founding of this country, because the pilgrims were
i-n-s-a-n-e. Kurt Andersen wrote a book about it called *Fantasyland:*

How America Went Haywire. It's really good. Accompanying the Enlightenment period and the democratization of science and data, and with the advent of investigative reporting and fact-checking, conspiracy theories became less and less relevant. It was harder to prove the government was putting fluoride in the water to enslave our minds when ABC and NBC weren't reporting it and, well ... science. But those dedicated to keeping the make-believe alive were really persistent. Ironically, in 2021, with science having progressed to its tallest heights and having the most educated population ever, conspiracy theories have made a huge comeback. A lot of it is fueled by anti-Semitism, racism, and general bigotry. By channeling popular discontent toward a series of unhinged conspiracy theories, right-wing propagandists have successfully distracted the electorate as they block urgently needed legislation and ram through their self-interested agenda.

***

TO BE CLEAR, EVERYONE—NO matter the party, race, creed, religion, or gender—is susceptible to believing them. If you've watched a YouTube video about 9/11 Truthers, you can tell they are quite sophisticated and believable.[1] However, if you are a Republican, chances are you are much more likely to believe in them than if you are a Democrat. In fact, Republicans have been leading the charge on conspiracy theories for the last sixty-five years. Today, the party is so thoroughly wrapped up in them that even the former president himself and a bunch of sitting members and candidates of Congress have pushed them; for example, take QAnon. This batshit theory professes a Democratic plot to destroy the world using pedophilia and Jews, which undergirds most of this lunacy. I encourage you to read more, but be forewarned.[2]

Several historians and journalists have described Ronald Reagan's retirement from politics and the end of the Cold War as catalysts for these conspiracy theories. "When Reagan left office and the Cold War ended," the journalist George Packer writes, "conservatism lost its best spokesman and its organizing principle. The movement's subsequent leaders—Gingrich, Rush Limbaugh, Jerry Falwell Jr., Ann Coulter, Sarah Palin, Ted Cruz—pursued power, celebrity, and their enemies on the Left without a trace of Reagan's optimistic gloss or William F. Buckley's intellectual dash."[3] They pushed conspiracy theories into pop culture and kept raising the bar of malice.

On August 22, 2020, @realDonaldTrump tweeted:

The deep state, or whoever, over at the FDA is making it very difficult for drug companies to get people in order to test the vaccines and therapeutics. Obviously, they are hoping to the delay the answer until after November 3rd. Must focus on speed, and saving lives! @SteveFDA

However, the conspiracy theories, in their current incarnation, appear to have begun with a guy named John Stormer and his book *None Dare Call It Treason*. Mr. Stormer, the original schemer, remade the conservative movement with the blessing of conservative Barry Goldwater in 1964. He demonstrated that a conspiracy theory can be a very powerful, profitable, and mesmerizing tool for the purpose of swinging an election. As he saw the popularity—or should I say, cult following—grow rapidly, he expanded his repertoire of theories to new wacky heights.

Nicole Hemmer, the author of *Messengers of the Right: Conservative Media and the Transformation of American Politics*, writes about Stormer's obsession not with Soviet Russia or outside influence but with the commie forces *inside* the United States seeking to subvert our American way of life. In other words, the deep state! Notice any parallels?

He argued that the State Department, *not* the Kremlin, had fomented every communist revolution of the twentieth century, including Russia's. Spies, dupes, and traitors in the US government had given Eastern Europe, China, and Cuba to the communists—and the

bomb to the Soviets. "Every communist country in the world literally
has a 'Made in the USA' stamp on it," he concluded.[4]

Nor were these traitors just abetting communists abroad. American leaders, manipulated by communist spies, were also quietly selling
their own people into slavery with the Soviets, ensuring that within
a generation, every American would be either Red or dead. "Once the
takeover comes, you, like millions of others . . . can be slaughtered like
diseased animals or worked to death in slave labor camps or brothels
for the Red Army," Stormer informed his readers. "The communists are
after your children or grandchildren who can still be molded into obedient slaves of the State." Totally normal, psychologically healthy stuff.

Stormer used this conspiracy along with others similar, suggesting,
for instance, that when Lyndon B. Johnson convened the Warren Commission to look into John F. Kennedy's assassination, he did so under
orders from the *Daily Worker*, a Communist Party newspaper.

It actually doesn't seem that crazy compared to the Trump–QAnon
manure-flinging we observe these days.

None Dare Call It Treason paperbacks sold like hotcakes. Conservatives ate this shit up. By Election Day in 1964, it had sold 6.8 million
copies—half the population of the Netherlands at the time. And that
wasn't the only skin-crawling deep state horror show that conservatives bought hook, line, and sinker. There were two others just like
Stormer's, both self-published, that became almost as popular. Here
are Hemmer's descriptions:

- Phyllis Schlafly's *A Choice Not an Echo* (1964)—about "a group of
  secret kingmakers" who had sold out the Republican Party

- J. Evetts Haley's *A Texan Looks at Lyndon* (1964)—an Infowars-
  level tract accusing Johnson of stolen elections and about a
  dozen murders

All in all, 16 million copies were sold, and conservatives successfully blended the borders of reality and lunacy. Hemmer continues,

"Conservatives treated them as campaign literature: handing them out at rallies, distributing them at the convention, mailing them to Republican delegates." The believers saw a natural fit with Goldwater's campaign because (you may have heard this one before), "the belief that established media were not covering Goldwater fairly also stoked the Right's appetite for conservative fare." Fake news!

Goldwater may have gotten his hat handed to him in the presidential election, but his candidacy was the launching pad for the happy marriage between conservative politics and conspiracy theories, just like libertarianism and segregation soon following Roosevelt's New Deal. Southern resistance to racial equality would be a natural ally to the conservative view of economics and federal governance.[5]

Allow me to regale you with those that followed. Stop me if you've heard them before. No need to summarize or attempt to provide witty commentary. I'll just cut and paste from Wikipedia, because the descriptions are hilarious as is:[6]

- *Black Helicopters*: This conspiracy theory emerged in the US in the 1960s. The John Birch Society originally promoted it, asserting that a United Nations force would soon arrive in black helicopters to bring the US under UN control. The theory reemerged in the 1990s during the presidency of Bill Clinton, and has been promoted by talk show host Glenn Beck. A similar theory concerning so-called "phantom helicopters" appeared in the UK in the 1970s.

- *The death of Vince Foster*—In 1997, crime reporter Dan Moldea was approached by Regnery Publishing House, a conservative group whose leadership was impressed by Moldea's published works, to publish a book on the Foster case. In researching Foster's death, Moldea found that documents relating to the Whitewater corporation were removed from Foster's office on July 22 and sent to the Clinton's personal attorney, and that the most oft-used conspiracy scenario could be traced back to Park Police Major

Robert Hines, who shared the idea with Reed Irvine (Accuracy in Media) and Christopher Ruddy (*New York Post*). Moldea concludes, and Maj. Hines publicly maintains, that Hines incorrectly told Irvine and Ruddy "... that there is no exit wound in Foster's head ... I don't think there was anything nefarious here; he was being approached by reporters and he wanted something to say." Still, the "missing exit wound" claim continued to surface.

- *The death of Seth Rich*—The 27-year-old Rich was an employee of the Democratic National Committee (DNC), and his murder spawned several right-wing conspiracy theories, including the false claim that Rich had been involved with the leaked DNC emails in 2016, contradicted by the law enforcement branches that investigated the murder.

- *Pizzagate*—In March 2016, the personal email account of John Podesta, Hillary Clinton's campaign manager, was hacked in a spear-phishing attack. WikiLeaks published his emails in November 2016. Proponents of the Pizzagate conspiracy theory falsely claimed the emails contained coded messages that connected several high-ranking Democratic Party officials and US restaurants with an alleged human trafficking and child sex ring. One of the establishments allegedly involved was the Comet Ping Pong pizzeria in Washington, DC.

- *QAnon*—Also called simply Q, this group holds a disproven and discredited far-right conspiracy theory alleging that a secret cabal of Satan-worshipping, cannibalistic pedophiles is running a global child sex-trafficking ring and plotted against former US president Donald Trump while he was in office. According to US prosecutors, QAnon is commonly called a cult. QAnon has many subscribers, including insurrectionists who stormed the Capitol building January 6, 2021, members of the Trump administration and sitting members of Congress.

- *9/11 Truthers*—The multiple attacks made on the US by terrorists using hijacked aircraft on 9/11 have proved attractive to conspiracy theorists. Theories may include reference to missile or hologram technology. By far, the most common theory is that the attacks were, in fact, controlled demolitions, a theory which has been rejected by the engineering profession and the 9/11 Commission.

- *COVID-19 is a hoax*—A number of conspiracy theories have been promoted about the origin and purported motive behind the SARS-CoV-2 virus and its spread. Some claimed that the virus was engineered, that it escaped or was stolen from a research laboratory, that it may have been a Chinese or United States bioweapon, a Jewish plot to force mass vaccinations or sterilizations, spread as part of a Muslim conspiracy, a population control scheme, or related to 5G mobile phone networks. While the origin has yet to be definitively proven, some of the latter sources are ludicrous.

- *Anti-vaxxers*—It is claimed that the pharmaceutical industry has mounted a cover-up of a causal link between vaccines and autism. The conspiracy theory developed after the publication in Britain in 1998 of a fraudulent paper by discredited former doctor Andrew Wakefield. The resulting anti-vaccine movement has been promoted by a number of prominent persons, including Rob Schneider, Jim Carrey, and US President Donald Trump, and has led to increased rates of infection and death from diseases such as measles in many countries, including the US, Italy, Germany, Romania, and the UK.

- *Chemtrails*—Also known as SLAP (Secret Large-scale Atmospheric Program), this theory alleges that water condensation trails (contrails) from aircraft consist of chemical or biological agents, or contain a supposedly toxic mix of aluminum, strontium, and barium, as a part of secret government policies. An estimated 17 percent of people globally believe the theory to be true or partly true. In 2016, the Carnegie Institution for Science published the first-ever peer-reviewed study of the chemtrail theory; 76 out of 77 participating atmospheric chemists and geochemists stated that they had seen no evidence to support the chemtrail theory, or stated that chemtrail theorists rely on poor sampling.

- *Clinton Body Count*—The Clinton Body Count refers to a conspiracy theory, parts of which have been advanced by Newsmax publisher Christopher Ruddy among others, that asserts that former US President Bill Clinton and his wife Hillary Clinton have assassinated fifty or more of their associates. Such accusations have been around at least since the 1990s, when a pseudodocumentary film called *The Clinton Chronicles*, produced by Larry Nichols and promoted by Rev. Jerry Falwell, accused Bill Clinton of multiple crimes including murder.

- *Fluoridation*—Water fluoridation is the controlled addition of fluoride to a public water supply to reduce tooth decay. Although many dental-health organizations support such fluoridation, the practice is opposed by conspiracy theorists. Allegations include claims that it has been a way to dispose of industrial waste or that it exists to obscure a failure to provide dental care to the poor. A further theory promoted by the John Birch Society in the 1960s described fluoridation as a communist plot to weaken the American population.

- *George Soros*—Hungarian-American investor George Soros has been the subject of conspiracy theories since the 1990s. Soros has used his wealth to promote many political, social, educational, and scientific causes, disbursing grants totaling an estimated $11 billion up to 2016. However, theories tend to assert that Soros is in control of a large portion of the world's wealth and governments and that he secretly funds a large range of persons and organizations for nefarious purposes, such as Antifa, which the conspiracy theorists claim is a single far-left militant group. Such ideas have been promoted by Viktor Orban, Donald Trump, Rudy Giuliani, Joseph diGenova, Bill O'Reilly, Roy Moore, Alex Jones, Paul Gosar, and Ben Garrison. Soros conspiracy theories are *directly* linked to anti-Semitic conspiracy theories. Those who spout them are deliberately connecting these outlandish events with the Jewish faith.

- *New World Order*—The New World Order theory states that a group of international elites controls governments, industry, and media organizations, with the goal of establishing global hegemony. They are alleged to be implicated in most of the major wars of the last two centuries, to carry out secretly staged events, and to deliberately manipulate economies. Organizations alleged to be part of the plot include the Federal Reserve System, the Council on Foreign Relations, the Trilateral Commission, the Bilderberg Group, the European Union, the United Nations, the World Bank, the International Monetary Fund, Bohemian Grove, Le Cercle, and the Yale University society Skull and Bones. New World Order is also related to anti-Semitism.

- *Birtherism and other Obama conspiracies*—Former US President Barack Obama has been the subject of numerous conspiracy theories. His presidency was the subject of a 2009 film, *The Obama Deception*, by Alex Jones, which alleged that Obama's administration was a puppet government for a wealthy elite. Another theory that came to prominence in 2009 is known as *birtherism*. It denies the legitimacy of Obama's presidency by claiming that he was not born in the US. This theory has persisted despite the evidence of his Hawaiian birth certificate and of contemporaneous birth announcements in two Hawaiian newspapers in 1961. Notable promoters of the theory are dentist–lawyer Orly Taitz and President Donald Trump, who has since publicly acknowledged its falsity but is said to continue to advocate for it privately. Other theories claim that Obama, a Protestant Christian, is secretly a Muslim. The birtherism conspiracy continued unabated with Vice President Kamala Harris, when conservatives attempted to claim she was born in Jamaica, not in Oakland (not true).

- *White genocide*—The White genocide, White extinction, or White replacement conspiracy theory is a White supremacist belief that there is a deliberate plot, often blamed on Jews, to promote miscegenation, mass non-White immigration, racial integration, low fertility rates, abortion, and governmental land-confiscation from Whites, organized violence, and eliminationism in White-founded countries in order to cause the extinction of Whites through forced assimilation and violent genocide.

- *False flag operations*—False flag operations are covert operations designed to appear as if they are being carried out by other entities. Some allegations of false flag operations have been verified or have been subjects of legitimate historical dispute (such as the 1933 Reichstag arson attack). Discussions of unsubstantiated allegations of such operations feature strongly in conspiracy theory discourse. Examples include the Parkland School mass shooting, Sandy Hook Elementary School (see below), and the Capitol riots of January 6, 2021.

- *Sandy Hook*—A 2012 fatal mass shooting at Sandy Hook Elementary School in Newtown, Connecticut, prompted numerous conspiracy theories, among which is the claim that it was a manufactured event with the aim of promoting gun control. Former Ku Klux Klan leader David Duke has theorized that Jewish Zionists were responsible. Theorists such as Alex Jones have suggested that the event was staged with actors. Harassment of the bereaved families by conspiracy theorists has resulted in actions for defamation. Rush Limbaugh also stated that the event happened because the Mayan Calendar phenomenon made shooter Adam Lanza do it.

- *Deep state*—While the term is occasionally used as a neutral term to denote a nation's bureaucracy, the conspiratorial notion of a deep state is a concept originating principally in Middle Eastern and North African politics with some basis in truth. The term has been known in the US since the 1960s. It has been revived under the Trump presidency. Deep state in the latter sense refers to an unidentified powerful elite who act in coordinated manipulation of a nation's politics and government. Proponents of such theories have included Canadian author Peter Dale Scott, who has promoted the idea in the US since at least the 1990s, as well as *Breitbart News, Infowars,* and US President Donald Trump. A 2017 poll by ABC News and *The Washington Post* indicated that 48 percent of Americans believe in the existence of a conspiratorial deep state in the US.

- *Cultural Marxism*—The intellectual group known as the Frankfurt School which emerged in the 1930s has increasingly been the subject of conspiracy theories which have alleged the promotion of communism in capitalist societies. The term *Cultural Marxism* has been notably employed by conservative American movements such as the Tea Party, and by Norwegian mass murderer Anders Behring Breivik.

- *Climate change is a hoax*—This global warming conspiracy theory typically alleges that the science behind global warming has been invented or distorted for ideological or financial reasons. Many have promoted such theories, including US President Donald Trump, US Senator James Inhofe, British journalist Christopher Booker, and Viscount Christopher Monckton.

- *Sutherland Springs*—The 2017 Sutherland Springs church shooting has also been the subject of multiple conspiracy theories. The shooter has been linked to multiple conspiracies, such as identifying him as a Democrat, Hillary Clinton supporter, Bernie Sanders supporter, alt-left supporter, Antifa member, or radical Muslim. Others claim that he carried an Antifa flag and told churchgoers: "This is a communist revolution." Some reports also falsely claimed that he targeted the church because they were White conservatives.

- 5G—There have been a number of concerns over the spread of disinformation in the media and online regarding the potential health effects of 5G technology. Writing in the *New York Times* in 2019, William Broad reported that RT America began airing programming linking 5G to harmful health effects which "lack scientific support," such as "brain cancer, infertility, autism, heart tumors, and Alzheimer's disease." Broad asserted that the claims had increased. RT America had run seven programs on this theme by mid-April 2019 but only one in the whole of 2018. The network's coverage had spread to hundreds of blogs and websites.

- *Sharia Law*—A ban on sharia law is legislation which prohibits the application or implementation of Islamic law (Sharia) in courts in any civil (nonreligious) jurisdiction. In the United States, various states have banned Sharia law, or passed some kind of ballot measure that prohibits the state's courts from considering foreign, international or religious law. As of 2014, these include Alabama, Arizona, Kansas, Louisiana, North Carolina, South Dakota, and Tennessee. In Canada, Sharia law is explicitly banned in Quebec, upheld by a unanimous vote against it in 2005 by the National Assembly, while the province of Ontario allows family law disputes to be arbitrated only under Ontario law.

- *Agenda 21*—Agenda 21 is a nonbinding action plan of the United Nations with regard to sustainable development. It is a product of the Earth Summit (UN Conference on Environment and Development) held in Rio de Janeiro, Brazil, in 1992. Far-right-wing groups, including the John Birch Society, assert that Agenda 21 is part of a scheme using environmental protection as a cover to impose a worldwide dictatorship.

- *Holocaust Denial*—Holocaust denial is the act of denying the Nazi genocide of Jews in the Holocaust. Holocaust deniers make one or more of the following false statements: 1) Nazi Germany's Final Solution was aimed only at deporting Jews and did not include their extermination. 2) Nazi authorities did not use extermination camps and gas chambers for the genocidal mass murder of Jews. 3) The actual number of Jews murdered is significantly lower than the accepted figure of five to six million, typically around a tenth of that figure.

Beyond the wild conspiracies, congressional Republicans have mastered the art of manufacturing outrage. Take a soundbite or a run-of-the-mill piece of news and *explode* it into some sinister "plot to destroy America." Well, that would actually be a conspiracy theory, in that case, so let's call these conspiracy-lite. They serve as red meat, outrage machines for their audiences.

- Over-hyped investigations (e.g., Benghazi, Fast & Furious, IRS, Solyndra).

- Cornwall Alliance for the Stewardship of Creation, calling environmental science the Cult of the Green Dragon.

- "Socialism!" and people coming to "take your guns!" or "abortions on demand!" and we're all going to live in a "liberal hellscape" if "demoRATS" are in charge.

The examples below are a case of right-wingers using something called Reductio ad Hitlerum to try to win support of their base, which is the practice of *playing the Nazi card*, an attempt to invalidate someone else's opinion on the basis that there are significant parallels to those held by Adolf Hitler or the Nazi Party. The Left is guilty of this as well, but I contend the similarities are actually legitimate, unlike the following:

- The venture capitalist Tom Perkins wrote about the parallels of fascist Nazi Germany to its war on its "one percent," namely its Jews, to the progressive war on the American one percent, namely the "rich."[7]

- Stephen Schwartzman, CEO of the financial titan Blackstone, equated Obama's attempt to raise taxes on hedge funds with "Adolph Hitler's invasion of Poland."

- Kenneth Langone, one of Home Depot's cofounders, warned that liberal arguments about income inequality reminded him of "Nazi propaganda."[8]

- Ben Carson, Trump's secretary of Housing and Urban Development stated that Obamacare is "the worst thing that has happened in this nation since slavery," and those who want to understand Obama should "read *Mein Kampf* and read the works of Vladimir Lenin."[9]

The Left, for the most part, does not engage in this type of absurdity. Sure, there are instances here and there of conspiracy theorizing and fearmongering (particularly with respect to the Trump administration), but not like this whacked-out version of it. Republicans are the party of conspiracy theories. They own it.

33

MCCARTHYISM

"I have here in my hand a list of 205 that were made known to the Secretary of State as being members of the Communist Party and who nevertheless are still working and shaping policy in the State Department."

—REPUBLICAN SENATOR JOSEPH MCCARTHY IN 1950, WHO NOT SO COINCIDENTALLY SOUNDS EXACTLY LIKE TRUMP AND THE GOP IN 2020

WHAT?

TO UNDERSTAND THE CURRENT craze of conspiracy theories that dominate the far-right discourse, it is necessary to look back to the McCarthyism era of the '50s. I'll let the Miller Center at University of Virginia define the madness:

"In the early 1950s, American leaders repeatedly told the public that they should be fearful of subversive Communist influence in their lives. Communists could be lurking anywhere, using their positions as schoolteachers, college professors, labor organizers, artists, or journalists to aid the program of world Communist domination. This paranoia about the internal Communist threat—what we call the Red Scare—reached a fever pitch between 1950 and 1954, when Senator Joe McCarthy of Wisconsin, a right-wing Republican, launched a series of highly publicized probes into alleged Communist penetration of the State Department, the White House, the Treasury, and even the US Army."[1]

The climate of fear and fearmongering that McCarthy created was unlike anything the country had ever seen. At the height of the era, it was impossible to confront McCarthy without being labeled disloyal and, by extension, a communist. Sound vaguely familiar? Large-scale paranoia? Loyalty to a leader lest you be labeled treasonous? Of course it does.

> **On July 7, 2017 @DonaldJTrumpJr retweeted a Drudge Report link regarding national security leaks and stated:**
> If there was ever confirmation that the Deep State is real, illegal & endangers national security, it's this. Their interests above all else.

WHY?

MCCARTHYISM AND ALL THE wild and ridiculous conspiratorial hogwash that runs with it weakens our democracy, for the primary reason that people begin to distrust our government. If the government is some nefarious secretive organization plotting to make us sicker or experiment on us like some lab, then naturally, people will lose faith in its function. With McCarthyism, in particular, it was a Soviet plot to take over and destroy capitalism and our free American way of life. People suddenly found themselves agonizing over the choice to vote for those who believe in government for good and those who will protect them from communists. In reality, it was a strategy to distract the workers from focusing on voting to improve their benefits and rights. It created red herrings and pulled their attention away from legitimate grievances. Ask yourself, why did Trump do his deep state shtick? Why did Reagan do his socialism thing? (More on that in chapter on Socialism.) Why do Republicans constantly accuse Democrats and the Left of this gigantic nebulous nonsense that no one can possibly defend? Because they are not grounded in reality (alert: alternative facts). There may be a small kernel of truth hidden somewhere, but, just like any other scandal in the last forty years, they manufacture the *hell* out of it. They do it to distract from Democratic legislative priorities that, for the most part, promote justice and equality. And since McCarthy, they've pulled the same baloney over and over and over—the culmination of their achievements being Trump and his absolutely psychotic QAnon theories.

THANK GOODNESS WE HAD a decent Republican president who thought McCarthy was a conspiratorial freak and who stood up to the fascist drunk. When C. D. Jackson, Dwight Eisenhower's speechwriter, approached him about a speech, he remembers, "The President read my text with great irritation, slammed it back at me and said he would not refer to McCarthy personally—'I will not get in the gutter with that guy.'"[2]

To be clear, real deep state spies did exist, and they helped the Soviets steal nuclear weapon secrets, like Julius and Ethel Rosenberg, but, in those cases, there was *evidence* against them, even if it was vague and inconclusive.

ROY COHN

None other than Roy Cohn, Esquire, was assisting McCarthy in these purges. He was counsel to the liquidations. He is the same Roy Cohn who was convinced homosexuality was a threat to national security, despite being gay himself and inviting his lover to work *alongside* him with McCarthy as a consultant. The same Roy Cohn who threatened to "wreck the Army" if his demands for special treatment of his lover were not met. The same Roy Cohn who was disbarred by the New York State Supreme Court for attempting to defraud a client who was on his deathbed by forcing him to sign a will amendment leaving him his fortune. And the same Roy Cohn who represented Donald Trump for his discrimination suit where he wouldn't rent to Black people. That piece of work, Roy Cohn.[3]

McCarthy (and Cohn) terrorized the United States. Under the guise of a "Communist Party takeover" of government, known colloquially as the Red Scare, he leveled false charges and accusations against thousands of people, created fear and paranoia and ruined countless lives. Sound familiar? He also launched a crusade against gay people, known then as the Lavender Scare. He made life miserable for them. The former US Senator Alan K. Simpson wrote, "The so-called 'Red Scare' has been the main focus of most historians of that period of time. A lesser-known element ... and one that harmed far more people was the witch hunt McCarthy and others conducted against homosexuals."[4]

BUSINESS LOVED MCCARTHY

Corporate America adored McCarthy and supported him throughout the monstrousness. Why? Because he was instrumental in impeding the progress of the labor movement. After all, unions were collectivist organizations that protected the rights of workers (read commie). Oh no! Corporate titan Robert E. Wood of Sears, Roebuck: "McCarthy is doing a job that had to be done to put traitors and spies out of our government. You can't be soft with these people."[5] Trump in 2019 is a spitting image of Wood: "You know what we used to do in the old days when we were smart, right? The spies and treason, we used to handle it a little differently than we do now."[6]

Of course, the conservative press fawned over McCarthy and the outstanding work he was doing by rooting out all those imaginary little red people, similar to how Soviet state press would report it. They propagated so much fear and paranoia; neighbors and friends were ratting on each other as they did in Soviet Russia. Law enforcement was looking into tons of bogus threats. While the Red Scare in America was nowhere near the extent of the Soviet skullduggery, I imagine McCarthy would not have minded a little fascist communism himself. "Joseph McCarthy, the Junior Republican Senator from Wisconsin," wrote Martha Gellhorn, in *The View from the Ground*, "ruled America like devil king for four years. His purges were an American mirror image of Stalin's purges, an unnoticed similarity."

William F. Buckley, the conservative intellectual and author, supported McCarthy and his purges *wholeheartedly*. As Kim Phillips-Fein notes, in his books Buckley put up "a vigorous defense of Joe McCarthy which argued that the opponents of the Wisconsin senator failed to fully apprehend the severity of the Red threat." And those books gave Buckley the authority that he needed to start a new magazine—*The National Review*—a magazine that he believed would be able to "revitalize the conservative position," demonstrating that "the conservative alternative to socialism at home and appeasement of the Soviet Union abroad is both plausible and profound, politically realistic and morally imperative."

Sign me up for zero subscriptions, thanks.

MCCARTHYISM KILLED BY HONEST REPUBLICANS

Unlike the yes-men Republican crew in Congress, whose only priority was to appease Trump during his term, Eisenhower was able to eventually stop McCarthy dead in his authoritarian tracks in 1954. The Senate passed a vote of condemnation 67–22, and McCarthy was stomped out like the cockroach he was. (The twenty-two Republican senators who voted "nay" were for censure, at least). He ended up passing away three years later from alcohol abuse, so I guess we have to feel some sympathy, but, then again, he ruined so many people's lives over paranoid delusions, with the help and support of conservative media and corporate America, so I am not shedding a tear.

34

THE JOHN BIRCH SOCIETY

"You should do your utmost to remove from public
office every official who violates the Constitution's
clear meaning if you want to save your own
freedom and help restore your republic."

—EX-CIA OFFICER AND CONSERVATIVE '60S RADIO HOST, DAN SMOOT.
IN THAT CASE, DAN, GET A LOAD OF DONALD TRUMP!

WHAT AND WHY?

THE JOHN BIRCH SOCIETY was (and still is) a ragtag collection of fanatics, radical rich, and somewhat prominent conservative politicians and media who have pushed conspiracy theories about—what else?—socialism, communism, and Democratic terrorists for nearly seventy years. It had, at one point, 100,000 dues-paying members around the country and sixty full-time staff. Fred Koch, the father Charles and David Koch (see my "Un-Koch Your Campus" chapter) was a founding member, so it was probably well-funded! Some of its original work you may remember, included "fluoridation in the water is a government

plot for mind control," and it took off from there. The Southern Poverty Law Center has published a must-read recap of the John Birch
Society and their bizarre theories—and, let's not forget, they've played
a major role in conservative politics for over sixty years.[1] The primary
reason for the existence of groups like John Birch is to inspire a deep
mistrust in government so that it could eventually cede control to
private interests.

LET US DELIBERATE A bit more on the fluoride plot with the author
Jesse Hicks, who writes that it had modest beginnings, initially spread
only by word of mouth and through neat little pamphlets passed
around at county fairs and the like. It then quickly blossomed into
radio, books, and TV, attracting audiences in the tens of millions.
And, by the late '50s, larger, better-funded, right-wing groups began
to support these conspiracy theories. The February 9, 1959, issue of
The Dan Smoot Report, for example, cited Aldous Huxley's dystopian
novel *Brave New World*, in which government-mandated drugs enthrall
and placate the populace. "How could ruling authorities ever manage
to give drugs to an entire population?" asked Smoot. His answer: via
water supplies, just like fluoridation.[2]

Smoot didn't blame the communists *directly*. Instead, he worried
about "the groundwork already being done by fine, civic-minded,
well-intentioned people who cannot be made to understand that they
are helping to open a Pandora's box of evil." Ah, yes, those unwitting
brainwashed communist aiders and abettors!

But then, as Hicks points out, the John Birch Society endorsed
Smoot's take and...blamed the witting communists. The March 31, 1960,
issue of *The Independent* ("A Died-in-the-Wool Yankee-Doodle Journal
of Patriotism for Vigilant Constitutionalists") declared, "Former Communists have stated that fluoridation is known to Communists as a

method of Red Warfare," while also implying that Communists had infiltrated the US Public Health Service.

Not long ago, John Savage from *Politico* sat down with a woman who belongs to today's incarnation of the John Birch Society and, to no one's surprise, found that the Birchers are just as absurd as they were back then. He writes, "She says that the John Birch Society—a group she was convinced could save the nation from a global conspiracy of Leftists and communists more than half a century ago—has come roaring back to life in the nick of time. The more she thinks about the situation, the more she sees parallels to the 1950s and 1960s: evil domestic and international terrorists threatening to undo all that is good and holy in the United States."[3] It would be good and holy if these people lost access to a microphone.

Did I mention they are hypocrites? Once upon a time, the John Birch Society was crazed over the Soviet infiltration of US government. Today? It wanted to *stop* the investigation into Russian meddling in the 2016 election of Trump. How convenient. At one point, the Society's founder Robert Welch called Dwight Eisenhower a "dedicated, conscious agent of the communist conspiracy." Or, in today's environment, perhaps a welcome comrade?

Despite its strong membership base and influential cadre of supporters, the John Birch Society, thankfully, *was* relegated to the sidelines by the mainstream media and its own party in the '60s. As the author Kurt Anderson notes, despite their extraordinary rise, their influence was basically marginalized.[4] The mainstream media played a critical role, but the most prominent rejection came from the intellectual and elite Right itself. Leaders of the conservative movement, unlike today's incarnation, fretted that these cranks might destroy their chance at the nomination and presidency in 1964.

But that didn't really stop the group. Anderson writes, "The marginalization of the Birch Society and brand didn't stop true believers in that mad vision of a globalist conspiracy involving liberals and elites from multiplying." He discusses Phyllis Schlafly's 1964 polemic *A Choice Not an Echo*, which sold millions of copies. "Most of what is ascribed to 'accident' or 'coincidence,'" she wrote, "is really the result of human plans." In that same year, a Missouri Republican named John Stormer self-published *None Dare Call It Treason*, which, Anderson writes, "explained how the federal government and the press and nonprofits were dominated by treasonous stooges and co-conspirators." Fantastic stuff. Stormer sold millions of copies, which led him to publish the sequel: *None Dare Call It Conspiracy*. "The conspirators come from the very highest social strata," he wrote. "They are immensely wealthy, highly educated and extremely cultured," a conspiracy of "the Insiders," "the elite of the academic world and mass communications media" intent on creating a "world supra-government." Totally sober and sensible.

Professor Christopher Towler examines the parallels between the John Birch Society and the racists in the Republican Party of today. He draws a line from their opposition to civil rights to how Tea Party supporters were scared of losing their country to an "anti-White Muslim" like Obama. Moreover, in their extensive examination of the Tea Party movement, political scientists Christopher Parker and Matt Barreto make the case that Obama's election provoked the rise of today's far Right. Towler writes, "Much like how the John Birch Society arose as a rejection of progress on civil rights, tea party supporters felt anxious about what they saw as the 'real' America slipping away when the country chose a Black man to be its president … Just as Birchers called Justice Warren a communist for overruling state and local segregation laws, the tea party labeled President Obama a socialist because of his plan to expand health insurance coverage."[5] And, consistent with Birch Society claims that the civil rights movement was a seditious plot to divide the country, Trump and his minions characterized the Black Lives Matter movement as a force working toward the collapse of social order. The parallels are obvious.

To recap, the John Birch Society is just the first in a long line of Republican groups who push conspiracy theories (see the chapter "Conspiracy Theories: The Whole Lot of Them"). They do this because 1) they've lost the battle of ideas, 2) they need a way to distract the base, 3) they believe politics and economics are zero-sum games, and 4) they want to enhance their financial standing. Mix in some anti-Semitism and racism, and sadly, it works.

MAKING THE REPUBLICAN PLATFORM PALATABLE THROUGH MANUFACTURED OUTRAGE AND DIVISION

CONGRESSIONAL REPUBLICANS HAVE BEEN exceedingly successful at one thing: getting their base riled up over very unpopular positions on critical issues by creating so much outrage around the issue, voters have no choice but to fall in line. For the sake of their survival, they must support the party platform lest the Maoists and neo-Marxists overrun the country and take every nonbeliever as political prisoner. Something like that. These are like wedge issues on steroids. And often times the Republican voters are voting against their economic benefit.

35

ABORTION ("BABY KILLERS!")

"If it's a legitimate rape, the female body
has ways to shut that thing down."

**—FORMER REPUBLICAN CANDIDATE FOR SENATE
AND FULL-TIME MORON TODD AKIN (2012)**

"Virtually every Democrat candidate has declared their
unlimited support for extreme late-term abortion,
ripping babies straight from the mother's womb,
right up until the very moment of birth."

—TRUMP (2020)

"Senate Democrats just voted against legislation to
prevent the killing of newborn infant children.
The Democrat position on abortion is now so extreme
that they don't mind executing babies AFTER birth."

—TRUMP (2019)

"Live birth abortion. Infanticide. Let's just call it what it is—
killing a baby after she or he is born. And it's wrong!"

—FORMER GOVERNOR SCOTT WALKER (2019)

WHAT?

THE AGE-OLD ISSUE OF abortion: when a woman *chooses* to end a pregnancy because it threatens her life, or because she doesn't believe she can care for the baby. Ninety percent of abortions occur in the first trimester, meaning before thirteen weeks. And about 1 percent happen at twenty-one weeks or later (third trimester).[1] A majority of congressional Republicans do not think women should be allowed to choose, despite the fact that abortion rates have been dropping every year since the 1970s, when abortion became legal. They also seem to believe women pine to receive abortions and are lining up to make appointments, just like they might at a hot new hair salon—or at least that's the way they talk about it.

WHY?

THIS IS THE PUREST form of manufactured outrage. White Evangelicals, the largest base of the Republican Party, who seem to make the loudest and smelliest stink about it, didn't really object to abortion at the time the landmark case *Roe v. Wade* was decided. Catholics have always seemed to object (though 56 percent of practicing Catholics are pro-choice).[2] And the Church itself has mostly leaned anti-abortion through its history. Evangelicals, though, not so much. As you will see, they use it as a cudgel and ruse for other bigger, more consequential stuff.

———

NOT UNTIL SEVEN WHOLE years after *Roe v. Wade* in 1973 did congressional Republicans start hammering away at the good sensibilities of their constituents. As you can see from the graph below, abortion became an ever-larger part of the Republican Party platform, judging by the number of mentions if garners election year after election year.

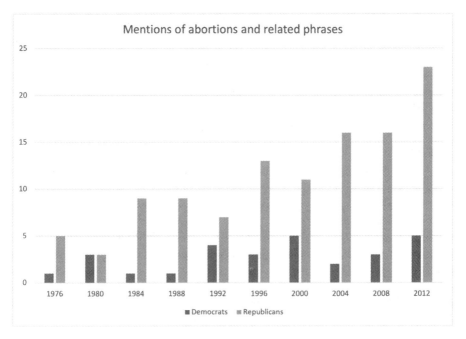

Source: The Guardian

Evangelicals didn't care about abortion at one point? That's weird. They are *fanatical* about it now. More importantly, they use the Bible, which is 2000-plus years old, to justify its evil. You would think they would have *always* been against it.

As a matter of fact, they didn't really feel that *infanticide* itch to scratch until they were able to use abortion as way to stop deseg-regation. That's correct. The issue that truly riled them up was desegregation. But by the 1970s, thankfully, they couldn't stand on a street corner and protest about Blacks-only schools and water foun-tains. A *Politico* piece, titled "The Real Origins of the Religious Right," by Randall Balmer, describes what happened: "It wasn't until 1979—a full

six years after Roe—that evangelical leaders, at the behest of conservative activist Paul Weyrich (founder of the Federalist Society), seized on
abortion not for moral reasons, but as a rallying-cry to deny President
Jimmy Carter a second term. Why? Because the anti-abortion crusade
was more palatable than the religious right's real motive: protecting
segregated schools. So much for the new abolitionism."[3]

If I told you that it was all about keeping Blacks segregated, would
you be surprised? Let's review the evidence. In 1968, the Christian
Medical Society and *Christianity Today*, the flagship magazine of evan-
gelicalism, sponsored a symposium where they not only *declined* to
call abortion "sinful" but rather cited "individual health, family welfare,
and social responsibility" as reasons for a woman to get one![4]

Three years later in 1971, delegates to the Southern Baptist Convention in St. Louis, Missouri, passed a resolution supporting "Southern
Baptists to work for legislation that will allow the possibility of abortion under such conditions as rape, incest, clear evidence of severe fetal
deformity, and carefully ascertained evidence of the likelihood of damage to the emotional, mental, and physical health of the mother."[5] That
very same convention re-doubled their support for that position in 1974
and 1976, three years after *Roe v. Wade* was decided. So conventions of
Baptists and the flagship Christian magazine not only did *not* denounce
it but they *encouraged* it? Whoa! This is some parallel universe.

And when *Roe v. Wade* became law, W. A. Criswell, the Southern Baptist Convention's former president and pastor of First Baptist Church
in Dallas, Texas—also one of the most famous fundamentalists of the
twentieth century—was happy. "I have always felt that it was only after a
child was born and had a life separate from its mother that it became an
individual person," he said, "and it has always, therefore, seemed to me
that what is best for the mother and for the future should be allowed."[6]

"Religious liberty, human equality and justice are advanced by
the Supreme Court abortion decision," wrote W. Barry Garrett, of
Baptist Press.[7]

Hang on there just a second. Religious liberty and human equality *and* justice are advanced by a woman's right to choose? What is going on!

This is the part where congressional conservatives traded abortion for segregation. Paul Weyrich was a smart guy. He knew he needed allies in this fight against multi-culturalism. "The new political philosophy must be defined by us [conservatives] in moral terms, packaged in non-religious language, and propagated throughout the country by our new coalition," Weyrich wrote in the mid-1970s. "When political power is achieved, the moral majority will have the opportunity to re-create this great nation."[8] Ah yes, political power to stifle dissent of the multicultural satanic liberals. The political possibilities were limitless. I used this quote previously because it is so poignant: "The leadership, moral philosophy, and workable vehicle are at hand just waiting to be blended and activated," he wrote. "If the moral majority acts, results could well exceed our wildest dreams." Even if you don't know what Weyrich looks like, can't you picture a balding, bespectacled, James Bond villain from the 1970s rubbing his cat and laughing maniacally?

The problem was, this "moral majority" needed something to spark it—something to rally around. Weyrich was trying on a bunch of different issues like porn, prayer in schools, the Equal Rights Amendment, and even abortion. Nada. "I was trying to get these people interested in those issues and I utterly failed," Weyrich recalled at a conference in 1990. But they finally found one in 1983. Segregation.

The court case that catalyzed the Moral Majority into action was *Bob Jones v. The United States*.[9] Though, I have to discuss at least one of the several cases predating *Jones* that lit the flame of antisegregation: *Green v. Connally* in 1968.[10] This was a case in Virginia that involved Kent County refusing to comply with the 1954 monumental court case *Brown v. The Board of Education*, which supposedly struck segregation from the books. Supposedly. It is common knowledge there have been plenty of cases since that have sought to effectively overturn it. In this case, the good ol' White people of Kent didn't want any race mixing in schools and in life, in general, but the SCOTUS, predictably, upheld *Brown*. The Bob Jones case was, as Balmer puts it "the final straw." Elmer L. Rumminger, the longtime administrator at Bob Jones University, told Balmer in an interview, the IRS actions against his school "alerted the Christian school community about what could happen with government interference" in the affairs of evangelical institutions. "That was really the major issue that got us all involved."

What happened at Bob Jones? Until 1971, good ol' Bob Jones had excluded Blacks from the university, under the pretense that interracial dating was a no-no. From 1971 to 1975, the university admitted Black students, but only if they were married—and after 1975, it admitted unmarried Black students, but only if they didn't engage in interracial dating. The United States took a while to catch up the industrialized world, but they finally told organizations like Bob Jones, if you want to get those tax breaks and subsidies, you gotta stop being overtly racist. Predictably, Bob Jones told the IRS to go hell. The infamous case began in a South Carolina district court and made its way to the US Supreme Court.

During this period, the right-wing machine of propaganda went to work. Weyrich pinned this forced-mixing policy on Jimmy Carter, though it actually began under Nixon, and started to draw in large swaths of voters who were angered by this decision and *Roe v Wade*. So he started championing anti-abortion positions. He began calling pro-life candidates "true cause for celebration," and Robert Billings, who was another prominent figure in the Moral Majority, predicted that opposition to abortion would "pull together many of our 'fringe' Christian friends." The only thing was that *Roe v. Wade* had been law for over five years at that point.

In the early months of 1979, Francis Schaeffer and Dr. C. Everett Koop, two significant twentieth century Christian figures, targeting an evangelical audience, toured the country with these films, which depicted the scourge of abortion in graphic terms—most memorably with a scene of plastic baby dolls strewn along the shores of the Dead Sea. Schaeffer and Koop argued that any society that countenanced abortion was captive to "secular humanism" and therefore caught in a vortex of moral decay.[11]

In 1967, as the governor of California, Ronald Reagan had signed into law the most liberal abortion bill in the country.[12] Even in August of 1980, when he addressed a rally of 10,000 evangelicals at Reunion Arena in Dallas and excoriated the "unconstitutional regulatory agenda" directed by the IRS "against independent schools," he made no mention of abortion.

The Supreme Court's decision in *Bob Jones v. The United States*, handed down on May 24, 1983, ruled against Bob Jones University in an 8-to-1 decision. Three years later, Reagan elevated the sole dissenter, William Rehnquist, to chief justice of the Supreme Court.

It's worth repeating how incredibly disingenuous evangelicals are in their biblical defense of anti-abortion, since they only dreamed it up seven years after it was federally legal. Colorado decriminalized abortion in 1967.[13] We didn't hear much from the Religious Right about that or the other states where it eventually became legal a few years later. And now we know their motivation: overturning desegregation.

Just as they do on other major issues, on abortion congressional Republicans take a small minority stance. You would think from their rhetoric and action that abortion is *wildly* unpopular. But let's take a look at what voters actually think. Only 29 percent of everyone (50 percent of Republicans) thinks we should overturn *Roe v. Wade*. And only 11 percent of people think abortion should be illegal in all circumstances, including rape.[14] Yet, Trump and congressional Republicans chose and confirmed Brett Kavanaugh, Neil Gorsuch, and Amy Coney Barrett so that they would destroy it.

36

GUN SAFETY

("They're Coming to Take Your Guns")

"President Obama is thinking about signing
an executive order where he wants to
take your guns away. I read it in the papers."
—A RESTRAINED TRUMP (2015)

"THE DEMS WANT TO TAKE YOUR GUNS."
—NORMAL TRUMP (AND NEARLY EVERY CONGRESSIONAL GOPER)

WHAT?

THE TERM "GUN CONTROL" is kind of a misnomer. No serious Democrat is trying to *control* guns by, say, limiting the number you can own or how many a manufacturer can produce. It's really about common-sense gun safety. This is not about taking away your guns, which is utter fear-mongering from the GOP. Responsible gun ownership and gun safety is a thing almost everyone in this country wants (literally, almost everyone). This is about universal background checks, an assault-rifle ban, getting guns out of the hands of clinically mentally ill people, reasonable waiting periods, closing gun show loopholes. You know, reasonable stuff. Yet we still have mass shooting after mass shooting, and Congress does absolutely nothing.

WHY?

THE NRA HAS BEEN *the* primary antagonist behind this lack of congressional action for years … decades! What was once a very reasonable organization with a legitimate mission (gun safety and education) became this three-headed succubus whose primary objective, beyond misusing donations for private jets and family trips, was fearmongering over the Second Amendment.[1] They are primarily responsible for the death of most critical gun safety legislation. To a great extent, the NRA has become a lobbying organization for gun manufacturers who have a different agenda—basically to sell as many weapons as possible—than gun owners, and with help from Russia, by the way.

IN REFERENCE TO THAT last part about Russia: the NRA effectively became a money and influence laundering operation for individuals connected to the Russian government. They used the NRA as a vehicle to penetrate the American political scene. Several GOP senators and congressmen flew to Russia over July 4th weekend 2018 to meet with Vladimir Putin.[2] The Justice Department indicted several Russian nationals along with NRA and GOP associates following the 2016 election.[3]

Much like the Sierra Club, the NRA keeps a legislative scorecard to show how loyal members of Congress have been to their cause.

Republicans basically get all As and Democrats straight Fs. If this were actual school, I'd be concerned. The grades would also be reversed, but that's another matter.

The truly sad part about the lack of gun-safety legislation, again, is that the public, the vast majority of us, including Republicans, want it. We really want it. Even Fox News polls say so:

PROPOSAL TO REDUCE GUN VIOLENCE
PERCENT SAYING "FAVOR"

REQUIRE BACKGROUND CHECKS	91%
REQUIRE MENTAL HEALTH CHECKS	84%
RAISE LEGAL AGE TO BUY TO 21	72%
PUT ARMED GUARDS IN SCHOOLS	69%
BAN ASSAULT WEAPONS	60%

MARCH, 2018
REGISTERED VOTERS ±3% PST

Proposal To Reduce Gun Violence

	Favor	Oppose
Require Background Checks	90%	7%
Take Guns From At-Risk People	81%	13%
Ban Assault Weapons	67%	27%

August, 2019
Registered Voters ±3% PST

But nothing gets done. Even people in positions of authority like Sheriff Richard Mack, the recipient of the NRA's Law Enforcement Officer of the Year Award (2013), believe in the tired old adage about "tyrannical government" coming to take our guns and enslave us. To him, government is the biggest terrorist. Literally. "The greatest threat we face today is not terrorists," Mack has said. "It is our own federal government. If America is conquered or ruined it will be from within, not a foreign enemy."[4]

Even worse, below is a transcript of a meeting with President Trump following the 2018 Parkland High School massacre, where a gunman killed seventeen students. Senator Chris Murphy, of Connecticut, basically pleads with Trump for simply passing popular sensible legislation that save lives![5]

Murphy, Feb. 28, 2018: Ninety-seven percent of Americans want universal background checks. In states that have universal background checks, there are 35 percent less gun murders than in the states that don't have them. And yet, we can't get it done. There's nothing else like that, where it works, people want it, And we can't do it.

Trump: But you have a different president now ... You went through a lot of presidents and you didn't get it done. You have a different president. And I think, maybe, you have a different attitude, too. I think people want to get it done.

Murphy: Well, listen, in the end, Mr. President, the reason that nothing has gotten done here is because the gun lobby has had a veto power over any legislation that comes before Congress. I wish that wasn't the case, but that is. And if all we end up doing is the stuff that the gun industry supports, then this just isn't worth it. We are not going to make a difference. And so I'm glad that you've sat down with the [National Rifle Association], but we will get 60 votes on a bill that looks like the Manchin-Toomey compromise on background checks, Mr. President, if you support it. If you come to Congress if you come to Republicans and say, "We are going to do a Manchin-Toomey-like bill to get comprehensive background checks," it will pass. But if this meeting ends up with just, sort of, vague notions of future compromise, then nothing will happen.

Trump: I agree We don't want that.

Murphy: And so I think we have a unique opportunity to get comprehensive background checks, and make sure that nobody buys a gun in this country that's a criminal that's seriously mentally ill, that's on the terrorist watch list. But, Mr. President, it's going to have to be you that brings the Republicans to the table on this because, right now, the gun lobby would stop in its tracks.

Trump: I like that responsibility, Chris. I really do. I think it's time. It's time that a president stepped up, and we haven't had them. And I'm talking Democrat and Republican presidents—they have not stepped up.

FactCheck.org fact-checked the entire meeting and follow up. Apparently two days later, Trump met discreetly with NRA officials, the White House "softened its tone"—as the *Washington Post* put it—on background checks. When questioned about the president's position on background checks, Sarah Huckabee Sanders, White House press secretary, told reporters he had something different in mind. "Not necessarily universal background checks, but certainly improving the background check system. He wants to see what that legislation, the final piece of it looks like. 'Universal' means something different to a lot of people." ARRRGHHH.

FactCheck continues with what the Democrats are doing about this unimaginable inertia at the hands of the congressional conservative bootlickers. After Democrats won control of the House in 2018, they passed the Bipartisan Background Checks Act on February 27—which, like the Manchin-Toomey legislation, proposed to expand federal background checks to gun purchases and transfers between private parties, including some sold at gun shows or over the internet not covered by current law. The bill passed 240–190 mostly along party lines, though eight Republicans voted for it.[6]

Then, the very next day, the House passed the Enhanced Background Checks Act of 2019, which sought to close the "Charleston Loophole" by lengthening background checks from three to ten business days.

Trump, of course, signaled he was going to veto both bills. A statement from the administration said that Bipartisan Background Checks Act "would impose burdensome requirements on certain firearm transactions, and would require that certain transfers, loans, gifts, and sales of firearms be processed by a federally licensed importer, manufacturer, or dealer of firearms," and "would therefore impose permanent record-keeping requirements and limitless fees on these everyday transactions."[7]

Oh, but there are more reasons they can't support this sensible gun-safety bill. It "contains very narrow exemptions from these requirements, and these exemptions would not sufficiently protect the Second Amendment right of individuals to keep and bear arms." Good Lord! These snowflakes and their Second Amendment!

37

IMMIGRATION

("A Caravan of Mexicans
Is Invading Your Neighborhood")

"When Mexico sends its people, they're not sending their best.
They're not sending you. They're not sending you.
They're sending people that have lots of problems,
and they're bringing those problems with us.
They're bringing drugs. They're bringing crime.
They're rapists. And some, I assume, are good people."

—CRIMINAL AND ALLEGED RAPIST DONALD TRUMP (2015)

WHAT?

IMMIGRATION. THE ISSUE THAT arguably got Trump elected. Some people want to shut it down completely. Even fewer people want *open borders*—but that's not what conservative media would have you believe. They even accuse President Biden of advocating for open borders. This is not such a good development for the majority of the American people, who actually like and support immigration and who don't want a porous border or a total shutdown but just a simpler, better system that allows for still millions of new entrants. But that can't happen, because we are held hostage by the radical wing of the GOP.

WHY?

THE PRIMARY EXPLANATION: RACISM. I mean, it's really xenophobia and White people seeking to preserve the White majority of this country, but po-tay-to, po-tah-to. White Trump supporters fear their impending minority status. If we examine what people think about immigration, we'll observe a different picture. According to Gallup, for the first time in at least fifty-four years, the percentage of people who think immigration should be *increased* is now higher than the people who think it should be decreased. *Fifty-four years!* Nearly 70 percent of people want to either increase immigration or keep it the same. Only 29 percent want to reduce it. And yet we have a party that wants to *drastically* reduce it. How in the world!

HEALTHY MAJORITIES, INCLUDING REPUBLICANS, also want to increase security on the border with Mexico, to establish a way for undocumented immigrants to stay here legally, and to take in refugees from war-torn countries. And yet none of this was reflected in the policy suggestions of the Trump administration and the Republican Congress except for a stupid expensive border wall with Mexico. According to Pew Research, 68 percent want more border security. (So do a majority of Democrats; it was part of Obama's big immigration plan that Republicans killed for really no other reason than it was written by Obama.) Sixty-seven percent of people want to establish a way for immigrants here illegally to stay legally, including 48 percent of Republicans. Seventy-three percent want to take in refugees escaping war and violence, including 58 percent of Republicans.[1] Meanwhile the GOP and Trump administration were trying to kick out illegal immigrants and block the entry of refugees *and* kick out those who have been here under protection from previous policies of Bush and Obama.

Take a trip down memory lane with me for a second. Republicans used to be a decent party on immigration. In 1982, at a ceremony on Ellis Island, Ronald Reagan spoke of immigrants who "possessed a determination that with hard work and freedom, they would live a better life and their children even more so."[2] Reagan signed the Immigration Reform and Control Act of 1986, which included stepped-up border enforcement and sanctions against employers who knowingly hire illegal workers. And that legislation legalized 2.8 million undocumented workers. A far cry from the previous occupant of the White House—Trump. In fact, more immigrants entered the United States legally during Reagan's term than under any previous administration since the nineteen teens under Theodore Roosevelt.

Even when he was on his way out, in January 1989, Reagan spoke of his compassion for immigrants: "I've spoken of the shining city all my political life, but I don't know if I ever quite communicated what I saw when I said it. But in my mind, it was a tall, proud city built on rocks stronger than oceans, windswept, God-blessed and teeming with people of all kinds living in harmony and peace; a city with free ports that hummed with commerce and creativity. And if there had to be city walls, the walls had doors and the doors were open to anyone with the will and heart to get here."[3]

Bush II was pretty cool on immigration, too. Don't take my word on this. Here's Stephen Miller, Trump's advisor and Golum stunt double, who called Bush's record on immigration an "astonishing betrayal."[4] If that guy is giving bad marks to an immigration record, you know it was good for the country.

In 2007, Bush tried to pass comprehensive immigration reform, which would have given a pathway to citizenship for the millions of illegal immigrants who had come into the United States during his presidency—but a majority of his own party in the House and Senate opposed it. This was about the time the radicals assumed *full* control of the party. Rush Limbaugh was on the airwaves bleating like a dying goat (not sorry) about "amnesty for illegals!" A study by the Project for Excellence in Journalism in 2007 writes, "If media attention translates into political pressure, the argument that talk radio helped kill the immigration bill in Congress has some support in the data … Thanks to energetic opposition from Rush Limbaugh, Sean Hannity, and Michael Savage, immigration was the biggest topic, at 16 percent, on conservative talk radio in the second quarter."[5]

President Obama tried to pass immigration reform in 2013, too. And Republicans rejected it again. The Senate actually passed the bill, and it nearly made it through the House, because there were enough Republicans—albeit a minority in their party—ready to join almost all of the Democrats to push it through. But Speaker Boehner wouldn't do it because he was effectively beholden to the hard-liners of the far Right.[6]

Republicans had repeatedly complained about an insecure border, even though border security had vastly increased under Obama, and net immigration from Mexico had actually fallen to zero, a decline also partly explained by the economic downturn. According to US Border Patrol, Obama increased funds for border security by nearly more than Presidents Clinton and Bush combined! Clinton increased the budget for the Border Patrol Program nearly $600 million, and Bush by $1.2 billion. Obama? It increased $1.4 billion, the point being, he was most certainly not weak on border security or for open borders.[7] But that's congressional Republicans for you. They are *great* at propaganda and manufactured outrage.

Not to mention, immigrant removals *peaked* under Obama. You read that right. During Bush II, the number hung around 200,000 to 350,000 per year. Obama increased that to nearly 450,000 per year.[8] Hardly a guy soft on illegal immigration.

"We can't have people pouring into our country like they have over the last 10 years."

THE REALITY Illegal border crossings have been declining for nearly two decades. In 2017, border-crossing apprehensions were at their lowest point since 1971.

Source: Washington Post

Yet more evidence Americans are bullish on immigration from Peter Dreier in the *American Prospect*:[9]

- Sixty-eight percent of Americans—including 48 percent of Republicans—believe the country's openness to people from around the world "is essential to who we are as a nation." Just 29 percent say that "if America is too open to people from all over the world, we risk losing our identity as a nation."

- Sixty-five percent of Americans—including 42 percent of Republicans—say immigrants strengthen the country "because of their hard work and talents." Just 26 percent say immigrants are a burden "because they take our jobs, housing and health care."

- Sixty-four percent of Americans think an increasing number of people from different races, ethnic groups, and nationalities makes the country a better place to live. Only 5 percent say it makes the United States a worse place to live, and 29 percent say it makes no difference.

- Seventy-six percent of registered voters—including 69 percent of Republicans—support allowing undocumented immigrants brought to the country as children (Dreamers) to stay in the country.

- Fifty-eight percent think Dreamers should be allowed to stay and become citizens if they meet certain requirements. Another 18 percent think they should be allowed to stay and become legal residents, but not citizens. Only 15 percent think they should be removed or deported from the country.

Needless to say, when it comes to immigration reform, congressional Republicans are not on the side of the American people.

38

ECONOMICS

("If We Cut Taxes for the Wealthy, It Will Trickle-Down to the All Americans")

"We're going to cut taxes massively. We'll cut business taxes massively. They're going to start hiring people. We're going to bring the $2.5 trillion that's offshore back into the country. We're going to start the engine rolling again because right now our country is dying at 1 percent GDP [growth]."

—TRUMP (BIG PROMISES FROM THE LEADER OF A FAILED ECONOMIC PLATFORM) (2016)

WHAT?

TAX CUTS. THAT'S IT. The singular legislative goal for conservatives and Republican congresspeople believe in: tax cuts. It's their singular goal in life. "Give me tax cuts or give me death!" Tax cuts are the answers to all our prayers. By cutting taxes, the economy will come back from the dead and roar ahead like a hungry lion giving chase. This is especially true if we cut taxes for the really rich and corporations, the theory goes: it will—surely—trickle down to the commoners. Surely. They've been saying that for forty years now. Oh, and slashing regulations. Let's not forget about that. The less government interference, the better (see why that's hogwash in the chapter on the Environment).

Ronald Reagan (1981):

> If, on the other hand, you reduce tax rates and allow people to spend or save more of what they earn, they'll become more industrious; they'll have more incentive to work hard, and money they earn will add fuel to the great economic machine that energizes our national progress. The result: more prosperity for all—and more revenue for government.

WHY?

LOWER TAXES AND LESS regulation mean more money and power for corporates and rich people. Simple.

GEORGE BUSH II HAS had enough of you criticizing tax cuts.

"I don't ever want to hear you use those words in my presence again. Bad policy. If I decide to [give a tax cut], by definition it's good policy. I thought you got that."—George W. Bush speaking to his chief of staff, Andy Card (2001).

Well, the verdict is in (actually it has been in for a while). Despite endless streams of congressional conservative promises, high and low, near and far, and lots of *shouting* about the *shared prosperity*, trickle-down economics has turned out to be one of the biggest failures and lies in American history. Its proponents claimed that by cutting taxes for the very wealthy and corporations, they could grow the economy, raise tax revenue, and create shared prosperity. None of that happened. We had less growth, less tax revenue, and a widening of inequality we haven't seen since the Gilded Age. Excellent news!

The graph on the left, from the AP, is what trickle-down proponents would like you to believe. As tax rate goes up, economic growth slows. But what really happens is the graph on the right. A *positive* correlation between raising taxes and economic growth. Whaddya know! When congressional conservatives blabber on about cutting taxes being good for the economy, turn off the TV.

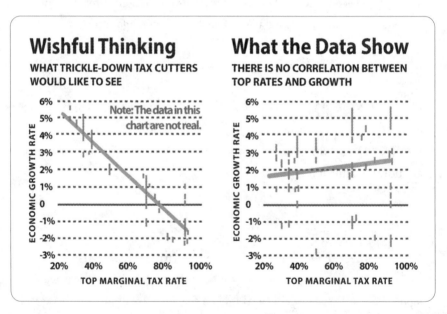

Source: the Associated Press

Here's what income inequality looked like as conservatives and corporations gained more and more traction in Washington in the 1970s into 2010s. As you can see, the distribution of income growth for the top 10 percent shot up like a rocket, while the bottom 90 percent saw their growth fall off a cliff and even turn negative recently.

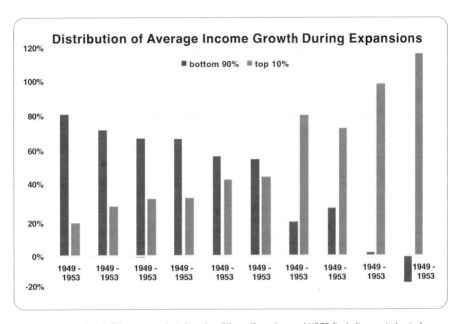

Source: Pavlina R. Tcherneva analysis based on Piketty/Saez data and NBER (including capital gains)

One can observe the same phenomenon with share of national income. In 1980, the top 1 percent earned roughly 11 percent and bottom 50 percent earned 21 percent of the national income. By 2018 the amounts were reversed with the top 1 percent earning 19 percent and the bottom 50 percent earning 13 percent of national income.[1]

Inequality stands at a one-hundred-year high as of this writing. One century. During his tenure, Obama attempted to lessen it (e.g., Affordable Care Act, Dodd–Frank, raising the highest tax bracket) and certainly did not do enough (but there was so much obstruction from Republicans, it was difficult to get anything past the Senate). How did Trump and the GOP approach this problem? Their signature Trump Tax Plan! Here's what it promised:

"Our focus is on helping the folks who work in the mailrooms and the machine shops of America," Trump told supporters in the fall of 2017. "The plumbers, the carpenters, the cops, the teachers, the truck drivers, the pipe-fitters, the people that like me best."[2]

"It will be rocket fuel for our economy."[3]

"The tax plan will pay for itself with economic growth," Treasury Secretary Steven Mnuchin told us.[4]

The White House website gloated over reducing the corporate tax rate from 35 to 20 percent, which would, according to the notable genius economic advisors of Trumpworld like Peter Navarro, "increase average household income in the United States by, very conservatively, $4,000 annually."[5] They haven't learned anything from the failure of trickle-down economics, or, more likely, they had and were simply lying to you. They had the chutzpah to insist that for the average American household, the value of corporate tax reform is "substantially higher than $4,000." This was simply laughable. Not only has recent nonpartisan analysis suggested it to be false but tax cuts for the majority of Americans will go in the opposite direction starting in 2021. Meaning, most people will be taxed *more* than they were in 2020.

"It was unbelievable at the time," writes Maya MacGuineas, the president of the Committee for a Responsible Federal Budget, "and it's proven to be absolutely untrue. The tax cuts were never going to—and have not—come anywhere close to paying for themselves."[6] Here's a compilation of what actually happened, according to MacGuineas:

- Corporate tax revenues fell 31 percent in the first year after the cut was passed. Overall tax revenues have declined as a share of the economy in each of the two years since the tax cut took effect. Let's repeat that with emphasis. Every year since the tax cut took effect, revenue to the government has declined. Contrast that to what Trump and every Republican politician on the planet pronounces: "It's going to get business humming and bring in so much more tax revenue for beautiful shared prosperity."

- The Federal deficit exploded (precoronavirus).

- Almost 80 percent of the gains will go to the top 1 percent. Definitely not "shared prosperity."[7]

- How about GDP Growth? Not really. In Obama's second term, growth averaged 2.3 percent. In Trump's first term, before the pandemic, growth averaged 2.5 percent.[8]

- Job Growth? That's another nope. Job growth was actually stronger under Obama than it was under Trump. On average, Obama created 43,000 more jobs per month than Trump.[9]

- Median household income? Nope. During Obama's last two years, 2014–2016, income grew faster in forty-eight states than it did under Trump's first two years. In fact, real household income grew at 5.6 percent on average across the nation under Obama, while under Trump it grew 2.7 percent.[10]

- Business investment? Yet another nope. This category is where Republicans bend over backwards to highlight when they want to cut taxes. "I would expect capital spending to really take off if the tax bill passes," Trump's chief economist Kevin Hassett told reporters just before the Trump Tax Plan passed. In reality, this phenomenon does not occur. Business investment moves instead according to cycles in the economy, despite what Republicans will tell you.[11]

SHARE BUYBACKS

Ah, stock buybacks! Now we're getting somewhere! That's where most of the corporate savings are going. If you're new to the concept of a stock buyback, it is essentially a way for a company to purchase its own shares on the stock market because they believe it is a good investment. But, if we're being honest, it's really more about driving the stock price higher. Because who owns the stock? Rich people, CEOs, board members, and other rich people. There are no laws against buying stock back, which is why it is, some would say, abused (my old finance friends would be mad at me for saying this and launch into a heated debate about "opportunity cost").

An analysis by the Center for Budget and Policy Priorities showed that most of the tax savings flowed to the shareholders. Some to job creation (though hardly any new jobs were created) and crumbs to workers and the others.[12]

And who owns stock in America? Mostly the top 1 percent and 10 percent. The top 1 percent own 50 percent of all stocks. The top 10 percent own a whopping 92.5 percent of all stocks. Over *90 percent!* The bottom 90 percent own the peanut shells: less than 8 percent of all stocks, which is less than half of what the top 0.1 percent of Americans own. Imagine that. Three hundred million Americans own less than half the amount of stock as the richest 300,000.[13] Unfathomable.

Just so we're clear, Trump, man of the people, the working class, the forgotten man, had a grand plan to improve their economic standing by … giving massive tax breaks that flowed to the top 1 percent. Jobs didn't come back. Businesses did not invest. GDP did not grow. Trump was simply carrying the mantle of Republican economic doctrine as it has been defined since the dawn of Ronald Reagan. Same empty promises. Year after year.

39

HEALTH CARE

("Obamacare is Soviet Communism")

"But if we have learned anything from Obamacare, we know more government is not the answer to America's health care problem. More government is the problem."

—SENATOR TED CRUZ (2020)

IN AN INTERVIEW ON Fox News in July 2013, Ted Cruz gave the game away. After ritualistically declaring that "Obamacare isn't working," he said this: "If we're going to repeal it, we've got to do so now or it will remain with us forever." Why? Because once the administration gets the health insurance "exchanges in place … the subsidies in place," people will get "hooked on Obamacare so that it can never be unwound."

WHAT AND WHY?

THAT'S IT. THAT'S THE Republican solution: Get the government out of health care. That's all they got. Sure, they have plans and drafts of plans on paper using fancy health care words, but all it actually says is, "Let the free market sort it out." Well, we tried that, and it didn't work. Or, it worked for only a small minority of the population. Framing the debate as *evil socialism vs the idyllic free market* is not only dishonest: It deliberately deprives people of life-saving care. Health care has been *the* most important issue for voters in the last two election cycles. People want accessible, affordable health care. Simply put, congressional Democrats believe this is a human right. Republicans do not. Because of this, the fight is over whether government should be the people's guarantor when they've got nowhere else to go. Leaving millions without health coverage makes our society weaker and sicker.

FIRST, WHAT IS THE current Republican plan for health care? As of this writing, they don't have one.

They tried repealing the popular Affordable Care Act (a.k.a. Obamacare) over seventy times between 2010 and today (*seventy times*), with the closest coming in 2017 when they were one Senate vote short (thank you, John McCain!). Mitch McConnell was very disappointed.[1]

Furthermore, Trump and the GOP wanted to yank health care from effectively hundreds of millions during a pandemic. Yes, you heard that right. Don't let a deadly pandemic and an economic crisis get in the way of radical conservative ideology.[2]

A bit of history. I am no health care historian, but I know that up through the early 1960s, health care was expensive and inaccessible to millions of middle- and low-income voters. Then, President Lyndon Johnson, in his famous campaign against poverty, promoted what was dubbed the Great Society, which created Medicare and Medicaid. You've probably heard of these. They are programs that insure access to health care for the poor and elderly. Despite tooth-and-nail efforts by congressional conservatives and wealthy corporates to defeat them, they have been a big success.

Johnson, in 1965, embarked on one of the largest health care expansions in our nation's history. The author Peter Feuerherd notes that historians largely agree that the Great Society made an impact.[3] Its programs increased Social Security benefits, which substantially aided the elderly poor; established Medicare and Medicaid, for which even conservatives today show their support; and helped African Americans in the 1960s, whose income rose by 50 percent in the decade. The percentage of families living below the poverty line also declined. Including programs such as food stamps, the Great Society propelled a 26 percent decrease in poverty rates today compared to before its enactment in 1960. Even today, programs that boosted support for struggling middle-class people, such as Medicare, remain highly popular. It's worth noting that congressional Republicans decried Medicare and Medicaid as socialist at the time of the Great Society.

When these programs were weakened by Presidents Reagan and Bush (and Clinton) in the decades following, President Obama stepped in with his signature Obamacare plan in 2010. Despite massive obstruction and opposition to the bill by the Tea Party and congressional conservatives (because, socialism), it has been a success.

The Commonwealth Fund has run the numbers. "Gaining insurance coverage through the expansions [of ACA Medicaid]," they found in 2017, "decreased the probability of not receiving medical care by between 20.9 percent and 25 percent. Gaining insurance coverage also increased the probability of having a usual place of care by between 47.1 percent and 86.5 percent. These findings suggest that not only has the ACA decreased the number of uninsured Americans but has substantially improved access to care for those who gained coverage."[4]

The ACA substantially improved access to health care *and* financial security. Between 2010 and 2018, the share of adults under 65:

- Fell by 17 percent for those who had a problem paying a medical bill
- Fell by 27 percent for those who didn't fill a prescription
- Fell by 24 percent for those who skipped a test or a treatment

- Fell by 19 percent for those who didn't visit a provider even though they needed care

Sounds good, if you ask me. But I care about people receiving health care who can't afford it, unlike congressional Republicans and the radical rich. I imagine rank-and-file Republicans care too—given that a lot of them benefit from the plan—but who knows.

Another critical component of the ACA was giving access to health care to people with preexisting conditions. They run the gamut from cancer to blood clots to migraines. Everyone has someone in their lives with a preexisting condition. Those people, sadly, would be turned away from coverage without the ACA. During a pandemic. And Republicans are still trying to dismantle it.

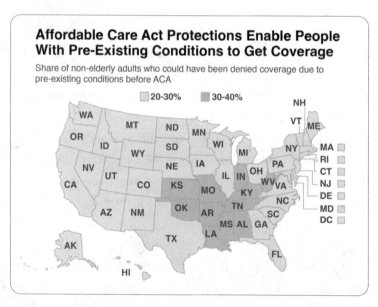

Source: Kaiser Family Foundation, The Commonwealth Fund and Center on Budget and Policy Priorities

A vast majority of people are satisfied (82 percent) with their coverage under the ACA. This number is *up* from 65 percent in 2014.

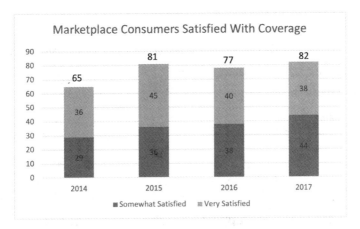

Source: Commonwealth Fund

But the GOP hates the program. And Trump berated it. "Obamacare is a disaster," he has said. "It's too expensive by far." For years, conservatives have been complaining about the cost of Obamacare. Years! Despite what they say, health care costs have slowed dramatically since the ACA's passing.

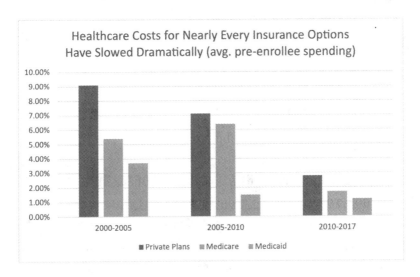

Premium growth for employer-provided family health coverage has slowed significantly, too. Total premiums fell from an average increase of 8 percent per year between 2000 and 2010 to 4.5 percent per year between 2010 and 2018. Worker's contributions? Fell from a 9.5 percent increase per year to 4.2 percent![5] Even employer's contributions fell. What the heck, Republicans? I thought costs were spiraling out of control!

And there is even really strong support (among both Republicans and Democrats) for the provisions of the ACA. Some over 80 percent!

There Is Strong Public Support for Major ACA Provisions

Affordable Care Act Provision	Percent in favor
Allows young adults to stay on their parents' insurance plans until age 26	82%
Creates health insurance exchanges where small businesses and people can shop for insurance and compare prices and benefits	82%
Provides financial help to low- and moderate-income Americans who don't get insurance through their jobs to help them purchase coverage	81%
Gradually closes the Medicare prescription drug "doughnut hole" so people on Medicare will no longer have to pay for the full cost of their medications	81%
Eliminates out-of-pocket costs for many preventive services	79%
Allows states to expand Medicaid to cover more low-income, uninsured adults	77%
Prohibits insurance companies from denying coverage because of a person's medical history	65%
Increases the Medicare payroll tax on earnings for upper-income Americans	65%

Source: Kaiser Family Foundation Health Tracking Poll (November 2018)

EVIDENCE OF THE EFFECTS OF PROPAGANDA

Incidentally, a sizable portion of the electorate supports the ACA but not Obamacare—even though, of course, they're the *same* thing. Gee, I wonder why? Could it be the endless stream of Obamacare bashing by congressional conservatives (and conservative media) since its inception? Here's an actual interview with a Republican about Obamacare that perfectly encapsulates the damage of manufactured outrage:[6]

"So you disagree with Obamacare?"

"Yes, I do."

"Do you think insurance companies should be able to exclude people with preexisting conditions?"

"No."

"Do you agree that young people should be able to stay on their parents' plans until they're 26?"

"They should be able to, yes."

"Do you agree that companies with 50 or more employees should provide health care?"

"I do."

"And so, by that logic, you would be for the Affordable Care Act?"

"Yes."

How frustrating and stupid!

According to a Morning Consult poll in 2017, if one knew of the policy consequences of repeal without replacement, they were likely to support on partisan lines. However, 53 percent of Republicans who wanted to repeal thought that expanded Medicaid coverage and private insurance subsidies would be not eliminated under repeal (compared with 21 percent of Democrats).[7]

People aren't that stupid. I give loads of credit to the right-wing media machine and their witting congressional participants who have been attacking Obamacare now for ten-plus years. Their *incessant* propaganda has meaningfully tipped the opinion scales. With Democrat-leaning votes, too.

For congressional Republicans and private industry (namely, insurance companies), it is not about solutions. It's about ideology. Forget what works, just get the government out of health care. Further proof of this:

"[Hillary Clinton] want[s] to move toward
mandated government medicine, socialized medicine."

—RUDY GIULIANI (2007)

"Creating a government-run plan—in any form—to compete
alongside the private sector for non-Medicare/Medicaid eligible
individuals is unnecessary to achieve comprehensive reform
and would have devastating consequences."

—SCOTT SEROTA, BLUE CROSS AND BLUE SHIELD ASSOCIATION (2009)

"Forcing free market plans to compete with these
government-run programs would create an unlevel
playing field and inevitably doom true competition."

—SENATORS MITCH MCCONNELL, ORRIN HATCH,
CHARLES GRASSLEY, MIKE ENZI, AND JUDD GREGG (2009)

"Yet research indicates that much of what Americans
spend on medical care, through both government programs
and a private sector heavily dominated by government
interference, offers no benefit to patients."

—CATO INSTITUTE'S 2017 HANDBOOK FOR POLICYMAKERS

"When listening to those advocating 'Medicare for All' it's good
to be skeptical about their promises. As head of the agency
that serves over 58 million Medicare beneficiaries, I deal
first-hand with the challenges of government-run health care."

—SEEMA VERMA, ADMINISTRATOR,
CENTERS FOR MEDICARE & MEDICAID SERVICES (2018)

At the end of the day, the wind is blowing in Obamacare's direction, and congressional conservatives are getting more desperate to repeal it. One by one, states are adopting more Obamacare. One Republican governor after another decided to buck conservative ideologues and take federal money to support their local hospitals and insure their most vulnerable citizens. Well, technically, the voters overruled the governor in some cases, but to-may-to, to-mah-to. It is pretty clear to me that if Republicans had tried to work with Obama rather than sabotage his health care plan, we, as a country, would be in a much better place than we are with health care (or any issue, for that matter).

One of the principal objections to the law, which I debunked earlier, was the increase in the cost of premiums. Would you be surprised if I said that Republicans were likely responsible for a sizable portion of the increase? Me neither. Naturally, they banded together to unilaterally (and illegally) block a provision to reimburse insurance companies for insuring sicker patients, per the law, known as the *risk corridor*, which was to take effect in 2014. That is, *seven years ago!* Insurers set premiums expecting these payments. Republicans labeled this *socialism* and illegally withheld the money by passing a spending-bill rider. The Supreme Court ruled in early 2020 that the government illegally denied assistance to health insurers who took part in the ACA. But the damage was already done. Had the money gone out when it was supposed to, it would have not led to insurers *increasing* premiums on other people and in general would have resulted in less complexity in dealing with the marketplaces. The government had to pay $12 billion it owed many years ago, way past the point it would have had a positive effect. There is a small possibility that insurers will be required to rebate some of the money to customers. A few early Obamacare participants, such as health co-ops established under the ACA, are no longer in existence, so hedge funds and state guaranty associations are likely to receive the money instead. Nevertheless, the premiums on Obamacare exchanges stabilized anyhow. This was just the latest in Republican efforts to sabotage the ACA, and it's costing taxpayers a boatload of money.

In fact, Louise Norris has detailed twelve different ways congressio-nal Republicans have obstructed Obamacare since its passage in 2010. These include umpteen legal challenges, short-changing health care co-ops, refusal to take ACA's Medicaid expansion funding, obstruct-ing enrollment efforts and various regulatory action to destabilize it.[8] If you ever wonder why we have the worst and most expensive health care coverage *in the industrialized world,* a good place to start is Republican shenanigans.

40

EDUCATION

("The Socialist Teachers Are Brainwashing Our Children")

"Our nation is witnessing a merciless campaign to
wipe out our history, defame our heroes,
erase our values and indoctrinate our children."

**—PRESIDENT TRUMP, WHO MOST LIKELY FLUNKED
EVERY HISTORY COURSE HE EVER TOOK (2020)**

WHAT?

REPUBLICANS' BASIC PREMISE ON education is the same as health care, the environment, and gun safety. "Get the government out! Let the private market sort it out." Mind you, we have one of the most privatized education systems in the world, and one of the most expensive, if not tops in both categories. And results are not all that great. We do have some of the best universities in the world, but those less fortunate who can't afford to attend those elite institutions are struggling in an ever-more-poorly-funded system. Just like Republican economics, the educational resources are not trickling down to the rest of the country. The state of education in this country is woeful, given how wealthy we are. This is in no small part due to the consistent attempts by the GOP to defund it over the last forty-plus years.

WHY?

CONGRESSIONAL REPUBLICANS SIMPLY DON'T value education. It represents an obstacle to their desired one-party rule. By keeping the *masses* deliberately undereducated, they are retaining the power for themselves. Effective self-government relies on a well-funded education system. By intentionally underfunding it, they take power out of the hands of the citizens and give it to the unelected wealthy among us. They seek to create more Republicans by defunding public school education and controlling what is taught.

I'D LIKE TO BEGIN by briefly mentioning critical thinking. It is, well, a critical component of education and life. We humans have to learn how to differentiate thoughtfully between ideas, know (conspiracy) theory from fact, and think through decisions with multiple streams of information. That is what critical thinking teaches us. Congressional conservatives don't seem to think so. Not only do they object to anything with the term "critical" in the title, like "critical race theory" or "critical legal theory," but they simply object to critical thinking altogether. From a 2012, Texas State standard school review: "Knowl-edge-Based Education—We oppose the teaching of Higher Order Thinking Skills (HOTS) (values clarification), critical thinking skills and similar programs that are simply a relabeling of Outcome-Based Education (OBE) (mastery learning) which focus on behavior modification and have the purpose of challenging the student's fixed beliefs and undermining parental authority."[1]

It is remarkable to me how congressional Republicans want to crush funding to states for education during the COVID-19 crisis. Their reasoning? No formal evaluation of how the money is being spent. OK... show me an evaluation of a stimulus for any amount spent anywhere. Did they track how hedge funds spent it? Trump's properties? Virginia Foxx of North Carolina, a Trump Republican and the ranking member on the Education and Labor Committee, said there's no way education is getting any more of our tax dollars. That's probably because they're reserved for her donor base. She argued, "Congress must first evaluate the impact of the billions of dollars in federal taxpayer education aid before rushing to further burden taxpayers with additional spending. Demanding additional funds at this time is premature and illogical."[2] You know what's illogical? How someone like her was elected to represent the interests of her constituents.

SCHOOL CHOICE

The concept of school choice was developed in 1955 by Milton Friedman. (As an aside, do you think it was any coincidence that he came up with this idea just a year after the Supreme Court desegregated schools with *Brown vs. the Board of Ed*? Just checking.) Under the guise of "liberty," it proposes parents being able to effectively not pay taxes to the government and spend the savings however they like for their child's education. Sounds nice on the surface, but it can lead to stuff like this: the first use of school vouchers came in the form of Virginia's

1956 Stanley Plan, which subsidized White-only private schools known as "segregation academies." At the time, several other states jumped on that bandwagon, always in the name of "choice."[3]

Research shows that school choice, while billed by conservatives, the radical rich, and other school-choice advocates as a way to level the educational playing field, actually burdens poor families. The researchers Angela Simms and Elizabeth Talbert looked at Cleveland's school-choice program in 2019. "Given entrenched racial residential segregation in the Cleveland region," they wrote, "we find introducing choice schools imposes a 'parenting tax' on Black parents because they expend resources—time and energy—to activate a public good most White parents can take for granted. Introducing 'choice' into a highly-racialized K-12 system exacerbates Black parents' disadvantages, which largely stem from Black communities' inadequate access to high-quality public goods generally."[4] They continue by recommending that better schooling options for Black children requires promoting equitable public resource distribution across different racial groups regardless of where those groups reside within a metropolitan area.

Now, not all states and cities are the same. School choice may work better in different locales, but so far, the data has shown that well-off families benefit and poor families suffer.

EDUCATION FUNDING

Let's discuss education funding (or the woeful lack of it). First, we have to establish that education is a cost center, meaning it is difficult to operate it like a for-profit private business (caveat: for-profit schools do exist in America). In other words, little Johnny and Susie who have special needs do not fuse so well with shareholder capitalism. They require additional resources, which cost money, and that expenditure will not produce additional value for the school (read, profit). So how does one rationalize that from a market perspective? On top of this, education continues to get more expensive each year. Not per pupil, but simply because the population of kids keeps growing. As the scholar Douglas Harris of the Brookings Institute has written, "Schools and colleges have to compete for labor with those sectors where productivity does improve—industries that pay higher salaries as productivity improves. This means the education sector has to spend more every year just to stand still."[5] Stick a pin in that one. As the population grows, we need to educate more and more people. Costs grow. Yet, education budgets are continuously slashed.

However, increasing spending is popular! Increasing school funding and increasing teacher salaries both have a net favorability of +37 percent. And that support is bipartisan, with Republicans at +18 percent.

It goes without saying that Trump and his yes-men doormats in the House and Senate did not do nearly enough to support students and teachers in the wake of COVID-19. They did not pass anything close to sufficient state aid, let alone employment and small-business benefits. At the time of this writing, President Biden and the Democratic Congress recently passed the largest COVID-19 relief bill, which provides much-needed aid to states and local municipalities.

Yet so many school districts have *still* not recovered from the 2008–2009 Great Recession. Consider the testimony given in 2020 to the House Education and Labor Committee by Michael Leachman, the vice president for state fiscal policy at the Center for Budget and Policy Priorities, a progressive nonpartisan research-and-policy organization. Across the nation, Leachman reported, schools were employing 77,000 fewer staff than before the Great Recession, despite serving 1.5 million more students. The $13 billion in federal education aid that Congress approved through the CARES Act, he said, was "far too little to meet the extreme fiscal challenges" that schools were facing.[6]

I pick on congressional Republicans because, based on their budgets, they value education less than Democrats do. Let's look at how states prioritize education funding. There seems to be a pattern for red states and for blue states. Let's see if you can spot it. In statistics, we call this a correlation. Below is per-pupil spending in 2019 courtesy of the Census Bureau. (I separate by different shades of gray based on which party controls the state legislature. The lighter being Democrat and the darker shade as Republican.)

STATE	TOTAL PER PUPIL SPENDING	TOTAL SPENDING (IN KS)
New York	$22,366	$61,447,337
District of Columbia	$19,159	$1,007,280
Connecticut	$18,958	$9,798,789
New Jersey	$18,402	$26,756,822
Vermont	$17,873	$1,652,676
Alaska	$17,510	$2,327,151
Wyoming	$16,442	$1,560,764
Massachusetts	$15,593	$15,466,496
Rhode Island	$15,532	$2,242,317
Pennsylvania	$15,418	$26,261,079
New Hampshire	$15,340	$2,778,905
Delaware	$14,713	$1,845,143
Maryland	$14,206	$12,516,025
Illinois	$14,180	$29,223,830
Hawaii	$13,748	$2,516,444
North Dakota	$13,373	$1,460,308
Maine	$13,278	$2,491,632
Minnesota	$12,382	$10,520,027
Nebraska	$12,299	$3,882,657
Ohio	$12,102	$20,561,122
United States	$11,762	$587,004,677
Michigan	$11,668	$15,860,412
Washington	$11,534	$12,569,546
California	$11,495	$72,641,244
Wisconsin	$11,456	$9,959,870

STATE	TOTAL PER PUPIL SPENDING	TOTAL SPENDING (IN KS)
Virginia	$11,432	$14,752,819
Montana	$11,348	$1,657,624
West Virginia	$11,291	$3,167,977
Iowa	$11,150	$5,694,316
Louisiana	$11,038	$7,305,990
Oregon	$10,842	$6,457,713
Missouri	$10,313	$9,417,531
South Carolina	$10,249	$7,746,894
Kansas	$9,960	$4,941,714
Kentucky	$9,863	$6,834,081
Indiana	$9,856	$9,959,771
Arkansas	$9,846	$4,750,938
Georgia	$9,769	$17,118,329
New Mexico	$9,693	$3,102,120
Colorado	$9,575	$8,519,780
Alabama	$9,236	$6,907,539
South Dakota	$9,176	$1,248,905
Texas	$9,016	$45,886,733
Nevada	$8,960	$3,978,436
Florida	$8,920	$25,339,845
Tennessee	$8,810	$8,886,616
North Carolina	$8,792	$12,917,195
Mississippi	$8,702	$4,246,156
Oklahoma	$8,097	$5,474,468
Arizona	$7,613	$7,276,067
Idaho	$7,157	$1,971,800
Utah·	$6,953	$4,095,444

AVERAGE FOR RED STATES: $10,498

AVERAGE FOR BLUE STATES: $14,369

Source: Census Bureau (2019)

And those states with below-average education funding have the highest incidence of child poverty.

STATE	UNDER 18 NUMBER	UNDER 18 PERCENT
Utah	87,445	9.5
North Dakota	17,145	9.9
New Hampshire	26,830	10.6
Maryland	152,237	11.6
Minnesota	149,502	11.7
Colorado	149,487	11.9
Hawaii	35,368	11.9
Vermont	13,712	12.1
Massachusetts	163,788	12.2
Washington	204,470	12.5
Nebraska	60,110	12.9
Iowa	97,222	13.5
New Jersey	264,253	13.7
Virginia	252,475	13.7
Wyoming	17,986	13.8
Wisconsin	175,243	14
Alaska	25,327	14.1
Connecticut	102,083	14.1
Idaho	62,855	14.3
Maine	34,878	14.5
Kansas	103,210	14.9
Oregon	134,383	15.7
Montana	35,999	16
Illinois	456,925	16.2
United States	11,869,173	16.2
South Dakota	34,201	16.4
Pennsylvania	434,736	16.8
California	1,541,067	17.4
Nevada	120,091	17.7

STATE	UNDER 18 NUMBER	UNDER 18 PERCENT
Indiana	275,370	18
Rhode Island	36,135	18
Missouri	247,209	18.3
New York	743,024	18.6
Delaware	37,283	18.7
Michigan	412,692	19.4
Ohio	495,616	19.5
Florida	819,256	19.7
Arizona	324,622	20.1
North Carolina	455,971	20.2
Georgia	504,745	20.5
Texas	1,545,362	21.1
Oklahoma	202,779	21.7
Tennessee	330,998	22.3
South Carolina	245,821	22.6
Kentucky	225,710	23
District of Columbia	29,048	23.1
Alabama	255,186	23.8
West Virginia	86,713	24.5
Arkansas	170,769	24.7
Louisiana	283,218	26.2
New Mexico	124,024	26.3
Mississippi	192,952	27.8
AVERAGE FOR RED STATES: 18.8		
AVERAGE FOR BLUE STATES: 15.3		

Source: Census Bureau (2019)

Furthermore, if we observe education-spending trends since the financial crisis, several states cut funding between 2008 and 2015, presumably while student population was growing. Mostly red states are cutting while blue states are increasing. Arizona cut funding by 36.6 percent, Florida by 22 percent, Alabama by 21.6 percent, Idaho by 18 percent.

Meanwhile, Vermont, Connecticut, and Illinois all *raised* spending, by 15.5 percent, 16.3 percent, and 30.8 percent, respectively.[7]

The Trump administration wanted to slash federal education spending by $8 billion, while Democrats want to increase it substantially, by $4.4 billion.

CONTENT

Let's move past funding and discuss content. What are we teaching students? A great window into the educational experience of children is to examine how settled science (evolution) is taught. It would be great if schools treated this topic uniformly—that is, according to a well-established record, so that we, as citizens, have shared truths about the past and better connections with our friends and neighbors. Bring the nation together one historical fact at a time. But that would be too inconvenient for a bunch of states that would rather indoctrinate their kids with alternative facts than search for truth. Actually, let's examine evolution, the scientific theory that the universe is billions of years old, and that humans evolved from amoebic creatures in the sea. We have the ability to test this hypothesis and record, with high certainty, that these events actually took place. Well, some states don't really agree with that. Texas, Wisconsin, Louisiana, Alabama, Florida, Georgia, Tennessee, and Arizona all have restrictions or curbs of some sort on the teaching of evolution, in most cases labeling it a "theory and not fact." Fact: scientific theory is basically fact.

According to Biomed Central, which reviews teaching curricula, a state-by-state comparison of middle-school science standards on evolution in the United States reveals that several states earn a grade of an F or D, which is like the equivalent of students learning about the origins of man from a televangelist. Actually, it's nearly half. They are nearly all Republican states, based on which party controls the legislature.[8]

41

CLIMATE CHANGE ("... IS A HOAX")

"It snowed over four inches this past weekend in New York City. It is still October. So much for Global Warming."
—DONALD TRUMP (2011)

DON'T YOU JUST WANT to smash your head against a desk? Yes.

WHAT?

TRUMP IS JUST THE tip of this gigantic, deformed, ugly, melting iceberg. Before him, congressional Republicans (at the behest of corporate America) were slowly murdering environmental policy. In fact, their record on the environment is such poop it deserves its own brand of toilet paper. Despite President Nixon having created the Environmental Protection Agency—because, you know, clean water and air—Republicans have been nothing but antagonistic towards anything resembling climate change (or should I say supportive). Beginning with President Reagan, followed by a brief positive interlude with President

Bush (revising and strengthening the Clean Air Act much to the dismay of radical rich conservative donors), which was a mere speed bump in their quest to trample on the planet, they've managed to thwart most if not all meaningful climate policy in the legislative and executive branches. They have mostly done this through promoting junk science and attacking the scientists personally.

WHY?

CLIMATE REGULATIONS DEMAND COMPLIANCE, and that means a higher cost burden to the owners of polluting companies. So it's no surprise that fossil-fuel executives financially support conservatives for Congress, because those conservatives don't support regulation. Their reasoning is simple: The less regulation restricting the pollution associated with the burning of fossil fuels, the less cost they have to incur. The less regulation on federal lands, the more they get to exploit our resources.

EVERY MAJOR REPUBLICAN FIGURE for the last thirty years has had a terrible record on the environment. The GOP is on the mound for kickball pitching a slow roll to fossil fuel executives with a foot like Ronaldo.

LEAGUE OF CONSERVATION OF VOTERS

The League of Conservation of Voters is an environmental group that lobbies to protect the planet from the sources of climate change. They also provide scorecards on various political actors—and on the whole they've given Republicans very poor grades, which are well-deserved.

In fact, every single Republican member of Congress has not received a score above 50% (out of 100) on environmental legislation in the past several years.

Saving the environment is a pretty popular policy item amongst voters, so in opposing that effort Republicans are once again embracing a really unlikable agenda. From a 2017 Quinnipiac Poll:[1]

- Seventy-six percent of voters are "very concerned" or "somewhat concerned" about climate change.

- Sixty-eight percent of voters think it is possible to protect the environment and protect jobs.

- Seventy-two percent of voters think it is a "bad idea" to cut funding for scientific research on the environment and climate change.

- Fifty-nine percent of voters say more needs to be done to address climate change.

Those numbers would probably be higher if there wasn't a gigantic stream of propaganda emanating from conservative media and politicians about supposed "job killing" regulations. Their argument is that environmental laws hurt employment (it doesn't):

"Rescind all the job-destroying Obama executive actions, including the Climate Action Plan."

—TRUMP (2016)

"President Trump Eliminates Job-Killing Regulations."

—PROMINENT SECTION ON THE TRUMP WH WEBSITE

Confronted with poor economic growth, President Reagan used to blame his predecessor, Jimmy Carter, for his "continuing devotion to job-killing regulation," when growth had probably slowed because of Reagan's having responded to stagflation with the "tough love" approach of raising interest rates through the roof.

> "On energy, I will cancel job-killing restrictions on the production of American energy, including shale energy and clean coal, creating many millions of high-paying jobs."
>
> **—TRUMP (2016)**

> "The regulatory overreach of the EPA has contributed to economic devastation in my state of West Virginia."
>
> **—SENATOR SHELLEY MOORE CAPITO, OF WEST VIRGINIA (2015)**

But guess what? The data says otherwise! Not only do regulations *not* kill jobs, but according to the research I've seen, they *create* jobs. Whaddya know!

The idea that environmental regulations are somehow bad for the economy and "cost millions of jobs," is just not the case. Better environmental stewardship from the government is *good* for businesses and the economy. Steven Meyers, a professor in political science at MIT, writes,

> "Given the high stakes involved, the reader might find it unsettling to learn that credible evidence supporting this policy shift is virtually non-existent. To be sure, anecdotes about companies ruined by environmental regulation abound. Yet they provide no clues regarding the likely economic benefits from deregulation. Moreover, there are an equal number of anecdotes about companies pulled back from the brink of bankruptcy by environmental efficiency. And stories about the growth of green

companies continue to proliferate giving rise to the argument that 'environmentalism'—vigorous policies of environmental protection—actually spurs economic growth. When we turn away from anecdotes and special interest (i.e., industry and environmental lobbies) 'studies,' the results from rigorous, independent, economic analyses strongly suggest that no lasting macro-economic gains will be forthcoming. Focusing on a number of different industries, using a variety of economic indicators, and covering different time periods these studies find that neither national nor state economic performance have been significantly or systematically affected by environmental regulation."[2]

In their book *Does Regulation Kill Jobs?*, Cary Coglianese, Adam M. Finkel, and Christopher Carrigan explore the question. While they acknowledge that regulations increased the cost burden, they also note that regulations don't seem to cause job losses or diminish pay and benefits. They note, too, that despite the GOP and Trump's endless obsession with "Obama's burdensome regulations" and how he was "killing the economy," Obama was actually something of a regulation killer himself. His Council on Jobs and Competitiveness also issued recommendations for "reducing regulatory burdens," which directed agencies to "be especially careful not to impose unjustified regulatory requirements."[3] Huh! Obama was not the ideological communist rule-maker like congressional conservatives made him out to be. Go figure.

Some nuance. Broadly speaking, according to the research, regulation does not hamper job growth. In certain sectors it may reduce jobs, and in others it may create them. For example, a factory that produces lead additives for gasoline might be closed down because regulations have banned lead additives. But that means new jobs will be created at a factory that produces catalytic converters, which are emissions-control devices for automobiles. In other words, some workers benefit from regulation, while others lose. Which is not to say that the losses aren't real and difficult for the people who had those jobs, but, in general, the picture is not one that congressional conservatives paint as "job-killing."

Coglianese points out, "If you look across the entire economy and you look in the aggregate as to jobs lost as well as jobs gained by regulation, it's generally speaking a wash."

Here's an interesting chart. And by interesting, I mean it demonstrates how media—particularly conservative media—plays a critical role in our perceptions of phenomena like how the economy is performing. The dotted line is the unemployment level and the solid line is media mentions of "job killing regulations." You can see how the frequency and intensity reached new heights following the 2008–2009 financial crisis, and, of course, while President Obama was in office. It was no surprise that voters became scornful of regulations and blamed them for the economic downtown.

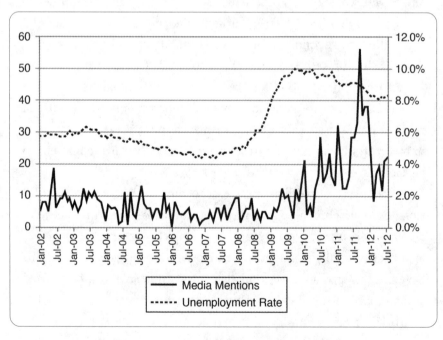

Source: *Does Regulation Kill Jobs?*

Jobs come and go. That's normal in any market economy. Some companies go out of business. Some get taken over. This has little to do with regulations. It's called capitalism. That doesn't mean, however, companies don't try to *blame* regulations. Coglianese notes a well-known case of copper smelter ASARCO, on the outskirts of Seattle which, after it had gone out of business, was all like, "It was the regulations"—even though it had gone out of business before the regulations took effect.

After Los Angeles tightened regulations on clean air, between 1979 and 1992, the researchers Eli Berman and Linda T. M. Bui found almost *zero* employment changes and, as a healthy bonus, "large reductions in NOx emissions." Sounds like a win-win! "We find no evidence that local air quality regulation substantially reduced employment," they wrote, "even when allowing for induced plant exit and dissuaded plant entry." They also found that regulations affected employment "only slightly— partly because regulated plants are in capital and not labor-intensive industries."[4] And their findings are robust across different regions.

In yet two additional studies, the economist and former EPA administrator Richard Morgenstern looked at census data between 1979 and 1991 to determine whether the regulation of some pollution-causing industries had destroyed jobs. He and another researcher, Anna Belova, also looked at thirty years of data in industries such as petroleum, plastics, pulp and paper, iron and steel, and found that there were net job *increases* with no significant job losses. "A million dollars of additional . . . [regulation] expenditure is associated with an insignificant change in employment," Morgenstern wrote.[5]

Sometimes, regulations simply cause jobs to shift from one area of the country to another, or one industry to another. When the researcher Michael Greenstone examined the effects of the EPA's Clean Air Act, he concluded that 40,000 jobs were lost in parts of the country that had "dirty air," but those losses were offset by jobs that shifted to cleaner areas of the country when factories relocated there.[6]

I don't mean to minimize how difficult it is for workers to uproot their lives and move to a place with better jobs. That's the kind of thing that the conservative columnist Ben Shapiro does. "If the sea level rises five or ten meters," he once told an audience, people can just "sell their homes and move."[7] Sweet advice, Ben. How absurd to suggest anybody can just pick up and go.

As a final point, the benefits of regulation *far* outweigh the costs. Following amendments to the Clean Air Act in 1990, the average worker in a newly regulated plant lost 20 percent of his/her income during relocation and retraining over the subsequent few years, which is equivalent to about $5.4 billion in earnings. However, this cost is small compared to the fact that the EPA has calculated that the health benefits of the environmental policy between 1990 and 2010, for example, were between $160 billion and $1.6 trillion. "In light of these benefits," the Berkeley economist W. Reed Walker has written, "The earnings losses borne by workers in newly regulated industries are relatively small."[8]

42

WELFARE

("Welfare Queens Are Bleeding this Country Dry")

"Public aid was paid for children born out of wedlock."

—PRESIDENTIAL CANDIDATE AND CONSERVATIVE GOD, BARRY GOLDWATER (1961)

"In Chicago, they found a woman who holds the record. She used 80 names, 30 addresses, 15 telephone numbers to collect food stamps, Social Security, veterans' benefits for four nonexistent deceased veteran husbands, as well as welfare. Her tax-free cash income alone has been running $150,000 a year."

GASPS FROM THE CROWD—RONALD REAGAN IN 1976, TALKING ABOUT LINDA TAYLOR, THE "WELFARE QUEEN," WHILE RUNNING FOR PRESIDENT

"The federal government declared a war on poverty, and poverty won."

—REAGAN AT HIS FINAL STATE OF THE UNION (1988)

WHAT?

WE DID LOSE THE war on poverty. When Reagan uses this one incredibly egregious example to evidence an entire system of mooches and thieves, of course he doesn't actually care about it working to *solve* poverty. You think by simply yanking away support for the poor, poverty will fix itself? This attitude is so defeating, ironically. Reams upon volumes of available research demonstrate that welfare, by and large, gives much-needed assistance to people who not only work but live at or below the poverty line. And *by and large* does not "demotivate" people from working.[1] Does all that corporate welfare discourage the wealthy or executives from working? Actually, ha, now that you ask, it kinda does. Between 1979 and 2007, when wages diverged substantially from bottom to top, poor people started working a lot more. Their annual hours increased by 22 percent, whereas the top 5 percent increased their hours by only 8 percent. And the hourly wages of the poor increased 8 percent, whereas wages of the wealthy increased 30 percent.[2]

But I digress.

WHY?

THE GOP'S WELFARE QUEEN routine was always deeply racist and driven by a desire to appeal to the worst instincts of its base: make White people believe that Black people were sucking the government dry so they would come to despise the system (that, incidentally, supported a heckuva lot more White people than African Americans). Reagan and his GOP acolytes demonized welfare, ultimately, because they wanted to shrink government and let the private market sort out poverty.

AND IT WORKED! By 1978, for example, 84 percent of Illinois voters considered welfare and Medicaid fraud to be matters of grave concern. The poor are out to rob us!

In *The Queen: The Forgotten Life Behind an American Myth*, Josh Leven writes about Linda Taylor and how she captured the imagination of so many (White) people. Well, by *captured*, I mean that Reagan and his propagandists—among them, Lee "You can't say 'Nigger' anymore, just state's rights" Atwater—incited a backlash against welfare recipients. "With [the welfare queen's] story," Levin writes, "Reagan marked millions of America's poorest people as potential scoundrels and fostered the belief that welfare fraud was a nationwide epidemic that needed to be stamped out. This image of grand and rampant welfare fraud allowed Reagan to sell voters on his cuts to public assistance spending. The 'welfare queen' became a convenient villain, a woman everyone could hate. She was a lazy Black con artist, unashamed of cadging the money that honest folks worked so hard to earn."[3]

What Reagan failed to mention was that Linda was an outright criminal. What he discovered was a woman who destroyed lives, a person eons more nefarious than even he could have imagined. In the 1970s, she was investigated for homicide, kidnapping, and baby trafficking. The police detective who was assigned her case tried to throw her behind bars for life, because, as Levin puts it, she was "responsible for one of Chicago's most legendary crimes, one that remains unsolved to this day." Homicide. Kidnapping. *Baby trafficking*! But, yeah, let's crucify her—and millions of others by extension—because of welfare fraud. Seems reasonable.

More proof that Reagan's welfare rhetoric was working: Levin notes that in 1964, just 27 percent of stories in newsmagazines about poor people in America showed images of Black people. By 1973, the number ballooned to 70 percent. As the journalist Jeremy Lyberger writes in the *Nation*, "Taylor embodied how the country imagined and identified poverty."[4] Indeed. Pictures are a powerful image, and the sea-change in how people view poverty may have spurred a bit of resentment and identity politics. Reagan's election victory in 1980 focused attention to White poverty in the wake of a fallen manufacturing sector. Pictures of trailer parks, rural devastation, and boarded-up Appalachian towns replaced the inner city as the primary backdrops for economic malaise. Lyberger continues, "Taylor was both the symbol of malicious entitlement and the reason why other Americans, White Americans, were denied the comforts they'd been promised." So on the one hand you had poor White people struggling, and on the other you had this lavish (Black) "welfare queen" robbing the system blind. White America was freaking pissed.

Reagan, at the time, insisted that while the (food stamp) program's original purpose had been "to ensure adequate nutrition for America's needy families," it was now functioning as "a generalized income-transfer program" unrelated to nutritional need. The president said that his proposal was "in accord with the Administration's efforts to target assistance to the most needy families and to restrain the uncontrolled growth of entitlement spending."[5]

So what did Reagan do? He aimed to reduce benefits and eligibility, of which the saddest suggestion that he and his administration came up with was to save $600 million by eliminating free lunch at schools for those families eligible. This would cost $12 a month for each school-age child: 44 cents for each meal ($1.10 in 2020). Well done, GOP! Well done!

Beyond that, it was mostly more of Reagan's cronies making a stink about benefits to poor people by citing—what else—fraud and abuse. William Shaker, the executive director of the National Tax Limitation Committee, a private advocacy group, told the Senate Agriculture Committee, "Food stamps score right at the top of the list in terms of misspent federal funds." The avowed racist Senator Jesse Helms of

North Carolina blamed poor Black people in his coded language: "I had one delegation [of Black people] come to see me, and they wanted some free money from Washington." That's the same Jesse Helms who hoped he'd make the first Black female senator cry by whistling the infamous confederate tune "Dixie" in an elevator with her.[6] That Jesse Helms.

With all this cutting of benefits, you would think poverty was improving, right? Slash programs because the picture's getting rosier? Not quite. Headline from the *New York Times* in 1983: "POVERTY RATE ROSE TO 15% IN '82, HIGHEST LEVEL SINCE MID-1960'S." From 1978 to 1982, people living in poverty increased by 40 percent. *Forty* percent![7] Or an additional 9.9 million people. Yet between 1959 and 1969, the poverty rates *declined*. Thanks, President Johnson!

Since then, congressional Republicans have been on a crusade to cut welfare spending from the budget at all costs. From Reagan to Gingrich to Bush/Cheney to Ryan, Boehner, McConnell, and Trump. Budget after budget of reducing benefits to the poor and working class. And they wonder, "Gee, we need more private market, less government to sort out this mess."

43

THE DEFICIT

("The Democrats Are Bankrupting this Country!")

"Trump's acting chief of staff, former Congressman
Mick Mulvaney, spent years ripping Obama about the deficit.
Asked recently why Trump's 2019 State of the Union
didn't mention the deficit, he replied, 'Nobody cares.'"

—ALEX SHEPHARD, IN THE *NEW REPUBLIC* (2019)

"All this talk about concern for the deficit and the
budget has been bogus for as long as it's been around."

—CONSERVATIVE RADIO HOST RUSH LIMBAUGH (2019)

"Sen. Mitt Romney (R-Utah), who made fiscal
responsibility a cornerstone of his 2012 presidential
bid against Obama, declined to comment Tuesday
on the pact or on the GOP's drift. 'I really don't
have anything for you today on that,' he said."

—ROBERT COSTA, IN THE *WASHINGTON POST* (2019)

WHAT AND WHY?

REPUBLICANS HAVE ALWAYS REGARDED themselves as and projected the sense that they are the party of fiscal responsibility. They've chastised Democrats for not adhering to fiscal restraint. But for all that talk about deficits, they sure do like to add to the national debt! As you probably guess, it is the Democrats who are responsible, and the Republicans who are profligate. The one exception on the democratic side was Barack Obama, who had to clean up Bush's mess in 2008.

SEE FOR YOURSELF:

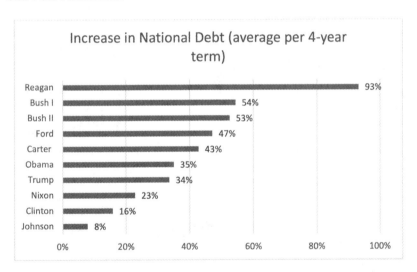

Increase in National Debt (average per 4-year term)

President	%
Reagan	93%
Bush I	54%
Bush II	53%
Ford	47%
Carter	43%
Obama	35%
Trump	34%
Nixon	23%
Clinton	16%
Johnson	8%

1. "The balanced budget is more important as symbolism than as accounting,"— Conservative bulwark, *National Review*.[1] Wow, you don't say?!

2. It was never about deficits. Republican presidents have exploded the deficit in recent history while Democrats have reduced it. Dick Cheney even said that Ronald Reagan proved "deficits don't matter."[2] It was just about limiting the power of the Democrats to govern.

3. For more on why the GOP is so hypocritical on deficits, please see the chapters "Radicalization" and "Chaos and Gridlock."

BUZZWORDS, MISDIRECTION, AND EUPHEMISMS

DISTINCT FROM THE PREVIOUS section, this part focuses more on the generalizations congressional Republicans hurl at the Democratic party (e.g., socialism, cancel culture, and radicalization). When the facts, the experts, history, common sense, and common decency are not on your side, it can be hard to convince anyone of your position. The congressional Republican solution? Use language not to communicate but to shut down dialogues with buzzwords, misdirection, and euphemism.

44

CANCEL CULTURE

"In many cases they have adopted the spirit of a Jacobin mob in the French Revolution, the Reign of Terror trying to completely erase our culture and our history. Unfortunately, many Democrats are vying to be the Robespierre for this Jacobin mob."

—GOP SENATOR TOM COTTON (2020)

"[There's] a new far-left fascism . . . driving people from their jobs, shaming dissenters and demanding total submission from anyone who disagrees."

—TRUMP (2020)

WHAT?

THE RIGHT, PREDOMINANTLY, ACCUSES the Left of something called *cancel culture,* which is mostly the idea that left-wing activists seek to destroy anything and everything that offends them. It refers to the popular practice of withdrawing support for (or canceling) celebrities or organizations after they have done or said something deemed to be wildly objectionable or offensive. Some conservatives might argue that this is simply the free market at work. If people don't like something or it offends them, they won't buy it, listen to it, watch it, have anything to do with it. Don't like it? Don't consume it. Makes perfect capitalistic sense, right? Well, not to congressional conservatives and right-wing media. They complain endlessly about the Left and how they want to "destroy America." Rather than debate each case of cancel culture in isolation, the outrage morphed into a sum-greater-than-the-parts, and the Left is now a grave danger to society, because it is trying to completely erase our country's culture and history, or some bullshit like that. I don't deny that there *are* problematic instances of cancel culture, but the idea that this is some horrifying, pervasive problem, on par with, say, the symptoms of an authoritarian dictatorship, is downright lunacy. Not only that, it is most certainly *not* one-sided. While the Right *complains* the most, they are actually just as, if not more, illiberal than the Left. Along the same lines as cancel culture, congressional conservatives trot out phrases like *identity politics, virtue signaling*, and *trigger warnings* as derogatory debate killers, seeking to make the other side look weak, as if the aforementioned are dirty words rather than benign and thoughtful strategies for dealing with our complex rhetorical problems.

WHY?

THE RIGHT NEEDS A boogeyman (as usual). Someone or something to complain and fear-monger about when the free market has rejected their ideas. To me, it's a clear sign they've lost the debate. Last time I checked, history and culture are constantly revised and shaped by updated facts and new societal sensibilities. No one is erasing anything. Why was the story of Christopher Columbus, and not Juneteenth, taught in school for so long? When important historical facts are ignored for decades, even centuries, and finally unearthed, that's not erasing history. That's learning a different perspective. In the '70s, people listened to Jefferson Airplane and wore bell bottoms. In the '00s, people texted and listened to Brittany Spears. That's culture changing. Like it or not.

AS I WROTE, THERE are plenty of problems with people seeking to *cancel* others for their words and actions, particularly if they are just mildly offensive. And there seem to be plenty of voices on social media with that point of view. But to say that the cancel-culture phenomenon has been blown out of proportion is putting it lightly.

Let's first examine the Right's trip down cancel-culture lane, starting with Trump, the genre's king. If you think some leftist Twitter randoms are the worst thing that's happened to free speech, get a load of a guy who actually had the power to make enormous consequential decisions on freedom of expression. Throughout the remainder of this chapter I will give examples of right-wing cancel culture and provide those that fall into exceedingly worse categories such as violence and threats. As the journalist Jane Mayer has reported in the *New Yorker*, Trump actually attempted to *block* a merger between AT&T and Time Warner because he didn't like the coverage about him on CNN. *Are you kidding me?* According to Mayer, a couple of months prior to the Justice Department's filing suit, apparently Trump ordered Gary Cohn, who was his director of the National Economic Council, to "pressure the Justice Department to intervene."[1]

Oh. My. God. A president putting his thumb on the scale of a private merger. Where are the libertarians?! The free marketeers?! Here's how it went down, according to a "well informed" source quoted by Mayer: "Trump called Cohn into the Oval Office along with John Kelly, who had just become the chief of staff, and said in exasperation to Kelly, 'I've been telling Cohn to get this lawsuit filed and nothing's happened! I've mentioned it fifty times. And nothing's happened. I want to make sure it's filed. I want that deal blocked!'"

Cohn promptly told Kelly, "Don't you fucking dare call the Justice Department. We are not going to do business that way." Of course, if he did it would look like the president was punishing a company for publishing unfavorable news coverage of him, but that didn't really matter, because Trump is the *ultimate* snowflake. Just, wow.

He threatened to revoke licenses of media companies. Some examples are below.

On October 11, 2017, @realDonaldTrump tweeted:
With all of the Fake News coming out of NBC and the Networks, at what point is it appropriate to challenge their License? Bad for country!

On the same day, @realDonaldTrump also tweeted:
Network news has become so partisan, distorted and fake that licenses must be challenged and, if appropriate, revoked. Not fair to public.

On September 4, 2018, @realDonaldTrump tweeted:
NBC FAKE NEWS, which is under intense scrutiny over killing the Harvey Weinstein story, is now fumbling around making excuses for their probably highly unethical conduct. I have long criticized NBC and their journalistic standards-worse than even CNN. Look at their license?

And since his own Federal Communications Commission would not pander to his patently unconstitutional tantrums, Trump urged his followers to literally *cancel* subscriptions to the news company that owns them.

> **On June 13, 2020 @realDonaldTrump tweeted:**
> Concast is known for its terrible service. On top of that they provide FAKE NEWS on MSDNC & @NBCNews. Drop them and go to a good provider!
>
> > **This tweet was a retweet of the following from @GovMikeHuckabee:**
> > Mafia better service than @comcast Sure they shoot you, but it's is over with and they don't charge you for the bullet.

He didn't like the *Washington Post* and their coverage of him, so he weaponized the Post Office against its owner, Jeff Bezos. Catherine Rampell wrote that in 2018, "Trump repeatedly urged the postmaster general to double the rates it charges Amazon."[2] According to an October 2019 memoir by a senior aide to former defense secretary James Mattis, Trump "called and directed Mattis to 'screw Amazon' by locking them out of a chance to bid" on a lucrative contract to build the Pentagon's cloud architecture.

> **On December 29, 2017, @realDonaldTrump tweeted:**
> Why is the United States Post Office, which is losing many billions of dollars a year, while charging Amazon and others so little to deliver their packages, making Amazon richer and the Post Office dumber and poorer? Should be charging MUCH MORE!

He's accused a TV host he doesn't like of being a murderer.

> **On May 24, 2020, @realDonaldTrump tweeted:**
> A lot of interest in this story about Psycho Joe Scarborough. So a young marathon runner just happened to faint in his office, hit her head on the desk, & die? I would think there is a lot more to the story than that? An affair? What about the so-called investigator?

He fired Lt. Colonel Alex Vindman for being a whistleblower and blocked his promotion to Colonel.[3] This was a gigantic deal at the time and the basis for Trump's first impeachment. He conducted himself like a mob boss who not only threatened to withhold military aid to Ukraine if it didn't dig up dirt on his opponent (Joe Biden) but he retaliated against a decorated military veteran by blocking his (well-deserved) promotion and eventually forcing him to resign. Disgusting.

He tried to block several books from being published that were negative about him and even jailed his former lawyer, Michael Cohen, for it![4]

He's attacked social-media companies, Colin Kaepernick, the NFL, NASCAR, Jemele Hill, Chuck Todd, Hillary Clinton, Justin Amash, Bob Corker, the Squad, Ambassador Gordon Sondland, and others who testified at his impeachment. The list goes on and on.

He has encouraged his supporters to beat the shit out of protestors. "If you see somebody getting ready to throw a tomato," he said at a 2016 rally during his campaign for the presidency, "knock the crap out of them, would you? Seriously, OK? Just knock the hell—I promise you I will pay for the legal fees. I promise, I promise."[5]

He gassed peaceful protestors for a photo op in front of the White House.[6]

He forced all his employees, before his presidential run, to sign NDAs so they can't say anything bad about him when they leave his gold-plated enterprise.[7]

But, it's not just Trump.

Fox News hardly has opposing viewpoints. As the long-time conservative columnist Max Boot notes, "Never-Trump conservatives such as Steve Hayes, George F. Will, and Bill Kristol are long gone at the network. Fox's prime-time programming is wall-to-wall Trump idolatry."[8] It happened at the *National Review*, too. In 2016, they ran a cover article titled "Against Trump" but, according to Boot, the magazine has since "become noisily pro-Trump." He continues, "When it does gingerly criticize Trump, it typically asserts that his opponents are way worse."

Plenty of other Republicans have had their issues with cancel culture:

- Senator Roy Blunt (R-Mo.), the fourth-ranking Republican in the Senate, dared to vote against Trump's declaration of a national emergency at the Southern border. In March 2019, he was disinvited from a local dinner by a Missouri county GOP committee.[9] CANCELED!

- Anthony Scaramucci, the president's former communications director, described Trump's attack on four congresswomen of color as "racist and unacceptable" in July 2019, so he was disinvited by the Palm Beach County GOP from its annual Lobsterfest fundraiser.[10] CANCELED!

- The Republican National Committee boycotted MSNBC and even the conservative *National Review*. A conservative group tried to boycott Burger King and Kit Kat for (what it claimed) were offensive ads.[11] TRIED TO CANCEL!

- Texas Sen. Ted Cruz and plenty of other congressional Republicans tried to cancel Nike and the NFL for honoring Colin Kaepernick.[12] TRIED AGAIN!

- Fox News fans tried to cancel Keurig for supporting social-justice initiatives by filming themselves smashing the company's coffee machines.[13] AND AGAIN!

- The Chicks (formerly known as The Dixie Chicks). Remember that one? During the lead-up to our senseless invasion of Iraq, the band said in March 2003 that they were "ashamed" that the guy who started the war, G. W. Bush, was from their home state of Texas. Conservatives denounced them as "Saddam's Angels," "Dixie Sluts," and "traitors," and banned them from hundreds of conservative radio stations across the country. In Bossier City, Louisiana, hundreds of pro-Bush protesters used a gigantic tractor to physically crush their CDs.[14] PHYSICALLY CRUSHED AND CANCELED!

- The list extends back decades. Conservatives have been canceling people who don't agree with them since the 1960s. In 1966, radical Christians tried to cancel John Lennon after he said the Beatles were "more popular" than Jesus. The band was greeted with plenty of death threats, and in Alabama, a shock jockey scheduled a bonfire and invited everyone to burn their records.[15] BURNED AND CANCELED!

A lot of the cancel culture on the Right exists because Republican governance and support for Trump have morphed into one. For example, guys like former Congressman Mark Sanford, who had an almost perfect voting record on conservative issues (93 percent) and Senator Jeff Flake (85 percent) were exiled from politics for, of all absolutely pathetic things, their criticism of Donald Trump. As Brent Orrell, a Koch-funded American Enterprise Institute scholar, has put it, Ben Sasse (83 percent) managed to survive cancelation by "moving to an undisclosed political location until he finished slogging nervously through his Republican primary."[16] Ha! This goes for former Attorney General Jeff Sessions, too. He put the rule of law before Trump and look what happened to him. Fired! While the nation is undergoing some of the worst crises in modern history—a pandemic, economic meltdown, protests over police killings—"the presidential personnel office," Orrell writes, "is busily conducting loyalty stress-tests on the administration's own appointees that focus on personal commitment to Trump rather than any particular administration policy." And the list goes on and on.

Then there's Mitt Romney. The primary Republican antagonist (or protagonist) of this Trump tragedy. He was the lone vote in the first impeachment trial to remove Trump from office, a move that caused hellfire to rain down on Romney and his family. Orrell notes, "This brought down the full force of Trumpian cancel-power. Relatives have changed their names. CPAC, engaging in what the late, great Florence King might have called the 'height of WASP rage,' made a point of announcing that it had not invited Romney this year on the theory that this constituted punishment rather than deliverance. Through this fire, Romney has emerged as the political equivalent of Harry Potter, 'the Boy Who Lived.' The moral here is that if you're going to state the obvious about Trump, survival depends on having a couple hundred million dollars in the bank, a lifetime of personal achievement, great hair, and a tan of a shade that occurs in nature."

To be clear, Democrats are guilty of cancel culture too, but Republicans *are* the party of cancel culture. They pay vomit-inducing fealty to a guy who tries to cancel everything he doesn't like, including dissent in the party. Is this a cult or what? Asking for 80 million people.

45

RADICALIZATION

"Radical left/democrats want to destroy you."
—TRUMP (2019)

"They would rather keep the radical left mob stirred up
and angry than lift a finger to fix the problem."
—KEVIN MCCARTHY (2020)

"I think the Democratic Party [sic], I think they have
been captured on the left by a group of people who see
socialism as just a step away from communism."
—FORMER SECRETARY OF STATE, MIKE POMPEO (2021)

WHAT?

SINCE THE DAWN OF time, it feels like, congressional Republicans have accused Democrats of being radicals, particularly socialists. In actuality, it's been since President Roosevelt's New Deal was ratified in the 1930s. Whether it is about insuring the poor, giving Black people the same rights as White people, providing appropriate funding for education, making the rich pay a fair tax rate, or issuing regulations to protect the environment, it's always, "They're radicals who want to destroy our great nation." I note that the practice of red-baiting—discrediting someone's otherwise logical argument by calling them a communist—often crossed party lines post-WWII.

WHY?

IT'S QUITE SIMPLE. ANY federal government expansion, particularly under Democrats, is portrayed as a zero-sum game. Liberals win, conservatives lose (they *hate* losing). There's no middle ground. Congressional conservatives are OK with defense and border wall spending, but anything that attends to the needs of the poor and middle class, or endeavors to shrink the colossal inequality chasm, is branded *radical socialism*! And, the key point here, the *very most important* key point is ... Republicans are actually genuinely, veritably, the radical party.

FIRST, LET'S COMPARE BOTH Democratic and Republican parties to other Western nations. I also use this chart in the chapter "Comparison to Western Countries," because it's so compelling. It is based on a study by the Manifesto Project that studies and sorts each statement in party manifestos, which are the source for a party's policy goals. Check out where the GOP falls in comparison. Who's the radical party, again?

Second, let's take a look at how much of the parties' representatives have moved from the center to the extreme. Between 1988 and 2015, the percentage of congressional Republicans that have migrated to the extremes has been nearly seven-fold (from 12 percent to 80 percent), while the number of congressional Democrats has stayed relatively in the middle-ground for decades.[1] So much for those *radical Democrats*.

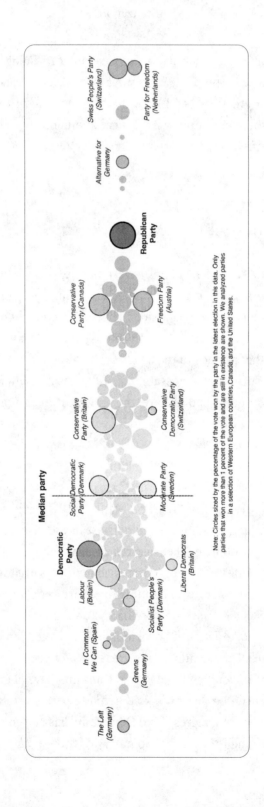

Median party

Democratic Party

The Left (Germany)

In Common We Can (Spain)

Greens (Germany)

Socialist People's Party (Denmark)

Labour (Britain)

Liberal Democrats (Britain)

Social Democratic Party (Denmark)

Moderate Party (Sweden)

Conservative Party (Britain)

Conservative Democratic Party (Switzerland)

Conservative Party (Canada)

Republican Party

Freedom Party (Austria)

Alternative for Germany

Swiss People's Party (Switzerland)

Party for Freedom (Netherlands)

Note: Circles sized by the percentage of the vote won by the party in the latest election in this data. Only parties that won more than 1 percent of the vote and are still in existence are shown. We analyzed parties in a selection of Western European countries, Canada, and the United States.

So when a vast majority of your party's representatives are conservative (or very conservative), but your base actually likes policies that Democrats like (see the chapter titled "People Actually Like Government"), where do you think that leaves the concept of compromise? Would you ever win an argument about the last piece of candy with a spoiled toddler over whom you have no authority? Compromise becomes nearly impossible, because the other side literally will not budge from their extreme position. As E. J. Dionne writes, "In a two-party system with separated powers that frequently produces divided government, the radicalization of the Right produces a zero-sum game. If it cannot take power, the GOP is committed, on principle, to preventing its adversaries from governing successfully."[2]

To continue, see the chapter "Compromise."

46

SOCIALISM

"Here, in the United States, we are alarmed by
new calls to adopt socialism in our country."
—DONALD TRUMP (2019)

"America will never be a socialist country."
—MIKE PENCE (2020)

"America needs strong borders—not socialism."
—MITCH McCONNELL (1983)

"Socialism only works in two places: Heaven, where they
don't need it, and hell, where they already have it."
—RONALD REAGAN

WHAT?

SOCIALISM. THE BOOGEYMAN OF all boogeymen about which the Right
has been screaming about from the rooftops since the dawn of time.
Hardly anyone knows what it actually means, and nobody can agree on

a definition, which means it can just become anything and everything government-related. What it actually means, according to its father, Karl Marx, is social ownership of the means of production. In other words, instead of Coca Cola being a private company with stockholders, it is owned by the government and operated as a public good like a school or a park. How the Right defines it, however, is anything the Democrats do to help the poor and the middle class. There are entirely legitimate reasons to fear socialism, but the Democratic platform ain't it.

WHY?

ANY LEGISLATION PROPOSED OR action taken by the Democrats financially burdens the radical rich. At least that's their thought. To them, it's a zero-sum game. If we expand government health care coverage, they are not able to profit from privatization. If we issue environmental regulations, it costs more for them to comply. If we give Black people the right to vote, it dilutes their voting power. Of course, we can debate the merits of this or that legislation, but that's not what they are interested in doing—or really have been interested in—as a party.

SOME OF THE EXAMPLES and supporting evidence I use in this section you may have read in a different section in one form or another. My intent is not to regurgitate the points but to paint a full picture of each section's topic.

Let's take a brief ride through the history of the Right's antisocialist crusade, starting with when rhetoric first arose in opposition to FDR's New Deal. Back then, a collection of businessmen and Southern Democrats (now Republicans) known as the American Liberty League (it's

always "liberty" with them) went to war with the Roosevelt administration over the policies that ultimately pulled the US out of the Great
Depression. Technically, World War II ended the Great Depression, but
the New Deal plucked millions from poverty and hardship and set the
country on a growth path.

The League coalesced around workers being treated like human
beings and not like indentured servants. "Five negroes on my place in
South Carolina refused work this spring," a former DuPont executive
named Ruly Carpenter wrote a former colleague and former chairman of the Democratic Party, John Raskob, in 1934, "and a cook on my
houseboat in Fort Myers quit because the government was paying him
a dollar an hour as a painter." Raskob wrote back, "You haven't much
to do, and I know of no one that could better take the lead in trying to
induce the DuPont and General Motors groups, followed by other big
industries, to definitely organize to protect society from the sufferings
it is bound to endure if we allow communistic elements to lead the
people to believe that all businessmen are crooks."[1]

Watch out for those "negroes" who want fair pay and their
rights upheld!

After World War II, congressional conservatives and the radical
rich were on the attack again over a Democratic plan to provide free
polio vaccines to children. As the historian Kevin Kruse has noted,
President Dwight Eisenhower's Secretary of Health, Education, and
Welfare Oveta Culp Hobby denounced a Democratic plan to provide
free polio vaccines to children as a *back door* that opened up the way
to socialized medicine.[2]

When Harry Truman introduced a national health-insurance program in 1945, the American Medical Association (AMA) poo-pooed
it as "socialized medicine" and called Truman's White House staffers
"followers of the Moscow party line." Health providers distributed
55 million pamphlets featuring a made-up quote attributed to Soviet
leader Vladimir Lenin: "Socialized medicine is the keystone to the arch
of the Socialist State."[3]

Then, a decade later, the AMA hired an actor named Ronald Reagan to be their spokesperson and official propaganda mouthpiece. Reagan bought into the whole economic-conservatism hogwash and became their number-one supporter, not to mention the future iconic symbol of what would turn out to be the biggest economic disaster—as far as exacerbating inequality is concerned—of the twentieth century: trickle-down economics.

In the late 1950s, the AMA launched Operation Coffee Cup, which, according to journalist Ian Millhiser, "asked doctors' wives to invite their friends over to drink coffee and listen to a recording called 'Ronald Reagan speaks out against SOCIALIZED MEDICINE.'" (Those capital letters are not mine.) Here's a snippet: "All of us can see what happens: Once you establish the precedent that the government can determine a man's working place and his working methods, determine his employment, from here it's a short step to all the rest of socialism—to determining his pay, and pretty soon your son won't decide when he's in school, where he will go, or what they will do for a living. He will wait for the government to tell him where he will go to work and what he will do." Reagan went on, "One of these days you and I are going to spend our sunset years telling our children, and our children's children, what it once was like in America when men were free."[4] Slavery is coming back, dear lord!

Then came the godfather of this modern-day extremism, I mean conservatism: Barry Goldwater. With a faithful, young, zippy Reagan coming out in support of him, Goldwater attacked everything about President Lyndon Johnson's Great Society. Medicare (socialism). War on Poverty (socialism). Civil Rights Act (socialism). JFK's assassination (communism). "The good Lord raised this mighty Republic to be a home for the brave and to flourish as the land of the free—not to stagnate in the swampland of collectivism, not to cringe before the bully of communism," Goldwater exclaimed from the rooftops.[5]

And yet, congressional conservatives used the power of the federal government (and state governments) to enact their own socialist agenda: corporate socialism and socialism for the rich. Stick a pin in this one. We'll return.

Reagan continued his attacks ad nauseam through the '70s, first as governor and then, during the '80s, as president. Socialist this, socialism that. In 1988, then-vice president George H. W. Bush deployed the smear against Democratic presidential candidate Michael Dukakis, claiming that Dukakis broke "with the American tradition of entrepreneurship and free enterprise" at the very moment when other world governments "are abandoning socialism."

Then came Speaker Newt Gingrich, Paul Ryan, Mitch McConnell and, of course, Trump, who said, "If Democrats win control of Congress this November, we will come dangerously closer to socialism in America." Everything is socialism. A tweet from the National Republican Congressional Committee used Joseph Stalin's likeness to describe wealthy Democratic leaders like Nancy Pelosi and Chuck Schumer.[6] Shocker.

Trump used the word over *260 times* while in office.

All of that was a long-winded but necessary historical account of how the Democrats are consistently labeled socialists by Republicans. The fiercest and loudest attacks come usually when congressional Republicans have mucked things up really badly and have to resort to nebulous cultural excoriations. But I'm here to tell you that not only are they bullshit artists, they're also Herculean hypocrites. Why? Because they practice the same brand of socialism that they accuse Democrats of. Not the real socialism (where government controls the means of production). I mean welfare, which you probably think of as programs that assist poor and middle-class Americans. The difference here is that Republican socialism subsidizes corporations and the wealthy. Those same halfwits screaming "COMMUNISM!" are more than happy to dole out many more billions to corporate entities, which represents the very idea they rail against.

Here are some examples:

Look at federal, state, and local subsidies for businesses that open factories or offices in a particular area. I know what you're saying:

"Jobs!" But rarely do the job-creation gains match the heft of the financial assistance that congressional Republicans provide to companies, usually large wealthy ones that already have plenty of capital. Have a look at this analysis conducted by Michigan state legislature of those who approved of subsidies, from most to least from 2001 through 2018:

Legislators that voted for the most business subsidies

Legislator	Subsidies approved	Precent approved	Party
Hildenbrand, Dave	$5,423,505,578	100%	R
Jones, Rick	$5,399,505,578	99.6%	R
Marleau, Jim	$5,399,505,578	99.6%	R
Hansen, Goeff	$5,349,505,578	99.6%	R
Proos, John	$5,349,505,578	99.6%	R
Booher, Darwin	$5,199,505,578	99.5%	R
Bieda, Steve	$4,961,886,878	99.4%	D
Hood, Morris, III	$4,961,886,878	99.4%	D
Hopgood, Hoon-Yung	$4,961,886,878	99.4%	D
Casperson, Tom	$4,872,898,064	97.6%	R
Anderson, Glenn	$4,606,471,700	97.5%	D
Whitmer, Gretchen	$4,546,699,800	98.1%	D
Allen, Jason	$4,524,761,686	99.8%	R
Bishop, Mike	$4,524,761,686	99.8%	R
Stamas, Tony	$4,524,761,686	99.8%	R
Van Woerkom, Gerald	$4,524,761,686	99.8%	R
Robertson, David	$4,515,498,064	97.5%	R
Brown, Cameron	$4,461,761,686	98.4%	R
Kuipers, Wayne	$4,461,761,686	98.4%	R
Jelinek, Ron	$4,456,188,686	98.4%	R
Jacobs, Gilda	$4,446,724,186	98.1%	D
George, Tom	$4,436,761,686	97.8%	R
Clarke, Hansen	$4,422,224,186	98.1%	D
Clark-Coleman, Irma	$4,378,596,086	98.0%	D
Birkholz, Patricia	$4,373,011,686	99.8%	R

Source: The Mackinac Center

Since 1994, when Republicans took control of Congress, earmarks— meaning government money dispensed to districts for pet projects or the like—have exploded. From the conservative group Citizens Against Government Waste:

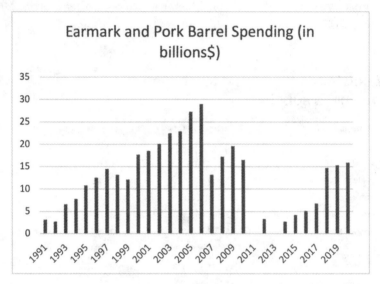

Source: Citizens Against Government Waste

Any Republican tax plan, particularly the most recent Trump Tax Plan, is a gift to corporations and their wealthy shareholders. That's where all tax savings are headed. As I explained in the chapter on Economics, stock buybacks are essentially ways for a company to purchase its own shares in the market, because they believe it is a good investment. However, it's really more about driving the stock prices higher. Again, who owns the stock? Mostly rich people.

According to research from the Center for Budget Policy Priorities:[7]

- Companies repatriated $2.6 *trillion* held in foreign cash reserves largely used to buy back stock.

- And companies that repurchased stock did better than the S&P 500 on average with a total return of 400 percent since 2009 versus 300 percent.

- In total, 61 percent of the tax cut went to shareholders, 20 percent went to job creation, 6 percent to workers, 6 percent to products, 4 percent to customers, and 3 percent to communities.

Finally, the abject and deliberate failure to pass bills that govern executive pay and board composition has led to the widest disparity and concentration of wealth since the Gilded Age. Since 1970, executive pay (+430 percent) has far outstripped corporate profits (+250 percent) and absolutely crushed average wages (+26 percent). Socialism!

And executive wages have decidedly mirrored almost exactly the rise of the S&P 500. The overlay of the S&P 500 and executive compensation is a near carbon copy. The extravagant pay relative to other employees is not based on how much value they add. It is decades of political and financial engineering.

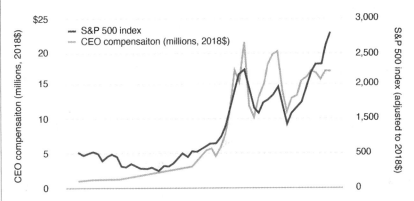

CEO realized direct compensation and the S&P 500 index (2018$), 1965-2018

Notes: CEO average annual compensation is computed using the "options realized" compensation series, which includes salary, bonus, restricted stock awards, options realized, and long-term incentive payouts for CEOs at the top 350 U.S. firms ranked by sales. Projected value for 2018 is based on the percent change in CEO pay in the samples available in June 2017 and in June 2018 (labeled first-half [FH] data) applied to the full-year 2017 value.

Source: Authors' analysis of data from Compustat's ExecuComp database and the Federal Reserve Economic Data (FRED) database from the Federal Reserve Bank of St. Louis

47

STATES' RIGHTS

"States' rights don't override federal rights."

—TRUMP SURROGATE GINA LOUDON (2018)

"We've got to take [sanctuary cities] to court, and we've got to start charging some of these politicians with crimes."

—ICE ACTING DIRECTOR THOMAS HOMAN, ON FOX NEWS (2018)

WHAT?

THE TERM STATES' RIGHTS originated in the 1850s when the federal government banned slavery and Southern states said, "Sorry, we don't abide by these unjust intrusive laws. We want to keep our slaves for whatever purpose we deem fit. States' rights!" States' rights are, basically, the idea that states should have power to govern ultimately over the federal government. The Tenth Amendment enshrines these rights in the Constitution and states, for the most part, are makers of their own destiny. Any power not reserved for the federal government is expressly reserved for the states.

WHY?

CONGRESSIONAL REPUBLICANS AND THE radical rich trotted this argument out each time they felt their rights were being taken away (they weren't). Each time a Democrat proposed an expansion of federal government powers, it was "States' rights!" From the New Deal to the Civil Rights Act to the Great Society to Obamacare and likely beyond: "States' rights!" To them, again, it's a zero-sum game. Either they win or the government wins. And they really *really* want to win. In that vein, they stopped at little to prevent and reverse any of the aforementioned programs. In reality, they didn't care about states' rights. Or the little guy. Instead, they employed the powers of the federal government whenever it suited them.

EZRA ROSSER IN THE *Hill* writes, "Conservative politicians love to celebrate states' rights, using a rhetorical commitment to local control as an excuse for blocking progressive policies. Standing behind the idea that states should have the final say has become an almost rote response of Republican members of Congress when they are pressed on social issues ... Conservatives emphasized on states' rights when it came to slavery and Jim Crow, and they continue to do so with regard to hot button issues such as gay marriage, abortion, and separation of church and state."[1]

States' rights increased in force during the run-up to the passage of the Civil Rights Act in 1964. The big bad federal government sought to grant Black people the right to vote and the right to drink at the same water fountains as White people, but that apparently was too much for conservatives and Southern Democrats, who trotted out the states' rights argument to protect themselves from the big meanies.

Republican states even went so far as to enshrine their love for states' rights after Obama took office in 2009, by introducing *state sovereignty resolutions*, or Tenth Amendment Resolutions, which are nonbinding ways for the state legislature to waste time and show they really don't care about governing. Such resolutions were introduced in the legislatures of 37 states and passed in seven states (Alaska, Idaho, North Dakota, South Dakota, Oklahoma, Louisiana, and Tennessee). During 2010, resolutions were introduced or reintroduced into the legislatures of twenty-one states, and passed in seven states (Alabama, Arizona, Kansas, Nebraska, South Carolina, Utah, and Wyoming). A state-sovereignty resolution was prefiled for the 2011 session of the Texas Legislature (a prior 2009 resolution did not pass).[2]

"The Trump administration is all in favor of states' rights," writes the author Michael Stratford. "Except when it's not."[3] As an example, in 2017, Attorney General Jeff Sessions disregarded state autonomy to file suit against California over its so-called sanctuary-city policies, which protect undocumented immigrants from deportation. He also untethered federal prosecutors to pursue marijuana businesses in the states that have legalized selling it. Separately, Interior Secretary Ryan Zinke, has crossed swords with governors in coastal states over his agency's proposal to open federal waters to offshore drilling. And Education Secretary Betsy DeVos informed states they did not have the authority to restrict predatory practices by some of the nation's largest student loan companies.

Now, it would stand to reason that if Republicans believed that the government "closer to the people" should pass and enforce the laws we are supposed to live by (which is the basis for states' rights), then state governments should defer to counties, cities, and towns in that same vein, right? Not even close. Republicans have passed a series of preemption laws in 2010 when they seized power in state governments. Preemption laws are basically federalism for states, which tell local governments that the governor has ultimate governing power. From NewAmerica.org: "Preemption is a legal concept where a higher level of government has the authority to limit, or even eliminate, the power of a lower level of government to regulate a certain issue."[4] What has become known as the *era of preemption* followed immediately on the heels of the Republican wave election of 2010. Moreover, most of the instances of preemption, including the most egregious, have transpired in Republican-majority states. Illinois State University professor Lori Riverstone-Newell highlighted the connection and concluded that "rising conservative dominance of state legislatures has provided the opportunity to thwart progressive local policies, and these efforts have been aided by various industry and conservative organized groups."

Here are a few highlights (or lowlights) from Alex Hertel-Fernandez's excellent book *State Capture*, which details how conservatives used state governments to do exactly what they were arguing against at the federal level.

He notes that the behemoths of the sharing economy, companies like Uber and Airbnb, have sent swarms of lobbyists to Chamber of Commerce meetings to aggressively push proposals that would limit how cities regulate businesses. These lobbyists have been instrumental in getting legislatures to tamp down on minimum wage and labor-market regulations. At one ACCE meeting, Hertel-Fernandez writes, a representative from the International Franchise Association advocated for a "two-pronged strategy to beat back higher wages."[5] The strategy included preemption efforts, which would make it more difficult—if not impossible—for local governments to pass labor-market regulation, including minimum-wage increases, which surpass state law, and intense litigation against cities to put a stop to these increases.

Progressives have repeatedly made earnest attempts at fair legislation, only to be beaten back by big business. And they fully embrace preemption in doing so. Enter American Legislative Exchange Council. ALEC for short. They are a nonprofit organization made up of conservative state legislators and private sector representatives who draw up and distribute extremely probusiness legislation to state governments, who, most of the time, do not even change a single word in the document before putting it forth for passage. ALEC has used pre-emption to stop cities from instituting strict regulations on business. By way of example, in the 1990s, ALEC, at the urgence of the tobacco industry, sponsored model bills that would prohibit cities from passing antismoking laws that exceeded the standards set by states. By 2000, more than half of all states had passed variants of that ALEC-drafted tobacco regulation preemption.

Below is a graph from *State Capture* that illustrates the percentage of the nation's population living in states with local minimum-wage preemption or local paid- or family-leave preemption. The dashed line in the center-right is 2011, the year when ALEC began disseminating labor-policy preemption bills to its puppet representatives. (Sometimes Republican legislators are so lazy that they don't even change the stationery a bill is drafted on. True story.)

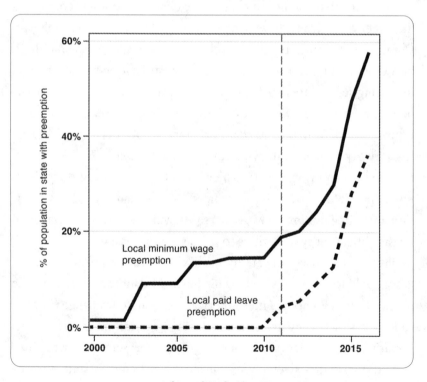

Source: State Capture

What you're looking at above is the destruction of fair-labor practices at the hands of big business, courtesy of advocacy groups who pay a group of powerful legislators to write bills for them.

Hertel-Fernandez closes with this: "In short, the combination of state power over preemption, coupled with the [radical rich and their puppets in legislatures] cross-state reach, severely curtails the ability of blue cities located within red states to take action on their own. While in some cases states have had to back off of preemption drives—as when North Carolina barred cities from prohibiting discrimination against LGBT people, including the use of bathrooms consistent with individuals' gender identities—more run-of-the-mill preemption of city efforts to raise working standards, improve the environment and deal with climate change, and address obesity and sugar consumption have generally been harder to reverse."

So, it's OK to scream "States' rights!" and "Local control!" when it's an issue you care about, but when the shoe is on the other foot, it's, "Sorry, you can't do that!" Sheer utter hypocrisy, but you already knew that.

REPUBLICANS

VS.

DEMOCRATS

48

CONVERTS

"What has happened to our party?
What has happened to the conservative movement?"

—FORMER GOVERNOR OF OHIO, JOHN KASICH (2015)

WHAT AND WHY?

THE GOP, AS AN establishment, has seen a ton of smart and decent members wave goodbye during the Trump years (2016–2020). Credit Trump, himself, for the mass exodus, but, to be fair, he's just the straw that broke the elephant's back. To understand how this racist conman became leader of the pack, you need to look deeper into the party itself. Trump would not be anyone without the full-throated support of Republicans. The sheer number of conservative converts is due primarily to what the entire party has become over decades of abhorrence, racism, and ignorance. To be clear, the Democratic Party has had its fair share of exits. However, I *seriously* doubt, that the collection of prominent card-carrying Republicans who have abandoned their party pales in comparison to those who have abandoned the Democrats.

THE COMMENTS BELOW SHOULD scare all of us. Mind you, they come from people who have spent their entire careers in Republican politics. Their relationships, both personal and professional, are imbued with Republicanism. If they, of all people, have decided to turn their backs on their party, that's pretty darn significant.

> "The GOP is less a political party than a cult—one that, as its founding charisma and spiritual mission have atrophied and ossified into unquestioned dogma, continually redoubles its efforts to enforce orthodoxy among the faithful."

—BRUCE BARTLETT, FORMER DOMESTIC POLICY ADVISER TO RONALD REAGAN AND A TREASURY OFFICIAL UNDER GEORGE H. W. BUSH (2018)

> "There is no Republican Party anymore—it's dead. Donald Trump killed it. He's like a parasite that ate its host from the inside out."

—RICK WILSON, SERVED ON GEORGE H. W. BUSH'S CAMPAIGN AS FLORIDA FIELD DIRECTOR AND WAS APPOINTED TO THE DEPARTMENT OF DEFENSE UNDER THEN-SECRETARY OF DEFENSE DICK CHENEY (2020)

> "Donald Trump has been the worst president this country has ever had. And I don't say that hyperbolically . . . When you listen to the President, these are the musings of an imbecile. An idiot . . . We've never seen a level of incompetence, a level of ineptitude so staggering . . . He's brought death, suffering, and economic collapse on truly an epic scale."

—STEVE SCHMIDT, SENIOR CAMPAIGN ADVISOR FOR PRESIDENT GEORGE W. BUSH, CALIFORNIA GOVERNOR ARNOLD SCHWARZENEGGER, AND ARIZONA SENATOR JOHN MCCAIN (2020)

"This Republican Party is unrecognizable to me."

**—NICOLLE WALLACE, FORMER WHITE HOUSE
COMMUNICATIONS DIRECTOR FOR GEORGE W. BUSH,
AND A SENIOR ADVISOR FOR JOHN MCCAIN'S
2008 PRESIDENTIAL CAMPAIGN (2019)**

"I was a Republican for 30 years,
but the GOP is now a sea of corruption."

**—RICHARD PAINTER, CHIEF WHITE HOUSE ETHICS LAWYER
IN THE GEORGE W. BUSH ADMINISTRATION (2020)**

"By August 2017, what was left of the philosophy formerly
known as conservatism beyond 'Fuck you, leftists'?"

**—DAVID FRUM, A FORMER GEORGE BUSH ADVISOR
AND SPEECHWRITER FOR NELSON ROCKEFELLER (2018)**

"I spent decades working to elect Republicans, including
Mr. Romney and four other presidential candidates, and I am
here to bear reluctant witness that Mr. Trump didn't hijack
the Republican Party. He is the logical conclusion of what the
party became over the past fifty or so years, a natural product
of the seeds of race-baiting, self-deception and anger that
now dominate it. Hold Donald Trump up to a mirror and that
bulging, scowling orange face is today's Republican Party."

**—STUART STEVENS, A ROMNEY CAMPAIGN ADVISOR, AND
THE AUTHOR OF *IT WAS ALL A LIE: HOW THE REPUBLICAN
PARTY BECAME DONALD TRUMP* (KNOPF, 2020)**

Those quotes just scratch the surface. The list of other conservatives and Republicans who have effectively turned their backs on their

party in recent years goes on and on. Among the people I could also
have quoted here are:

- John Dean, former White Counsel to Richard Nixon

- Gordon J. Humphrey, former US Senator from New Hampshire

- Joe Scarborough, former US Representative from Florida

- Paul Mitchell, US Congressman from Michigan

- Joe Walsh, former US Congressman from Illinois

- Bill Kristol, long-time conservative, the son of Irving Kristol, the founder of *Washington Examiner*, associated with and the founder of a number of conservative think tanks

- Charlie Sykes, long-time conservative author and commentator

- George Will, Reagan speechwriter and advisor, Pulitzer Prize–winning conservative author

- Jennifer Rubin, long-time conservative political columnist

- Max Boot, senior foreign-policy adviser for the presidential campaigns of John McCain, Mitt Romney, and Marco Rubio

- David Jolly, Former US Congressman from Florida

49

COMPROMISE

"All legislation, all government, all society is founded upon the principle of mutual concession, politeness, comity, courtesy; upon these everything is based."

—HENRY CLAY (1850)

WHAT AND WHY?

COMPROMISE IS CRITICAL TO any functioning democracy. It's critical to working in any company. It's critical to any relationship between two people, let alone a system of government for 330 million people. I mean, seriously, where the *hell* would we be without compromise? Most, if not all, deals, transactions, agreements, whatever—not under extreme duress or coercion from one side—would have never been completed without compromise. That big corporate acquisition you read about in the *Wall Street Journal* yesterday. The car you bought from the dealership when the salesman said he would throw in those whitewall tires and satellite radio. What you're eating for dinner! Of course, not all scenarios are an explicit back-and-forth. We already sort of do a *pre*-compromise with our spouses, for example, because we know their likes and dislikes and consider them *before* negotiating. Knowing your wife hates seafood, you're probably not going to debate Red Lobster, are you? Well, suggesting the fishiest smelling restaurant is exactly what the GOP does in negotiations with Democrats. Being uncompromising, in fact, is in Republican DNA!

THEIR INABILITY OR UNWILLINGNESS—WHATEVER makes you feel better to call it—to compromise is destroying democracy, because democracy is predicated on compromise. Reaching agreements to produce an outcome that is acceptable to all parties is at its core. In 2013, Pew Research asked whether respondents preferred elected officials who "make compromises with people they disagree with" or those who "stick to their positions." Among Democrats, 59 percent preferred compromise-seekers; among Republicans, only 36 percent did.[1]

A BRIEF HISTORY OF COMPROMISES

American history is full of compromises. How about, um, the US Constitution? It's called a "bundle of compromises" because it required so much input from such a broad swath of interests. Here's Ben Franklin to elaborate:

> "I agree to this Constitution with all its faults, if they are such; because I think a general Government necessary for us, and there is no form of Government but what may be a blessing to the people if well administered, and believe farther that this is likely to be well administered for a course of years [...] For when you assemble a number of men to have the advantage of their joint wisdom, you inevitably assemble with those men, all their prejudices, their passions, their errors of opinion, their local interests, and their selfish views. From such an assembly can a perfect

production be expected? [...] Within these walls they were born, and here they shall die. If every one of us in returning to our Constituents were to report the objections he has had to it, and endeavor to gain partizans in support of them, we might prevent its being generally received, and thereby lose all the salutary effects & great advantages resulting naturally in our favor among foreign Nations as well as among ourselves, from our real or apparent unanimity."

Franklin and the Founders understood the need to compromise, perhaps better than anyone. The excitement at the prospect of self-government pushed these "partizans" to drive a hard bargain. They would have to live with the rules for a long time. Here are some more fairly well-known compromises:

- The "Great Compromise," which laid out the bicameral nature of our government (a Senate and a House)

- Commerce Compromise, which imposed tariffs on imports and regulated interstate commerce

- Electoral College, which elects our president every four years

In fact, there's an entire Wikipedia page dedicated to compromises since our founding.[2]

But compromise becomes impossible when it is equated with selling out, as Republicans have branded it in the past forty-five-plus years. The refusal to agree is not even ideologically based, which is the worst part. Most Republicans in Congress do not want to budge or even negotiate simply because the other side are Democrats. Matter-of-factly, Republicans view Democrats as an illegitimate political party. Obama? Illegitimate. Pelosi? Illegitimate. The lowest ranking Freshman member in the House? Illegitimate. Frankly, they don't care about the plight of the poor or working people, so their strategy is mostly based on how to make the other side fail. Michael Grunwald, who wrote about Obama and Republican obstructionism, said that during the stimulus negotiations of 2009, a Republican aide told him, "If this thing works and the economy is booming and everybody is happy, your vote against the stimulus won't be held against you. In good times, people get reelected." On the flip side, Grunwald noted, "If the economy wasn't booming by 2010, Republicans could return from the wilderness."[3] So, when the stimulus passed, they ran home to their constituencies and bragged to have voted against it. Zero House Republicans supported it. Z-E-R-O.

But when Trump became president, the $2 trillion stimulus, double what Obama passed, flew through the Senate and House like the wind. It garnered *ninety* out of one hundred votes in the Senate. Christ Almighty! The journalist Adam Serwer brilliantly notes,

> "The supposedly insurmountable ideological divides in Washington parted like saloon doors, as congressional leaders from both parties negotiated a compromise that left neither side fully content . . . Mitch McConnell, who had demanded to know 'how we're going to pay for' the $831 billion American Reinvestment and Recovery Act, enthusiastically supported the $2 trillion CARES Act. Lindsay Graham, who had complained that $800 billion was far too much spending in 2009, said last month's bill would 'help save the country.' Chuck Grassley bragged about having 'beefed up' funding for small businesses and unemployment insurance. Lamar Alexander declared, 'We are here not as Democrats and Republicans, but we are here to work together to do whatever we can to address COVID-19.' The soaring spirit of civic responsibility that was altogether absent during the Great Recession suddenly reasserted itself, even as the overriding concern about excess government spending disappeared."

But, you say, Republicans *had* to vote for the stimulus *this* time around because the economic meltdown was no one's fault, per se; it was a natural disaster, of sorts. I would say, just hang on two seconds there, chief. The difference between 2009 and 2020 is not due to combatting the virus. No, no. Most Republicans voted *for* the bank bail-outs *prior* to voting against Obama's stimulus (but voted for Trump's stimulus). You see what happened here? They voted to help those most responsible for the Great Recession (big banks), then voted to shaft those whose lives were most affected by the financial hardship (middle class and poor). And the Republican stymieing of Obama to address the crisis was not merely hypocrisy. In most cases, Democrats want better protection and support for individual workers while Republicans want more for big business and the wealthy. These ideological differences shouldn't stand in the way of compromise. Republicans' and Demo-crats' view of the role and size of the federal government shouldn't really stand in the way either. These are the differences that have his-torically produced compromise. Again, as Serwer puts it, it "stems from the ideological conviction, held by much of the Republican Party, that the Democratic Party is inherently illegitimate and has no right to gov-ern." Mitch McConnell and his Republican lackeys viewed prolonging the Great Recession not as a threat to millions of Americans and their livelihoods but as a political opportunity to be milked. The lengthier and more painstaking the economic recovery, the easier it would be to bounce Obama from the White House and Democrats from Congress, even if their own constituents suffered as a result. The Democrats, on the other hand, did not try to block help for Americans figuring their way out of the financial devastation of the coronavirus. Au contraire, they fought for *more* generous provisions, *despite* the knowledge that Trump had recently been impeached for trying to blackmail a for-eign country into framing his Democratic presidential challenger and knowing, full well, he would take the credit for the aid and use it as a talking point for his own reelection, which he did. You'll notice at the signing ceremony for the CARES Act, Trump was surrounded solely by Republicans. Democrats didn't get the invite. Shameless.[4]

When I see the GOP acting like this, it sends waves of intense anger through my entire body. That these charlatans would help bail out the wealthiest of society, leave the have-nots out to dry, then support the stimulus bill just because it pleases the president is the grossest thing. Having people like this lead our country is just mind-numbingly outrageous.

But it didn't start in 2009 against Obama. There was a lot of the same partisan obstructionism prior to that.

Quotes:

"The single most important thing we want to achieve is for President Obama to be a one-term president."

—MITCH MCCONNELL (2010)

"We're going to do everything—and I mean everything we can do—to kill it, stop it, slow it down, whatever we can."

—JOHN BOEHNER, SPEAKER OF THE HOUSE BETWEEN 2010 AND 2015

"There will be no compromise on stopping runaway spending, deficits and debt. There will be no compromise on repealing Obamacare."

—REP. MIKE PENCE (R-IND.), IN AN INTERVIEW ON THE CONSERVATIVE HUGH HEWITT'S RADIO SHOW (2010)

"When it comes to spending, I'm not compromising. I don't care who, what, when or where, I'm not compromising."

—KEN BUCK, THE REPUBLICAN SENATE NOMINEE IN COLORADO, IN THE WASHINGTON POST (2010)

"Well, we didn't get very much done. Listen, I'll be the first to admit that when the Tea Party wave, of which I was

one, got here in 2011, the last thing we were interested
in was giving President Obama legislative successes."

—MICK MULVANEY (2019)

"Trump's America and the post-American society that the
anti-Trump coalition represents are incapable of coexisting.
One will simply defeat the other. There is no room for compromise.
Trump has understood this perfectly since day one."

—NEWT GINGRICH (2018)

PRESIDENT CLINTON'S HEALTH CARE PLAN

The Republicans coordinated an attack on Bill Clinton's health care plan *despite the fact* that it was originally similar to a plan adopted by conservatives from the Heritage Foundation. Theda Skocpol, a professor of public policy at Harvard, writes in *Health Affairs*, "Toward the end of 1993 right-wing Republicans realized that their ideological fortunes within their own party, as well as the Republican partisan interest in weakening the Democrats as a prelude to winning control of Congress and the presidency, could be splendidly served by first demonizing and then totally defeating the Clinton plan."[5] Irving Kristol, the chief ideologue of the Project for the Republican Future, began to dole out instructions, urging all-out partisan warfare. Like clockwork, public support for the plan started to erode, thanks to what Kristol called "an aggressive and uncompromising counterstrategy." That ultimately killed the plan and convinced people who would benefit (i.e., middle- and lower-income Americans) that there really wasn't a crisis in American health care at all (there was). Kristol persistently communicated the message that "mandatory health alliances and government price controls will destroy the character, quality, and inventiveness of

American medical care." Whatever the hell that means. Skocpol continues, "During 1994, the hardline conservative attack on the Clinton plan
brought together more and more allies and channeled resources and
support toward antigovernment conservatives within the Republican
Party. Ideologues and think tanks launched lurid attacks on the plan.
Small-business members of the National Federation of Independent
Business (NFIB) and other associations mobilized against the proposed
employer mandate." Then the conservative bull horn Rush Limbaugh
took to the airwaves about "socialism," and the plan was as good as
dead. Moderate congressional Republicans who initially supported the
deal were pressured to kill any cooperation they forged with the Clinton administration, because working with it was a mortal sin worthy of
being primaried in the next election.

OBAMACARE

Obamacare prompted the most absurd and fierce obstruction of them
all. Originally an idea from the Heritage Foundation and Mitt Romney—
yes, that's right, the "there are 47 percent of the people who will vote
for the president no matter what"[6] Mitt Romney and the antigovernment crusading Heritage—this plan was actually implemented under
Romney in Massachusetts in 2006. And it worked! What's more, the
difference between the Republican Party's response to the enactment
of Medicare and its reaction to the passage of the Affordable Care Act
could hardly be more significant. They absolutely lost their shit with
Obamacare. As E. J. Dionne writes, "Republicans rapidly came to terms
with Medicare, even if they have in recent years tried to pare it back
or partially privatize it. Obamacare, on the other hand, has been under
constant attack from the Right—on the floor of Congress, in the courts,
and in many of the states Republicans control. Republicans talked of
'repealing and replacing' the Affordable Care Act, but all their efforts
focused on wiping it off the books."[7] *Seventy times* the GOP tried to

repeal Obamacare, including when they had the presidency and both chambers of Congress. Seventy![8]

What a waste of time and disservice to their constituents, especially poor folk and people with preexisting conditions, who depend on the ACA, Medicare, and Medicaid. And they didn't even have a replacement. Republicans want to return to the system we had: overcharging patients and a woeful lack of coverage. Even worse, because they weren't able to repeal it, they've been sabotaging the ACA since it passed.

OBAMA'S ECONOMIC RECOVERY PLAN

In describing the Obama Administration's efforts to end the Great Recession, the journalists Andrew Fieldhouse and Josh Bivens write, "From the start, the GOP sought to block measures that a wide swath of economists agreed would provide help to boost the economy and bring down unemployment."[9] This kind of obstructionism and unnecessary gridlock was a consistent theme throughout the Obama years, and it continues today during Joe Biden's first term. Zero Republicans in the House or the Senate voted for the $1.9 trillion stimulus package. (For more on this, see "Chaos and Gridlock.")

The list goes on and on. Republicans do not miss an opportunity to stymie any legislation, no matter if it was painstakingly compromised and negotiated. Because ultimately, the Republican Party believes that Democrats are illegitimate and they, Republicans, alone should be allowed to govern.

50

POLARIZATION

"The Republican Party sharply turned away
from the center line and hasn't looked back."

—JOURNALIST CHRISTOPHER INGRAHAM (2015)

WHAT?

IF YOU HAVEN'T BEEN living under a rock since 2016 or on a really long silent meditation retreat, you know we are a very polarized nation. Trump has elevated the acrimony and warring to dizzying heights, but the divisiveness didn't start in 2016. We've been at odds with each other since the founding of this country (Federalists vs. Democrat-Republicans), and, particularly during the Civil War. In modern times, however, since the early '90s—I'll keep returning to this decade—it's been a dumpster fire. Voters began to be divided on everything from guns to abortion to voting rights to the environment. Thanks to former Republican Speaker Newt Gingrich, his acolytes, radical rich donors, and conservative media, the fire grew massive and out of control.

WHY?

POLARIZATION BENEFITS THOSE WHO thrive on chaos and dysfunction (i.e., conservative media, congressional Republicans, and the radical rich). Of course, the mainstream media loves controversy, but the primary source of the dysfunction is the absurd and totally uncompromising positions the congressional Republicans have intentionally staked out with seemingly endless backing and support (very sophisticated and well-funded, I might add) of conservative media and the radical rich. The more polarization in Washington and throughout the country, the better. There are people with wealth and power who benefit most when the government is in shambles, meaning, when the government cannot act on behalf of its citizens.

EVEN MORE TROUBLING, WHILE the country has become increasingly liberal/progressive in its views, congressional Republicans and their wealthy benefactors have become increasingly conservative/Trumpian.

In fact, Republicans have pulled away from Democrats in their extremism—thanks, primarily, to conservative media radicalizing their audience. I'm sure you've heard the cries of "Socialism!" "Infanticide!" "Coming for your guns!" ad nauseum, but, if you haven't, consider yourself lucky. From 1930 through 1980, parties' ideologies stayed relatively constant between Republicans and Democrats. Beginning in 1980, however, Republicans started to speed away from the center. The number of Republicans calling themselves conservative or very conservative is triple that of Democrats who call themselves liberal. Democrats in 2019, according to Gallup, view themselves as 49 percent liberal, 38 percent moderate, 14 percent conservative. Republicans? They came in at 73 percent conservative, 21 percent moderate, and 4 percent liberal.[1]

It is worth showing this graph again (previously in the chapter "Radicalization"). Observe the ideology among the House members. There is a meteoric rise in extremism around the time of, you guessed it, Newt Gingrich (see arrow)! Nearly every congressional Republican is not ideologically moderate but extremely conservative. While Democrats are a fraction of radical.

Party Polarization 1879–2013
Distance Between the Parties First Dimension

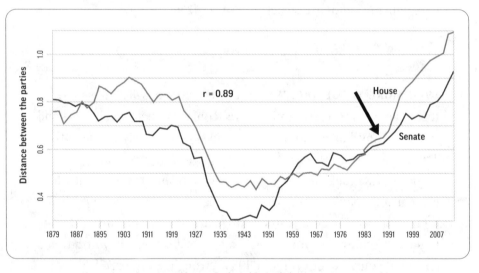

Source: Poole and Rosenthal

Even after the rise of Bernie Sanders and the election of 2018, progressives represent a small fraction of House Democrats. And let's be frank, progressives are not extremists. Wanting Medicare for All and a Green New Deal is in line with European ideals, while the current incarnation of conservatism—QAnon, White supremacy, and authoritarianism—is abhorrent and fucking contemptible.

In their book *It's Even Worse Than It Looks*, the scholars Thomas Mann and (the conservative) Norm Ornstein describe the GOP as "ideologically extreme," "scornful of compromise," and "dismissive of the legitimacy of its political opposition." Breaking with traditional Washington norms that have sought "solutions that move both sides to the center," Republicans have adopted positions that are "simply untenable," when it comes to compromise, because "one side is so far out of reach. The Republican Party has become an insurgent outlier in American politics—ideologically extreme; contemptuous of the inherited social and economic policy regime; scornful of compromise; unmoved by conventional understanding of facts, evidence and science; and dismissive of the legitimacy of its political opposition." What happened to Republicans?

It's obvious to me what happened. A bunch of radical rich, conservative, and religious goons decided they had enough of Washington telling them they should integrate, be taxed fairly, give poor people health care, and generally follow the rules to protect a healthy governing society. So they took over our political system like a coup in a developing country. Now they are holding it hostage. Fuck. Them.

SECTION 9

LOOKING
FORWARD

with it). The war in Vietnam was a gift to congressional conservatives and the radical rich.

But, as the author Donald Cohen of In the Public Interest—a national resource and policy center on privatization and responsible contracting—writes, progressives are guilty too: "We also must acknowledge the implicit cooperation of progressives in solidifying distrust of government after LBJ's lies about Vietnam, Nixon's abuse of power, and the actions of industry-connected and antigovernment public officials since then."[1] To remedy this, he continues, we need to develop ways for "how to talk about government failures and corruption without reinforcing negative attitudes toward the idea of government."

WHY?

IT IS IMPERATIVE PROGRESSIVES and liberals regain their faith and trust in government, because we need it to deal with the injustices and problems facing our country. Private enterprise is not going to step up. They can't take on these massively expensive endeavors (like health care, poverty, and education). We need a strong central government whose constituents believe in its mission and leaders. The author and Vietnam War veteran Karl Marlantes writes, "You don't finish the world's largest highway system, build huge numbers of public schools and universities, institute the Great Society, fight a major war, and go to the moon, which we did in the 1960s—simultaneously—if you're cynical about government and politicians."[2]

WE ARE CERTAINLY NOT getting any help from Republicans. They are actively obstructing the mission to restore faith and trust in the government. And I mean *actively*. As I have demonstrated through direct quotes and actions (see Conservatives War on Government and Chaos and Gridlock), they seek to slow it down, throw sand in its gears, shrink it, and eventually get it small enough to drown it in a bathtub.

As you can see, Vietnam was the cliff. Then it was slow roll down the hill with a brief positive interlude under Bill Clinton, then off the GW Bush Bridge.

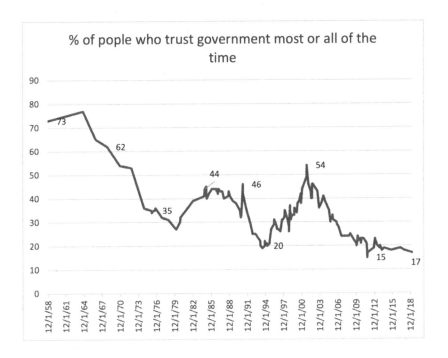

Don't misunderstand me, we should still be critical of government. After all, it (more like *they*, the individuals running it) has perpetrated some really heinous shit (and so has private enterprise, by the way). For example, the national security and industrialized-military apparatus has threatened our freedoms (while also protecting them), our criminal-justice system unfairly burdens poor and minorities, and lax government enforcement has allowed corporate America to crush what's left of the labor movement. Public-sector unions have also stood in the way of meaningful reforms. The author and professor Jacob Hacker writes, "The point is not to be uncritical of the public sector . . . Sometimes better governance will mean more expensive government, but in many cases, more effective government could cost less, especially in the long run. We should be committed to rooting out rent seeking and remedying government missteps in all their forms."[3] In other words, let's not throw the baby out with the bathwater. Let's start by paying more attention to those bad actors and policies that do the most harm and throw them out by their britches. Give 'em the hook! Just because your brother tells poorly timed tasteless jokes at dinner with your wife's family (true story) doesn't mean you are going to ex-communicate him. Work on his tact and give him a Jim Gaffigan joke book to memorize.

Cohen agrees. He declares it a necessity to distinguish between good and bad actors in government and weed out the latter. Like criminal justice and police—or any—reform. We can't take a blanket view of "bad government," because that's totally counterproductive. He also emphasizes the need to talk about the people who committed these actions and not the "government" as some giant irredeemable entity. He writes, "While it's critically important to wage campaigns that expose and challenge corporate and Wall Street control of public institutions, doing so fosters cynicism and the (well-deserved) belief that governments serve the powerful—another source of discontent . . . When we talk about 'the government' or refer to things the 'government did' we divert our attention from the people and forces in control of government."

If progressives and liberals want to regain the narrative about good government and use it effectively to heal the injustices in our society, we must begin talking about it in a positive way. Think happy thoughts, like Tinkerbell and Peter Pan. Cohen has the outline of a plan (obviously the implementing part requires a lot of resources and human capital, but it's a start):

- reclaim freedom: reengage in the battle of ideas
- keep up the assault on failed ideas (and the interests that they serve)
- turn our ideas and values into a new conventional wisdom
- be defenders and reformers, not attackers
- distinguish between the control of government and the democratic idea of government
- add it up to more than the sum of its parts
- embrace strategic incrementalism: chart a path toward the future we want
- build the base: gain power through numbers
- culture and music aren't the add-ons—they are the heart and soul
- plant before harvesting: focus on the work that gives meaning to elections

CAMPAIGN AGAINST GOVERNMENT

And the campaign against government is far larger, more sustained, and better-funded than any campaign against private enterprise. Cohen writes,

> While there is some generalized disdain for free-market capitalism among progressive activists, there isn't a clearly articulated alternative. We need an ideology and an economic theory to convincingly demonstrate that democratic public institutions and public power (e.g., regulatory, social insurance) are uniquely capable of doing what needs to be done to advance and protect the common good and that markets alone are inherently incapable of delivering basic public goods.

A few examples:

- FedEx can deliver packages, but it won't deliver an envelope to any address in the United States for the same price.

- Auto companies can build cars, but they need rules to ensure our air isn't polluted.

- Health insurers sell policies to those who can afford them, but only government can ensure that every American has access to health care.

Beyond a governing philosophy, we should be able to describe the role and purpose of government in American democracy. For example, here's one view of those basic roles:

- Provide public services that we all rely upon to live, work, play, and become educated, productive members of society

- Provide subsidies and investments that grow the economy and give everyone a fair shot at a decent life

- Regulate corporate and individual behavior to prevent excessive concentrations of power and exploitation, to create shared prosperity, and to protect public health, safety, and the planet

- Promote public safety and fair justice

- Protect and ensure equal human and civil rights

52

PEOPLE ACTUALLY
LIKE GOVERNMENT

"By wide margins, Americans support universal health care,
the minimum wage, strong regulations on financial industry,
background checks for gun owners, and are worried about
climate change and the influence of money in politics.
But, trust in government—the only institution that can
solve those problems—is at all-time lows."

—AUTHOR DONALD COHEN (2018)

WHAT?

WHILE PEOPLE GENERALLY DISLIKE government as a singular entity,
parts of it are quite popular. The paradox! A majority of Americans,
both Republican and Democrat, are fans of a wide range of government programs. And, get this, they think they are well run, too. Whaaaa?
How is this possible? Ronald Reagan assured me that government *is*
the problem! Could it be that the stink conservatives have purposely

produced around the literal word *government* has created an automatic gag reflex? Is it possible that demonizing government for forty-plus years has led people to hate the sum way more than the parts?

WHY?

THIS IS NOT A positive development for conservatives. If people increasingly like the parts of government, then their desire to destroy it becomes less of a reality.

THE SUM: 11 PERCENT of Americans trust government "most or all of the time."

The parts: the following is a survey of those who say the government should have a major role in supplying and those who say the government is doing a good job for that role.

	Major role for Government	Government doing a good job
Keeping country safe from terror	94%	72%
Responding to natural disasters	88%	79%
Ensuring safe food and medicine	87%	72%
Managing immigration system	81%	28%
Maintaining infrastructure	76%	52%
Protecting the environment	75%	59%
Strengthening the economy	74%	51%
Ensuring access to high quality education	70%	52%
Ensuring basic income for 65+ year olds	69%	48%
Setting workplace standards	66%	76%
Ensuring access to healthcare	61%	56%
Helping people get out of poverty	55%	36%
Advancing space exploration	47%	51%

Source: Pew Research, Aug 27 - Oct 4, 2015

Private industry, on the other hand, has never really had well-funded enemies, outside or inside. While there have been sporadic campaigns against big business, the mistrust they've engendered is primarily self-inflicted. According to Pew, people who've had a "great deal" to "quite a lot" of confidence have steadily eroded since 1999 from 30 percent to today at 19 percent.

Voters even pass tax hikes and large debt issuances to fund social-welfare projects. (Don't tell your conservative uncle, who angrily types into the Facebook cosmos "TAXATION IS THEFT! Now give me my Social Security and infrastructure!") Cohen notes that in 2016:

- Thirty-four transit bonds passed (two-thirds of all those on the ballot), raising billions of dollars for important public-transit infrastructure projects. (Center for Transportation Excellence, "2016 Election Results")

- Voters adopted large numbers of bond measures for afford-able housing, water infrastructure, and school construction and renovation. Wisconsin alone passed fifty-three local school-bond measures. (*The Wheeler Report*, "School Referendum Results, 2016")

- A number of municipalities passed sales, income, and soda taxes to pay for preschools, K-12 schools, health programs, homeless services, community colleges, and even general city revenues to fund basic services.

Now, I'm no expert, but it seems to me that the ideas of brainwashed conservatives, who parrot their antitax hero Ronald "government is the problem" Reagan, do not actually line up with what's happening in reality.

I'd like to close this chapter with a quote from Barack Obama: "If you were successful, somebody along the line gave you some help. There was a great teacher somewhere in your life. Somebody helped to create this unbelievable American system that we have that allowed you to thrive. Somebody invested in roads and bridges. If you've got a business—you didn't build that. Somebody else made that happen. The Internet didn't get invented on its own. Government research created the Internet so that all the companies could make money on the Internet."[1]

The point is, government is not the "problem" or an "evil institution" looking to suck the motivation and entrepreneurship out of the country. It's a big part of the solution. If only congressional conservatives (and plenty of Democrats) would stop pandering to corporate interests perhaps we could return to the days of better growth and shared prosperity.

EPILOGUE

WE ARE IN A scary place. The institutions that many of us grew up trusting are at risk. In this book, I have attempted to show that the vulnerable state of our democracy is not the result of one administration—incompetent and depraved as Trump was—but rather a decades-long siege by the GOP. This book is by no means exhaustive. I've barely discussed how the ultraconservative Heritage Foundation and Federalist Society have transformed the judiciary into an arm of the Republican Party. Or how we lack the proper checks and balances as we watched congressional Republicans acquiesce to every Trump demand and cower at the thought of an insulting Trump tweet hurled in their direction. Or how Trump completely defiled the highest office in the land. In other words, I've only scratched the surface of how fucking dreadful the GOP is.

What's here, I hope, is a solid repository of critical issues and events that have shaped our country, mostly for the worse. It is seriously helpful to understand them and how they led us to the place (near civil war) we are today. Without the insidious efforts by prominent congressional conservatives and their radical-rich benefactors to destroy the government, spread conspiracy theories and misinformation, and enact gigantic power grabs, this country would be a vastly more sane and prosperous place. For *everyone*. Believe that! Those bad actors understand full well that their constituency, old White conservatives, is rapidly dwindling. That's why they continue marching towards authoritarianism (while accusing the Democrats of being dictators) and attempting to shut the doors of this country to younger, more diverse, forward-thinking, educated members of our electorate.

The solution is to vote for the Democrats. They're far from perfect, but they are the party of the future. In every respect. So we now have to send a message to the GOP every two years at the ballot box. Let's put a stop to this bullshit and reclaim our country.

Call to Action:

Even though elections are every two years, there are actions we can take in the meantime to engage our neighbors and strengthen democracy. As I mentioned in the acknowledgements, I cofounded an organization called Fight for a Better America. We support local grassroots organizations that are engaged in year-round voter contact and issue advocacy, particularly in those all-important swing states and districts. While supporting traditional campaigns is important, we believe that we need complementary solutions to tackle the colossal amount of misinformation and general disengagement of the electorate. Further, early in-person contact around issues affecting the community has shown to make a significant difference. Please visit our website www.fightforbetter.org for more information on how you can help today!

NOTES

INTRODUCTION

1. Diaz, Jaclyn. "One of the Men Charged in the Michigan Governor Kidnap Plot Gets 6 Years in Prison." NPR, August 26, 2021. https://www.npr.org/2021/08/26/1031172713/kidnap-plot-prison-michigan-governor.

2. John Dewey, "The Need for a New Party II: Breakdown of the Old Order," 1931.

3. Peters, Jeremy W. "Grover Norquist, Author of Antitax Pledge, Faces Big Test ..." *New York Times*, November 19, 2012. https://www.nytimes.com/2012/11/20/us/politics/grover-norquist-author-of-antitax-pledge-faces-big-test.html.

CHAPTER 1

1. "Palace of Justice Siege." Wikipedia. Wikimedia Foundation, November 7, 2021. https://en.wikipedia.org/wiki/Palace_of_Justice_siege#:~:text=The%20Palace%20of%20Justice%20siege,trial%20against%20President%20Belisario%20Betancur.

2. "Farewell Address to the Nation." Farewell Address to the Nation | The Ronald Reagan Presidential Foundation & Institute. Accessed November 30, 2021. https://www.reaganfoundation.org/ronald-reagan/reagan-quotes-speeches/farewell-address-to-the-nation-1/.

3. Theodore Roosevelt on "The New Nationalism" (1910)

4. Abraham Lincoln, "The Gettysburg Address" (1863)

5. The President's Special Message to Congress Regarding a National Highway Program, February 22, 1955

6. Edward Epstein, "Congress Goes Home with Budget Work Unfinished; Lawmakers Fail to Approve 9 of 11 Appropriations Bills," San Francisco Chronicle (Dec. 8, 2006), A-12.

7. Cooper, Kenneth J. "Gingrich Pledges Major Package of Spending Cuts Early next Year." The Washington Post. WP Company, December 13, 1994. https://www.washingtonpost.com/archive/politics/1994/12/13/ gingrich-pledges-major-package-of-spending-cuts-early-next-year/ bba4244a-6494-4d73-8aa6-9591a83825a6/.

CHAPTER 2

1. "Welcome to the American Presidency Project: The American Presidency Project." The American Presidency Project, November 29, 1803. https://www.presidency.ucsb.edu/.

2. Coppins, McKay. "The Man Who Broke Politics," November, 2018.

3. Root, Danielle, and Sam Berger. "Structural Reforms to the Federal Judiciary." Center for American Progress, May 3, 2019. https:// www.americanprogress.org/article/structural-reforms-federal-judiciary/.

4. Samuelsohn, Darren. "Obama's Vanishing Administration." POLITICO, January 5, 2016. https://www.politico.com/story/2016/01/ obamas-vanishing-administration-217344.

5. Drum, Kevin, and Jaeah Lee. "3 Charts Explain Why Democrats Went Nuclear on the Filibuster." Mother Jones, November 22, 2013. https://www.motherjones.com/kevin-drum/2013/11/ charts-explain-why-democrats-went-nuclear-filibuster/.

6. Grunwald, Michael. "The Victory of 'No.'" POLITICO Magazine, December 4, 2016. https://www.politico.com/magazine/story/2016/12/ republican-party-obstructionism-victory-trump-214498/.

7. Rauch, Jonathan. "How American Politics Went Insane." Atlantic. Atlantic Media Company, April 19, 2018. https://www.theatlantic.com/magazine/ archive/2016/07/how-american-politics-went-insane/485570/.

CHAPTER 3

1. Dionne, E. J. *Why the Right Went Wrong: Conservatism—From Goldwater to the Tea Party and Beyond*, (Simon & Schuster, 2016).

2. Anderson, Kurt. *Fantasyland: How America Went Haywire: A 500-Year History* © 2017.

CHAPTER 4

1. Niskanen, William. "Reaganomics." Econlib, June 10, 2021. https://www.econlib.org/library/Enc/Reaganomics.html.

2. Cohen, Donald. "Dismantling Democracy." In the public interest. Accessed November 30, 2021. https://www.inthepublicinterest.org/wp-content/uploads/DonaldCohen_DismantlingDemocracy_2018.pdf.

3. Ronald Reagan, A Time for Choosing, aka The Speech, 1964.

4. "U.S. Economic Performance under Democratic and Republican Presidents." Wikipedia. Wikimedia Foundation, November 8, 2021. https://en.wikipedia.org/wiki/U.S._economic_performance_under_Democratic_and_Republican_presidents.

5. "The Second American Revolution: Reaganomics." The Ronald Reagan Presidential Foundation & Institute. Accessed November 30, 2021. https://www.reaganfoundation.org/ronald-reagan/the-presidency/economic-policy/.

6. Plotnick, R D. "Changes in Poverty, Income Inequality, and the Standard of Living in the United States during the Reagan Years." *International Journal of Health Services*. U.S. National Library of Medicine. Accessed November 30, 2021. https://pubmed.ncbi.nlm.nih.gov/8500951/.

7. Smith, Hedrick. "Reagan's Effort to Change Course of Government." *New York Times*, October 23, 1984. https://www.nytimes.com/1984/10/23/us/reagan-s-effort-to-change-course-of-government.html.

8. Attanasio, John. "Auctioning the American Dream." Inequality.org, October 16, 2018. https://inequality.org/research/auctioning-america-campaign-finance-inequality/.

9. Smith, Hedrick. "Reagan's Effort to Change Course of Government." *New York Times*, October 23, 1984. https://www.nytimes.com/1984/10/23/us/reagan-s-effort-to-change-course-of-government.html.

10. Copeland, Curtis W. "Federal Rulemaking: The Role of the Office of Information and Regulatory Affairs," June 9, 2009. https://sgp.fas.org/crs/misc/RL32397.pdf.

11. Schwen, Christine. "Fox News Is BP Oil Spill Misinformation Clearinghouse." Media Matters for America, June 24, 2010. https://www.mediamatters.org/fox-news/fox-news-bp-oil-spill-misinformation-clearinghouse.

12. "Cabinet Aide Greeted by Reagan as 'Mayor'." *New York Times*, June 19, 1981. https://www.nytimes.com/1981/06/19/us/cabinet-aide-greeted-by-reagan-as-mayor.html.

13. Roberts, Chris. "The Great Eliminator: How Ronald Reagan Made Homelessness Permanent." *SF Weekly*, June 30, 2016. https://www.sfweekly.com/news/the-great-eliminator-how-ronald-reagan-made-homelessness-permanent/.

14. Johnston, Robert C. "Terrel Bell, Known for Defending Federal Role in Education, Dies." Education Week, July 10, 1996. https://www.edweek.org/policy-politics/terrel-bell-known-for-defending-federal-role-in-education-dies/1996/07.

15. Ronald Reagan, A Time for Choosing, aka The Speech, 1964

16. Bump, Philip. "The Story Behind Obama and the National Debt, in 7 Charts." *Washington Post*. WP Company, January 7, 2015. https://www.washingtonpost.com/news/the-fix/wp/2015/01/07/the-story-behind-obama-and-the-national-debt-in-7-charts/.

17. Danziger, Sheldon, and Robert Haveman. "The Reagan Administration's Budget Cuts: Their Impact on the Poor." Accessed November 30, 2021. https://www.irp.wisc.edu/publications/focus/pdfs/foc52b.pdf.

18. Olsen, Henry. "How the Right Gets Reagan Wrong." *POLITICO Magazine*, June 26, 2017. https://www.politico.com/magazine/story/2017/06/26/how-the-right-gets-reagan-wrong-215306/.

CHAPTER 5

1. Pareene, Alex. "Newt Gingrich on Obama the 'Kenyan Anti-Colonial' Con Man." Salon. Salon.com, September 13, 2010. https://www.salon.com/2010/09/13/newt_dsouza_obama_kenyan_con/.

2. Murphy, Tim. "Your Daily Newt: Politicians Can't Be Bought." *Mother Jones*, December 15, 2011. https://www.motherjones.com/politics/2011/12/your-daily-newt-politicians-cant-be-bought/.

3. Coppins, McKay. "The Man Who Broke Politics." *Atlantic*. Atlantic Media Company, November 2018. https://www.theatlantic.com/magazine/archive/2018/11/newt-gingrich-says-youre-welcome/570832/.

4. "A 1978 Speech by Gingrich." PBS. Public Broadcasting Service, 1978. https://www.pbs.org/wgbh/pages/frontline/newt/newt78speech.html.

5. Osborne, David. "The Swinging Days of Newt Gingrich." *Mother Jones*, November 1, 1984. https://www.motherjones.com/politics/1984/11/newt-gingrich-shining-knight-post-reagan-right/.

6. Sadowski, Jathan. "The Much-Needed and Sane Congressional Office That Gingrich Killed Off and We Need Back." *Atlantic*. Atlantic Media Company, October 26, 2012. https://www.theatlantic.com/technology/archive/2012/10/the-much-needed-and-sane-congressional-office-that-gingrich-killed-off-and-we-need-back/264160/.

7. Mooney, Chris. "Requiem for an Office." Bulletin of the Atomic Scientists, September 1, 2005. https://thebulletin.org/2005/09/requiem-for-an-office/.

8. Coppins, McKay. "The Man Who Broke Politics." *Atlantic*. Atlantic Media Company, November 2018. https://www.theatlantic.com/magazine/archive/2018/11/newt-gingrich-says-youre-welcome/570832/.

9. Eilperin, Juliet. "The Education of Newt Gingrich: A First-Person View of Events." *Washington Post*. WP Company, April 7, 1998. https://www.washingtonpost.com/archive/politics/1998/04/07/the-education-of-newt-gingrich-a-first-person-view-of-events/759593a9-deea-44d8-bde6-7a48e3bf51fc/.

10. Seitz-Wald, Alex. "How Newt Gingrich Crippled Congress." *Nation*, January 30, 2012. https://www.thenation.com/article/archive/how-newt-gingrich-crippled-congress/.

11. Purdum, Todd S. "Gingrich Shut Down the Government In a Tantrum 23 Years Ago." *Atlantic*. Atlantic Media Company, December 22, 2018. https://www.theatlantic.com/politics/archive/2018/12/newt-gingrichs-1995-shutdown-came-fit-pique/578923/.

12. "GOPAC Republican Handout." Gopac Republican handout. Accessed November 30, 2021. https://uh.edu/~englin/rephandout.html.

13. Dionne, E. J. *Why the Right Went Wrong: Conservatism—From Goldwater to the Tea Party and Beyond*. (Simon & Schuster, 2016).

14. Dionne, E. J. *Why the Right Went Wrong: Conservatism—From Goldwater to the Tea Party and Beyond*. (Simon & Schuster, 2016).

CHAPTER 6

1. Martin, Isaac William. *Rich People's Movements: Grassroots Campaigns to Untax the One Percent*.

2. Grunwald, Michael. "The Victory of 'No'." *POLITICO Magazine*, December 4, 2016. https://www.politico.com/magazine/story/2016/12/republican-party-obstructionism-victory-trump-214498/.

3. CNBC.com. "Rick Santelli's Shout Heard 'Round the World." CNBC. CNBC, February 22, 2009. https://www.cnbc.com/2009/02/22/rick-santellis-shout-heard-round-the-world.html.

4. "Glenn Beck's Greatest Hits: An Odyssey of Outrageousness (Video)," Tim Kenneally (June 2011)

5. Nesbit, Jeff. "The Secret Origins of the Tea Party." *Time*. Accessed November 30, 2021. https://time.com/secret-origins-of-the-tea-party/.

6. Dionne, E. J. *Why the Right Went Wrong: Conservatism—From Goldwater to the Tea Party and Beyond*, (Simon & Schuster, 2016).

7. Hacker, Jacob S. "No Cost for Extremism." *American Prospect*, April 20, 2015. https://prospect.org/power/cost-extremism/.

CHAPTER 7

1. Hacker, Jacob S. "Don't Dismantle Government-Fix It." *American Prospect*, April 1, 2016. https://prospect.org/power/dismantle-government-fix/.

CHAPTER 8

1. Smart, Tim. "Who Owns Stocks in America? Mostly, It's the Wealthy and White." U.S. News & World Report, 2021. https://www.usnews.com/news/national-news/articles/2021-03-15/who-owns-stocks-in-america-mostly-its-the-wealthy-and-white.

2. "OECD Dataset on the Size and Composition of National State-Owned Enterprise Sectors." OECD, 2012. https://www.oecd.org/corporate/oecd-dataset-size-composition-soe-sectors.htm.

3. "Is the Private Sector more efficient: A cautionary tale," Global Centre for Public Service Excellence, 2015.

4. "Public and Private Sector Efficiency," PSIRU, May 2014.

5. "Mythbusters: The private sector is more efficient than the public sector," Tax Justice Network, 2013.

6. Wainwright, Hilary. "The Tragedy of the Private the Potential of the Public," 2014.

7. William J. Pier, Robert B. Vernon and John H. Wicks. "An Empirical Comparison of Government and Private Production Efficiency," 1974.

8. Starr, Paul. "The Limits of Privatization." *Proceedings of the Academy of Political Science* 36, no. 3 (1987): 124–37. https://doi.org/10.2307/1174103.

9. Ford, Chris, Stephenie Johnson, and Lisette Partelow. "The Racist Origins of Private School Vouchers." Center for American Progress, July 12, 2017. https://americanprogress.org/article/racist-origins-private-school-vouchers/.

10. Cohen, Donald. "Dismantling Democracy," 2018.

11. Goodman, John B., and Gary W. Loveman. "Does Privatization Serve the Public Interest?" *Harvard Business Review*, 1991. https://hbr.org/1991/11/does-privatization-serve-the-public-interest.

CHAPTER 10

1. Watson, Libby. "Sunlight Foundation." Sunlight Foundation Blog, April 19, 2016. https://sunlightfoundation.com/2016/04/19/what-is-shadow-lobbying-how-influence-peddlers-shape-policy-in-the-dark/.

2. McCabe, David. "Opposition to Net Neutrality Was Faked, New York Says." *New York Times*, May 6, 2021. https://www.nytimes.com/2021/05/06/technology/internet-providers-fake-comments-net-neutrality-new-york.html.

3. CQ Almanac Online Edition. https://library.cqpress.com/cqalmanac/document.php?id=cqal78-1238478.

4. Drutman, Lee. "How Corporate Lobbyists Conquered American Democracy." *Atlantic*. Atlantic Media Company, April 20, 2015. https://www.theatlantic.com/business/archive/2015/04/how-corporate-lobbyists-conquered-american-democracy/390822/.

5. "The Trust Buster." ushistory.org. Independence Hall Association. Accessed November 30, 2021. https://www.ushistory.org/us/43b.asp.

6. Powell, Lewis F. "Attack on American Free Enterprise System," August 23, 1971. https://law2.wlu.edu/deptimages/Powell%20Archives/PowellMemorandumPrinted.pdf.

7. Wessel, David. "Is Lack of Competition Strangling the U.S. Economy?" *Harvard Business Review*, April 2018. https://hbr.org/2018/03/is-lack-of-competition-strangling-the-u-s-economy.

8. "Tech Giants Will Pay $415 Million to Settle Employees' Lawsuit." NPR, January 16, 2015. https://www.npr.org/sections/alltechconsidered/2015/01/16/377614477/tech-giants-will-pay-415-million-to-settle-employees-lawsuit.

9. Wessel, David. "Is Lack of Competition Strangling the U.S. Economy?" *Harvard Business Review*, April 2018. https://hbr.org/2018/03/is-lack-of-competition-strangling-the-u-s-economy.

10. Kopf, Dan. "Jobs Are Plentiful, so Why Aren't Wages Rising?" Quartz, August 19, 2018. https://qz.com/1355878/jobs-are-plentiful-so-why-arent-wages-rising/.

11. Abdela, Adil, and Marshall Steinbaum. "The United States Has a Market Concentration Problem." RooseveltInstitute.org. Creative Commons, September 2018. https://www.ftc.gov/system/files/documents/public_comments/2018/09/ftc-2018-0074-d-0042-155544.pdf.

12. Klukowski, Ken. "Conservatives Unite Against H.R. 1, 'Ultimate Fantasy of the Left'." Breitbart, January 28, 2019. https://www.breitbart.com/politics/2019/01/28/conservatives-unite-against-h-r-1-ultimate-fantasy-of-the-left/.

13. Nilsen, Ella. "Lobbyists Are Already Mounting an Opposition Strategy to Democrats' Anti-Corruption Bill." Vox, January 29, 2019. https://www.vox.com/policy-and-politics/2019/1/29/18200973/lobbyists-oppose-house-democrats-anti-corruption-bill-hr1.

14. Jones, Sarah. "With pro Act, Democrats Commit to Dramatic Labor Reforms." *Intelligencer*, May 3, 2019. https://nymag.com/intelligencer/2019/05/pro-act-democrats-in-congress-back-dramatic-labor-reforms.html.

15. Nilsen, Ella. "Mitch McConnell Calls House Democrats' Anti-Corruption Bill a 'Power Grab.'" Vox, January 18, 2019. https://www.vox.com/2019/1/18/18188150/mitch-mcconnell-house-democrats-anti-corruption-bill-hr1.

16. Dean, John Wesley. Broken Government: *How Republican Rule Destroyed the Legislative, Executive, and Judicial Branches*. New York, NY: Penguin Books, 2008.

CHAPTER 11

1. Coppins, McKay. "The Man Who Broke Politics." *Atlantic*. Atlantic Media Company. November 2018. https://www.theatlantic.com/magazine/archive/2018/11/newt-gingrich-says-youre-welcome/570832/.

2. Patrick, Kate. "Who Dominates Dark Money Spending: Democrats or Republicans?" InsideSources. September 13, 2019. https://insidesources.com/who-dominates-dark-money-spending-democrats-or-republicans/.

3. Dionne, E. J. *Why the Right Went Wrong: Conservatism—From Goldwater to the Tea Party and Beyond*, (Simon & Schuster, 2016).

4. "Koch Brothers Could $1.4 Billion Tax Cut From The Law They Helped Pass." Americans For Tax Fairness. January 24, 2018. https://americansfortaxfairness.org/issue/koch-brothers-1-billion-tax-cut/.

CHAPTER 12

1. Friedersdorf, Conor. "Remembering Why Americans Loathe Dick Cheney." *Atlantic*. August 30, 2011. https://www.theatlantic.com/politics/archive/2011/08/remembering-why-americans-loathe-dick-cheney/244306/.

2. "Summary Of Findings | Costs Of War." The Costs Of War. 2021. https://watson.brown.edu/costsofwar/papers/summary.

3. Stein, Jonathan, and Tim Dickinson. "Lie By Lie: A Timeline Of How We Got Into Iraq." *Mother Jones*. September/October 2006. https://www.motherjones.com/politics/2011/12/leadup-iraq-war-timeline/.

4. Borger, Julian. "Bush Decided To Remove Saddam 'On Day One.'" *Guardian*. January 11, 2004. https://www.theguardian.com/world/2004/jan/12/usa.books.

5. "FINAL VOTE RESULTS FOR ROLL CALL 455." Clerk.House.Gov. October 10, 2002. https://clerk.house.gov/evs/2002/roll455.xml.

6. "U.S. Senate: U.S. Senate Roll Call Votes 107Th Congress - 2Nd Session." Senate.Gov. October 11, 2002. https://www.senate.gov/legislative/LIS/roll_call_lists/roll_call_vote_cfm.cfm?congress=107&session=2&vote=00237.

7. Leopold, Jason. "Under Cheney, Halliburton Helped Saddam Siphon Billions From UN's Oil-For-Food Program." CounterPunch. October 12, 2004. https://www.counterpunch.org/2004/10/12/under-cheney-halliburton-helped-saddam-siphon-billions-from-un-s-oil-for-food-program/.

8. Mayer, Jane. "The Hidden Power." *New Yorker*. June 25, 2006. https://www.newyorker.com/magazine/2006/07/03/the-hidden-power.

9. Burleigh, Nina. "George W. Bush's White House "Lost" 22 Million Emails." *Newsweek*. September 12, 2016. https://www.newsweek.com/2016/09/23/george-w-bush-white-house-lost-22-million-emails-497373.html.

10. Dean, John W. *Broken Government: How Republican Rule Destroyed the Legislative, Executive, and Judicial Branches*. (New York: Viking Adult, 2007).

11. Friedersdorf, Conor. "Remembering Why Americans Loathe Dick Cheney." *Atlantic*. August 30, 2011. https://www.theatlantic.com/politics/archive/2011/08/remembering-why-americans-loathe-dick-cheney/244306/.

12. Friedersdorf, Conor. "Remembering Why Americans Loathe Dick Cheney." *Atlantic*. August 30, 2011. https://www.theatlantic.com/politics/archive/2011/08/remembering-why-americans-loathe-dick-cheney/244306/.

13. Ornstein, Norman J., and Thoman E. Mann. "When Congress Checks Out." *Foreign Affairs*. November/December 2006. https://www.foreignaffairs.com/articles/united-states/2006-11-01/when-congress-checks-out.

14. Dionne, E. J. *Why the Right Went Wrong: Conservatism—From Goldwater to the Tea Party and Beyond*, (Simon & Schuster, 2016).

CHAPTER 13

1. Rabouin, Dion. "Record-low science funding could slow research for coronavirus cure." Axios. May 11, 2020. https://www.axios.com/coronavirus-record-low-science-funding-b8fa8455-aee4-476d-a01d-3966c1493934.html.

2. "The third industrial revolution." *The Economist*. April 21, 2012. https://www.economist.com/leaders/2012/04/21/the-third-industrial-revolution.

3. Graham, John R., Campbell R. and Harvey, and Shiva Rajgopal. "Value Destruction and Financial Reporting Decisions." September 6, 2006. https://www0.gsb.columbia.edu/mygsb/faculty/research/pubfiles/12924/Rajgopal_value.pdf.

CHAPTER 14

1. Bradner, Eric, and Tal Kopan. "Scott Walker: U.S-Canada wall a 'legitimate' idea." CNN Politics. August 31, 2015. https://www.cnn.com/2015/08/30/politics/scott-walker-northern-border-immigration-2016/index.html.

2. Cooper, David. "As Wisconsin's and Minnesota's lawmakers took divergent paths, so did their economies." Economic Policy Institute. May 8, 2018. https://www.epi.org/publication/as-wisconsins-and-minnesotas-lawmakers-took-divergent-paths-so-did-their-economies-since-2010-minnesotas-economy-has-performed-far-better-for-working-families-than-wisconsin/.

CHAPTER 15

1. Eilperin, Juliet. "Trump establishes task forces to eliminate 'job killing regulations.'" *Washington Post.* February 24, 2017. https://www.washingtonpost.com/news/powerpost/wp/2017/02/24/trump-establishes-task-forces-to-eliminate-job-killing-regulations/.

2. "Good Enough to Eat." Oxfam. January 14, 2013. https://www.foodsafetynews.com/files/2014/01/Good-Enough-To-Eat-Media-brief-1.pdf.

3. Tikkanen, Roosa, and Melinda K. Abrams. "U.S. Health Care from a Global Perspective, 2019: Higher Spending, Worse Outcomes?" The Commonwealth Fund. January 30, 2020 https://www.commonwealthfund.org/publications/issue-briefs/2020/jan/us-health-care-global-perspective-2019.

4. Miller, Lee J., and Wei Lu. "These Are the World's Healthiest Nations." Bloomberg. February 24, 2019. https://www.bloomberg.com/news/articles/2019-02-24/spain-tops-italy-as-world-s-healthiest-nation-while-u-s-slips.

5. Piller, Charles. "Exclusive: FDA enforcement actions plummet under Trump." *Science.* July 2, 2019. https://www.science.org/content/article/exclusive-fda-enforcement-actions-plummet-under-trump.

6. Ritchie, Hannah, and Max Roser. "Drug Use." *Our World in Data.* December 2019. https://ourworldindata.org/drug-use.

7. Schneider, Eric C., Arnav Shah, Michelle M. Doty, Roosa Tikkanen, Katharine Fields, and Reginald D. Williams II. "Mirror, Mirror 2021: Reflecting Poorly." The Commonwealth Fund. August 4, 2021 https://www.commonwealthfund.org/publications/fund-reports/2021/aug/mirror-mirror-2021-reflecting-poorly.

8. "2016 TIInternational Out-of-Pocket Cost Survey." *TIInternational.* https://www.tlinternational.com/access-survey16/.

9. Carliner, Michael, and Ellen Marya. "Rental Housing: An International Comparison." Joint Center for Housing Studies of Harvard University. September 1, 2016. https://www.jchs.harvard.edu/research-areas/working-papers/rental-housing-international-comparison.

CHAPTER 16

1. Dickson, Caitlin. "Poll: Two-thirds of Republicans still think the 2020 election was rigged." Yahoo! News. August 4,2021. https://news.yahoo.com/poll-two-thirds-of-republicans-still-think-the-2020-election-was-rigged-165934695.html?guccounter=1.

2. Swenson, Ali. "Family of Hugo Chavez does not own Dominion Voting Systems." AP News. December 1, 2020. https://apnews.com/article/fact-checking-9809670730.

CHAPTER 17

1. "In Changing U.S. Electorate, Race and Education Remain Stark Dividing Lines." Pew Research Center. June 2, 2020. https://www.pewresearch.org/politics/2020/06/02/in-changing-u-s-electorate-race-and-education-remain-stark-dividing-lines/.

CHAPTER 18

1. Newkirk, Vann R. "How Redistricting Became a Technological Arms Race." *Atlantic*. Atlantic Media Company. October 28, 2017 https://www.theatlantic.com/politics/archive/2017/10/gerrymandering-technology-redmap-2020/543888/.

CHAPTER 19

1. Bump, Philip. "How Broken Is the Senate? The Gun Bill Blockers Only Represent 38% of America." *Atlantic*. Atlantic Media Company. April 18, 2013. https://www.theatlantic.com/national/archive/2013/04/senate-filibusters-vs-represented-population/316110/.

2. Yglesias, Matthew. "American democracy's Senate problem, explained." Vox. December 17, 2019. https://www.vox.com/policy-and-politics/2019/12/17/21011079/senate-bias-2020-data-for-progress.

3. "In Changing U.S. Electorate, Race and Education Remain Stark Dividing Lines." June 2, 2020. Pew Research Center. https://www.pewresearch.org/politics/2020/06/02/in-changing-u-s-electorate-race-and-education-remain-stark-dividing-lines/.

4. Yglesias, Matthew. "American democracy's Senate problem, explained." Vox. December 17, 2019. https://www.vox.com/policy-and-politics/2019/12/17/21011079/senate-bias-2020-data-for-progress.

5. McAuliffe, Colin. "The Senate is an Irredeemable Institution." Data For Progress. December 17, 2019. https://www.filesforprogress.org/memos/the-senate-is-an-irredeemable-institution.pdf.

CHAPTER 20

1. "Slavery in the Lower South (AL, FL, GA, LA, MS, SC, TX)." Gale Library of Daily Life: Slavery in America. Encyclopedia.com. https://www.encyclopedia.com/humanities/applied-and-social-sciences-magazines/slavery-lower-south-al-fl-ga-la-ms-sc-tx.

CHAPTER 21

1. Sherman, Amy. "Candace Owens' false statement that the Southern strategy is a myth." Politifact. April 10, 2019. https://www.politifact.com/factchecks/2019/apr/10/candace-owens/candace-owens-pants-fire-statement-southern-strate/.

2. Haldeman, H.R.. "H.R. Haldeman Diaries Collection: Audio Diary Entry – April 28, 1969." Richard Nixon Presidential Library and Museum. April 28, 1969. https://www.nixonlibrary.gov/sites/default/files/virtuallibrary/documents/haldeman-diaries/37-hrhd-journal-vol02-19690428.pdf.

3. Plott, Elaina. "Trump's 'Law and Order': One More Deceptive Tactic Is Exposed." *New York Times*. January 16, 2021. https://www.nytimes.com/2021/01/16/us/politics/trump-law-order.html.

4. Maxwell, Angie. "What we get wrong about the Southern strategy." *Washington Post*. July 26, 2019. https://www.washingtonpost.com/outlook/2019/07/26/what-we-get-wrong-about-southern-strategy/.

5. Maxwell, Angie. "What we get wrong about the Southern strategy." *Washington Post.* July 26, 2019. https://www.washingtonpost.com/outlook/2019/07/26/what-we-get-wrong-about-southern-strategy/.

6. Carter, Dan T. *From George Wallace to Newt Gingrich: Race in the Conservative Counterrevolution, 1963–1994.* (Louisiana State University Press, 1999).

7. Kramer, Curtlyn. "Vital Stats: Southern congressmen are regaining committee chairmanships, but that means something different than it used to." Brookings. January 17, 2017. https://www.brookings.edu/blog/fixgov/2017/01/17/vital-stats-southern-committee-chairs-congress/.

CHAPTER 22

1. Kamarck, Elaine. "A short history of campaign dirty tricks before Twitter and Facebook." Brookings. July 11, 2019. https://www.brookings.edu/blog/fixgov/2019/07/11/a-short-history-of-campaign-dirty-tricks-before-twitter-and-facebook/.

2. Kennedy, Merrit. "'Pizzagate' Gunman Sentenced To 4 Years In Prison." NPR. June 22, 2017. https://www.npr.org/sections/thetwo-way/2017/06/22/533941689/pizzagate-gunman-sentenced-to-4-years-in-prison.

3. Steinhauer, Jennifer. "Confronting Ghosts of 2000 in South Carolina." *New York Times.* October 19, 2007. https://www.nytimes.com/2007/10/19/us/politics/19mccain.html.

4. Reyes, G. Mitchell. "The Swift Boat Veterans for Truth, the Politics of Realism, and the Manipulation of Vietnam Remembrance in the 2004 Presidential Election." *Rhetoric and Public Affairs* 9, no. 4 (2006): 571–600. http://www.jstor.org/stable/41940103.

5. Hudson, John. "GOP Operative Enlists the Homeless to Fight Dems." *Atlantic.* Atlantic Media Company. September 7, 2010. https://www.theatlantic.com/politics/archive/2010/09/gop-operative-enlists-the-homeless-to-fight-dems/344272/.

6. "Wisconsin voters, beware of dirty tricks." NBC News. June 4. 2012. https://www.nbcnews.com/news/world/wisconsin-voters-beware-dirty-tricks-flna813488.

7. Schwartz, David M. "Zeldin mailer uses wrong deadline for absentee ballots." *Newsday*. October 23, 2018. https://www.newsday.com/long-island/politics/spin-cycle/zeldin-gershon-mailer-1.22304894.

8. Labash, Matt. "Roger Stone, Political Animal." *Washington Examiner*. November 5, 2007. https://www.washingtonexaminer.com/weekly-standard/roger-stone-political-animal-15381.

9. Bort, Ryan. "Republicans Are Doing a Good Job Blocking Efforts to Fight Russian Meddling in 2020." *Rolling Stone*. July 26, 2019. https://www.rollingstone.com/politics/politics-news/republicans-block-action-to-fight-russian-election-meddling-863864/.

10. Koncewicz, Michael. "How Republican dirty tricks paved the way for Russian meddling in 2016." *Washington Post*. March 9, 2018. https://www.washingtonpost.com/news/made-by-history/wp/2018/03/09/how-republican-dirty-tricks-paved-the-way-for-russian-meddling-in-2016/.

11. Rowl, Evans and Robert Novak. "Behind Those Dukakis Rumors." *Washington Post*. August 8, 1988. https://www.washingtonpost.com/archive/opinions/1988/08/08/behind-those-dukakis-rumors/dbdf4dab-5557-41fa-9bd1-1c6020b9d809/.

12. "The way the Bush administration operates." https://www.cs.cornell.edu/gries/howbushoperates/ethicscampaign.html.

13. Panetta, Grace. "Trump admits he's refusing to fund the US Postal Service to sabotage mail-in voting." Business Insider. August 13, 2020. https://www.businessinsider.com/trump-admits-he-wants-block-usps-funding-sabotage-mail-voting-2020-8.

14. Tiffany, Kaitlyn. "How a conspiracy theory about Democrats drinking children's blood topped Amazon's best-sellers list." Vox. March 6, 2019. https://www.vox.com/the-goods/2019/3/6/18253505/amazon-qanon-book-best-seller-algorithm-conspiracy.

15. Allassan, Fadel. "GOP Sen. Marsha Blackburn blocks three election security bills." Axios. February 11, 2020. https://www.axios.com/gop-senator-election-security-blocks-3f432161-42f4-4fa2-9207-d281ec857058.html.

CHAPTER 23

1. Wagner, John, and Scott Clement. "'It's just messed up': Most think political divisions as bad as Vietnam era, new poll shows." *Washington Post*. October 28, 2017. https://www.washingtonpost.com/graphics/2017/national/democracy-poll/?utm_term=.43c2cebb6d13.

2. "Americans' view on Money in Politics." *New York Times*. June 2, 2015. https://www.nytimes.com/interactive/2015/06/02/us/politics/money-in-politics-poll.html.

3. "ECU Memo 8.18.16 Revised." Normington, Petts & Associates. August 18, 2016. https://endcitizensunited.org/wp-content/uploads/2016/04/ECU-Poll-memo-8-18-16.pdf.

4. "ECU Memo 8.18.16 Revised." Normington, Petts & Associates. August 18, 2016. https://endcitizensunited.org/wp-content/uploads/2016/04/ECU-Poll-memo-8-18-16.pdf.

5. Hacker, Jacob S., and Nathan Loewentheil. "How Big Money Corrupts the Economy." *Democracy Journal*. 2013. https://democracyjournal.org/magazine/27/how-big-money-corrupts-the-economy/.

6. Koerth, Maggie. "How Money Affects Elections." FiveThirtyEight. September 10, 2018. https://fivethirtyeight.com/features/money-and-elections-a-complicated-love-story/.

7. "S.751 - Fair Elections Revenue Act of 2009." Congress.gov. https://www.congress.gov/bill/111th-congress/senate-bill/751/text.

8. "H.R. 1, the For The People Act, Passes In House With Significant Amendments By Jayapal." Pramila Jayapal Congresswoman for WA-07. March 8, 2019. https://jayapal.house.gov/2019/03/08/h-r-1-the-for-the-people-act-passes-in-house-with-significant-amendments-by-jayapal/.

9. Waldman, Paul. "How Our Campaign Finance System Compares to Other Countries." *American Prospect*. April 4, 2014. https://prospect.org/power/campaign-finance-system-compares-countries/.

10. Khazan, Olga. "Why Germany's Politics Are Much Saner, Cheaper, and Nicer Than Ours." *Atlantic*. Atlantic Media Company. September 30, 2013. https://www.theatlantic.com/international/archive/2013/09/why-germany-s-politics-are-much-saner-cheaper-and-nicer-than-ours/280081/.

11. Dreier, Peter. "Most Americans Are Liberal, Even If They Don't Know It." *American Prospect.* November 10, 2017. https://prospect.org/power/americans-liberal-even-know/.

CHAPTER 24

1. Smith, Jamil. "Exclusive: In Leaked Audio, Brian Kemp Expresses Concern Over Georgians Exercising Their Right to Vote." *Rolling Stone.* October 3, 2018. https://www.rollingstone.com/politics/politics-news/brian-kemp-leaked-audio-georgia-voting-745711/.

2. Smith, Jamil. "Jamil Smith: Watch the Georgia Minority Vote Disappear Before Your Eyes." *Rolling Stone.* October 11, 2018. https://www.rollingstone.com/politics/politics-news/georgia-voter-suppression-736362/.

3. Scanlan, Quinn. "Kemp signs sweeping elections bill passed by Georgia legislature. Here's what's in it." ABC News. March 25, 2021. https://abcnews.go.com/Politics/kemp-sign-sweeping-elections-bill-passed-georgia-legislature/story?id=76677927.

4. Johnson, Theodore R. "The New Voter Suppresion." Brennan Center For Justice. January 16, 2020. https://www.brennancenter.org/our-work/research-reports/new-voter-suppression.

5. Dionne, E. J. *Why the Right Went Wrong: Conservatism—From Goldwater to the Tea Party and Beyond,* (Simon & Schuster, 2016).

6. Bialik, Kristen. "How Americans view some of the voting policies approved at the ballot box." Pew Research Center. November 15, 2018. https://www.pewresearch.org/fact-tank/2018/11/15/how-americans-view-some-of-the-voting-policies-approved-at-the-ballot-box/.

7. McReynolds, Amber, and Charles Stewart III. "Let's put the vote-by-mail 'fraud' myth to rest." *Hill.* April 28, 2020. https://thehill.com/opinion/campaign/494189-lets-put-the-vote-by-mail-fraud-myth-to-rest.

8. "What ID is required when voting?" Tennessee Secretary of State Tre Hargett. https://sos.tn.gov/elections/faqs/what-id-is-required-when-voting.

9. Gaskins, Keesha. "The Challenge of Obtaining Voter Identification." Brennan Center For Justice. July 18, 2012. https://www.brennancenter.org/our-work/research-reports/challenge-obtaining-voter-identification.

CHAPTER 25

1. Gajanan, Mahita. "Kellyanne Conway Defends White House's Falsehoods as 'Alternative Facts.'" *Time*. January 22, 2017. https://time.com/4642689/kellyanne-conway-sean-spicer-donald-trump-alternative-facts/.

2. "We Fact-Checked the Science Behind the Republican Party Platform." Live Science. July 21, 2016. https://www.livescience.com/55481-analysis-of-rnc-2016-platform.html.

3. Chait, Jonathan. "American Death Cult: Why has the Republican response to the pandemic been so mind-bogglingly disastrous?" *Intelligencer*. July 20, 2020. https://nymag.com/intelligencer/2020/07/republican-response-coronavirus.html.

4. Oreskes, Naomi, and Erik M. Conway. *Merchants of Doubt: How a Handful of Scientists Obscured the Truth on Issues from Tobacco Smoke to Global Warming*, (Bloomsbury Press, 2010).

5. Waldman, Scott. "Political appointees once kept a scientist 'hit list.'" E&E News. May 14, 2018. https://www.eenews.net/articles/political-appointees-once-kept-a-scientist-hit-list/.

6. Mooney, Chris. *The Republican War on Science*. (Basic Books, 2005).

7. Vladeck, David. "Paralysis by Analysis: How Conservatives Plan to Kill Popular Regulation." *American Prospect*. November 19, 2001. https://prospect.org/environment/paralysis-analysis-conservatives-plan-kill-popular-regulation/.

8. "Childhood Obesity Facts: Prevalence of Childhood Obesity in the United States." Centers for Disease Control and Prevention. https://www.cdc.gov/obesity/data/childhood.html.

9. Urrutia-Rojas, Ximena, and John Menchaca. "Prevalence of risk for type 2 diabetes in school children." *The Journal of school health* vol. 76,5 (2006): 189-94. doi:10.1111/j.1746-1561.2006.00093.x. https://pubmed.ncbi.nlm.nih.gov/16635203/.

10. Atkin, Emily. "The War on Science Is Over. The Republicans Won." The New Republic. April 5, 2018. https://newrepublic.com/article/147729/war-science-over-republicans-won.

11. Brayton, Ed. "What Marketing Pitches Reveal About the Religious Right." Patheos. November 29, 2012. https://www.patheos.com/blogs/dispatches/2012/11/29/what-marketing-pitches-reveal-about-the-religious-right/.

12. Chotiner, Isaac. "The Contrarian Coronavirus Theory That Informed the Trump Administration." *New Yorker*. March 29, 2020. https://www.newyorker.com/news/q-and-a/the-contrarian-coronavirus-theory-that-informed-the-trump-administration.

13. Ryckaert, Vic. "Pence's decades-old 'smoking doesn't kill' statement resurfaces after coronavirus appointment." *Indianapolis Star*. February 27, 2020. https://www.indystar.com/story/news/politics/2020/02/27/pence-smoking-cancer-donald-trump-coronavirus-response/4890066002/.

CHAPTER 26

1. Morley, Jefferson. "The Washington Intellectual." The New Republic. August 10, 1986. https://newrepublic.com/article/91589/the-washington-intellectual.

2. Motta, Matt. "Republicans are increasingly antagonistic toward experts. Here's why that matters." *Washington Post*. August 11, 2017. https://www.washingtonpost.com/news/monkey-cage/wp/2017/08/11/republicans-are-increasingly-antagonistic-toward-experts-heres-why-that-matters/.

3. Nichols, Thomas M. *The Death of Expertise: The Campaign against Established Knowledge and Why it Matters*. (Oxford University Press, 2017).

4. Hagen, Lisa. "Trump on Booker: 'I know more about Cory than he knows about himself.'" *Hill*. July 25, 2016. https://thehill.com/blogs/ballot-box/presidential-races/289206-trump-on-booker-i-know-more-about-cory-than-he-knows.

CHAPTER 27

1. Schwartzman, Jack. "Natural Law and the Campus." The Freeman. December 3, 1951. https://cdn.mises.org/Freeman51-12_3.pdf.

2. Banwart, Doug. "Jerry Falwell, the Rise of the Moral Majority, and the 1980 Election." Western Illinois Historical Review. 2013. http://www.wiu.edu/cas/history/wihr/pdfs/Banwart-MoralMajorityVol5.pdf.

3. Newsinger, John. "America's Christian Right, Republicans and Donald Trump – 3." InDepthNews. https://www.indepthnews.net/index.php/opinion/3326-america-s-christian-right-republicans-and-donald-trump-3.

4. Christerson, Brad, and Richard Flory. "How a Christian movement is growing rapidly in the midst of religious decline." The Conversation. March 15, 2017. https://theconversation.com/how-a-christian-movement-is-growing-rapidly-in-the-midst-of-religious-decline-73507.

5. Jain, Kalpana. "Trump prophecy and other Christian movements: 3 essential reads." The Conversation. October 1, 2018. https://theconversation.com/trump-prophecy-and-other-christian-movements-3-essential-reads-104091.

6. Balmer, Randall. "The Real Origins of the Religious Right." Politico. May 27, 2014. https://www.politico.com/magazine/story/2014/05/religious-right-real-origins-107133/.

7. Campbell, David E, and Robert D. Putnam. "God and Caesar in America." *Foreign Affairs.* March/April 2012. https://www.foreignaffairs.com/articles/united-states/2012-02-12/god-and-caesar-america.

8. "In U.S., Decline of Christianity Continues at Rapid Pace." Pew Research Center. October 17, 2019. https://www.pewforum.org/2019/10/17/in-u-s-decline-of-christianity-continues-at-rapid-pace/.

9. Merritt, Jonathan. "The Religious Right Turns 33: What Have We Learned?" *Atlantic.* Atlantic Media Company. June 8, 2012. https://www.theatlantic.com/politics/archive/2012/06/the-religious-right-turns-33-what-have-we-learned/258204/.

10. Stewart, Katherine. "The Religious Right's Hostility to Science Is Crippling Our Coronavirus Response." *New York Times.* March 27, 2020. https://www.nytimes.com/2020/03/27/opinion/coronavirus-trump-evangelicals.html.

11. Sharlet, Jeff. ""He's the Chosen One to Run America": Inside the Cult of Trump, His Rallies are Church and He is the Gospel." Hive. *Vanity Fair.* June 18, 2020. https://www.vanityfair.com/news/2020/06/inside-the-cult-of-trump-his-rallies-are-church-and-he-is-the-gospel.

12. "Bob Jones University, Petitioner v. United States. Goldsboro Christian Schools, Inc., Petitioner v. United States." Legal Information Institute. https://www.law.cornell.edu/supremecourt/text/461/574.

13. "FirstDraft Jan. 29, 2015." *New York Times.* https://www.nytimes.com/politics/first-draft/2015/01/29/today-in-politics-85/.

14. Johnson, Daryl. "Holy Hate: The Far Right's Radicalization of Religion."
    Southern Poverty Law Center. February 10, 2018. https://www.splcenter.org/
    fighting-hate/intelligence-report/2018/holy-hate-far-right%E2%80%99s
    -radicalization-religion.

CHAPTER 28

1. Henderson, Cydney. "'I wasn't expected to be alive': Emotional
   Rush Limbaugh thanks listeners amid cancer battle." *USA Today*.
   December 24, 2020. https://www.usatoday.com/story/entertainment/
   celebrities/2020/12/24/rush-limbaugh-thanks-listeners-amid-cancer-battle-
   gets-emotional/4037752001/.

2. Silverstein, Jason. "Rush Limbaugh now has a Presidential Medal of Freedom.
   Here are just 20 of the outrageious things he's said." CBS News. February 6,
   2020. https://www.cbsnews.com/news/rush-limbaugh-presidential-medal-
   of-freedom-state-of-the-union-outrageous-quotes/.

3. *The Loudest Voice in the Room: How the Brilliant, Bombastic Roger Ailes Built
   Fox News-and Divided a Country* by (Random House, 2014).

4. Savillo, Rob. "Fox News pushed coronavirus misinformation
   253 times in just five days." MediaMatters For America. July, 16,
   2020. https://www.mediamatters.org/coronavirus-covid-19/
   fox-news-pushed-coronavirus-misinformation-253-times-just-five-days.

5. Yglesias, Matthew. "The hack gap: how and why conservative nonsense
   dominates American politics." Vox. October 23, 2018. https://www.vox.
   com/2018/10/23/18004478/hack-gap-explained.

6. Quealy, Kevin. "The Complete List of Trump's Twitter Insults (2015–
   2021)." *New York Times*. January 19, 2021. https://www.nytimes.com/
   interactive/2021/01/19/upshot/trump-complete-insult-list.html.

CHAPTER 29

1. Easton, Nina J. "Chapter One." Essay. In Gang of Five: Leaders at the Center of
   the Conservative Ascendancy. New York, NY: Simon & Schuster, 2000.

2. Strauss, Valerie. "Donald Trump Jr.: 'You don't have to be indoctrinated by these loser teachers that are trying to sell you on socialism.'" *Washington Post.* February 12, 2019. https://www.washingtonpost.com/ education/2019/02/12/donald-trump-jr-you-dont-have-be-indoctrinated- by-these-loser-teachers-that-are-trying-sell-you-socialism/.

3. Walsh, David Austin. "Conservative Philanthropy in Higher Education." Urban Institute. June 2019. https://www.urban.org/sites/default/files/2019/06/27/ conservative_philanthropy_in_higher_education.pdf.

4. Blakely, Jason. "A History of the Conservative War on Universities." *Atlantic.* Atlantic Media Company. December 7, 2017. https://www.theatlantic.com/education/ archive/2017/12/a-history-of-the-conservative-war-on-universities/547703/.

5. Lieberman, Dan. "Death threats are forcing professors off campus." CNN. December 28, 2017. https://www.cnn.com/2017/12/21/us/university- professors-free-speech-online-hate-threats/index.html.

6. Parker, Kim. "The Growing Partisan Divide in Views of Higher Education." Pew Research Center. August 19, 2019. https://www.pewresearch.org/ social-trends/2019/08/19/the-growing-partisan-divide-in-views-of -higher-education-2/.

7. Jaschik, Scott. "Professors and Politics: What the Research Says." Inside Higher Ed. February 27, 2017. https://www.insidehighered.com/ news/2017/02/27/research-confirms-professors-lean-left-questions- assumptions-about-what-means.

8. Tyson, Alec, and Shiva Maniam. "Behind Trump's victory: Divisions by race, gender, education." Pew Research Center. November 9, 2016. https://www.pewresearch.org/fact-tank/2016/11/09/ behind-trumps-victory-divisions-by-race-gender-education/.

CHAPTER 30

1. "About Heritage." The Heritage Foundation. https://www.heritage.org/ about-heritage/mission.

2. "Increased Funding, Increased Influence: Koch University Funding Update 2005-2019." UnKoch My Campus. May 2021. http://www.unkochmycampus. org/funding-report.

3. Walsh, David Austin. "Conservative Philanthropy in Higher Education." Urban Institute. June 2019. https://www.urban.org/sites/default/files/2019/06/27/conservative_philanthropy_in_higher_education.pdf.

4. Alterman, Eric. "Money Well Spent." *Nation*. September 9, 2010. https://www.thenation.com/article/archive/money-well-spent/.

CHAPTER 31

1. Stahl, Jason. *Right Moves: The Conservative Think Tank in American Political Culture Since 1945*. (University of North Carolina Press, 2016).

2. "How Charles Koch Is Buying Credibility With Academic Investments." Desmog. September 12, 2020. https://www.desmog.com/2020/09/12/charles-koch-academic-george-mason-utah-state-university/.

3. Powell, Lewis F. "Confidential Memorandum: Attack on American Free Enterprise System." August 23, 1971. https://law2.wlu.edu/deptimages/Powell%20Archives/PowellMemorandumTypescript.pdf.

4. Mayer, Jane. *Dark Money: The Hidden History of the Billionaires Behind the Rise of the Radical Right*. (Doubleday, 2016).

5. Dionne, E. J. *Why the* Right *Went Wrong: Conservatism—From Goldwater to the Tea Party and Beyond*. (Simon & Schuster, 2016).

CHAPTER 32

1. "How 9/11 'Truther' conspiracy fueled the war on reality | Opinion." *Washington Post*. YouTube, September 9, 2021. https://www.youtube.com/watch?v=itBC228XSh4.

2. "Qanon." Wikipedia. Wikimedia Foundation, last modified December 5, 2021. https://en.wikipedia.org/wiki/QAnon.

3. Packer, George. "The Demise of the Moderate Republican." *New Yorker*, November 5, 2018. https://www.newyorker.com/magazine/2018/11/12/the-demise-of-the-moderate-republican.

4. Hemmer, Nicole. *Messengers of the Right: Conservative Media and the Transformation of American Politics*. University of Pennsylvania Press, 2016.

5. Phillips-Fein, Kim. *Invisible Hands: The Making of the Conservative Movement from the New Deal to Reagan.* New York: W. W. Norton & Company, 2009.

6. "List of conspiracy theories." Wikipedia. Wikimedia Foundation, last modified December 3, 2021. https://en.wikipedia.org/wiki/List_of_conspiracy_theories.

7. Wallace, Gregory. "Investor compares U.S. wealth debate to Nazi Germany." CNN Business, January 26, 2014. https://money.cnn.com/2014/01/26/investing/tom-perkins-nazi-kristallnacht.

8. Weissmann, Jordan. "And Another Billionaire Just Compared Liberals to Nazis." *Slate*, March 18, 2014. https://slate.com/business/2014/03/ken-langone-nazis-billionaire-compares-liberals-to-hitler.html.

9. Sullivan, Sean. "Ben Carson: Obamacare worst thing 'since slavery.'" *Washington Post*, October 11, 2013. https://www.washingtonpost.com/news/post-politics/wp/2013/10/11/ben-carson-obamacare-worst-thing-since-slavery/.

CHAPTER 33

1. "McCarthyism and The Red Scare." Miller Center. University of Virginia, accessed December 6, 2021. https://millercenter.org/the-presidency/educational-resources/age-of-eisenhower/mcarthyism-red-scare.

2. "Daily Notes by C.D. Jackson, Speechwriter and Special Assistant to the President, December 2, 1953." Dwight D. Eisenhower Presidential Library, Museum & Boyhood Home, December 2, 1952. https://www.eisenhowerlibrary.gov/sites/default/files/research/online-documents/mccarthyism/1953-12-21-cd-jackson.pdf.

3. "Roy Cohn." Wikipedia. Wikimedia Foundation, last modified December 4, 2021. https://en.wikipedia.org/wiki/Roy_Cohn.

4. McDaniel, Rodger. "Prologue," in *Dying for Joe McCarthy's Sins: The Suicide of Wyoming Senator Lester Hunt*, xiii–xxi. WordsWorth Press, 2013.

5. Phillips-Fein, Kim. *Invisible Hands: The Making of the Conservative Movement from the New Deal to Reagan.* New York: W. W. Norton & Company, 2009.

6. Pettypiece, Shannon. "Trump says those who gave info to the whistleblower are like spies, reports say." NBC News, September 26, 2019. https://www.

nbcnews.com/politics/white-house/trump-says-our-country-stake-
whistleblower-account-made-public-n1059011.

CHAPTER 34

1. Terry, Don. "Bringing Back Birch." *Intelligence Report*, March 1, 2013.
   https://www.splcenter.org/fighting-hate/intelligence-report/2013/
   bringing-back-birch.

2. Hicks, Jesse. "Pipe Dreams: America's Fluoride Controversy." Distillations.
   Science History Institute, June 24, 2011. https://www.sciencehistory.org/
   distillations/pipe-dreams-americas-fluoride-controversy.

3. Savage, John. "The John Birch Society is Back." *Politico Magazine*,
   July 16, 2017. https://www.politico.com/magazine/story/2017/07/16/
   the-john-birch-society-is-alive-and-well-in-the-lone-star-state-215377.

4. Andersen, Kurt. "How America Lost Its Mind." *Atlantic*, 76–91. September
   2017. https://www.theatlantic.com/assets/media/files/theatlantic20170901_
   compressed.pdf.

5. Towler, Christopher. "The John Birch Society is still influencing American
   politics, 60 years after its founding." The Conversation, December 6, 2018.
   https://theconversation.com/the-john-birch-society-is-still-influencing-
   american-politics-60-years-after-its-founding-107925.

CHAPTER 35

1. "Abortion Surveillance—Findings and Reports." Centers for Disease Control
   and Prevention (CDC), last modified November 22, 2021. https://www.cdc.
   gov/reproductivehealth/data_stats/abortion.htm.

2. Fahmy, Dalia. "8 key findings about Catholics and abortion." Pew
   Research Center, October 20, 2020. https://www.pewresearch.org/
   fact-tank/2020/10/20/8-key-findings-about-catholics-and-abortion/.

3. Balmer, Randall. "The Real Origins of the Religious Right." *Politico Magazine*,
   May 27, 2014. https://www.politico.com/magazine/story/2017/07/16/
   the-john-birch-society-is-alive-and-well-in-the-lone-star-state-215377.

4. Stipe, Claude, Richard H. Bube, Earl J. Reeves, and Russell L. Mixter. "A Protestant Affirmation on the Control of Human Reproduction." *Journal of the American Scientific Affiliation* 22 (1970): 46–47. https://www.asa3.org/ASA/PSCF/1970/JASA6-70Christian.html.

5. "Southern Baptists Approve Abortion in Certain Cases." *New York Times*, June 3, 1971. https://www.nytimes.com/1971/06/03/archives/southern-baptists-approve-abortion-in-certain-cases.html.

6. Balmer, Randall. "The Real Origins of the Religious Right." *Politico Magazine*, May 27, 2014. https://www.politico.com/magazine/story/2017/07/16/the-john-birch-society-is-alive-and-well-in-the-lone-star-state-215377.

7. Wax, Trevin. "Baptist Press Initial Reporting on Roe v. Wade." The Gospel Coalition, May 6, 2010. https://www.thegospelcoalition.org/blogs/trevin-wax/baptist-press-initial-reporting-on-roe-v-wade/.

8. Taliesin, Julia. "Profile on the Right: The Heritage Foundation." Political Research Associates, June 22, 2018. https://politicalresearch.org/2018/06/22/profile-right-heritage-foundation.

9. *Bob Jones University v. United States*. 461 U.S. 574 (1983). Legal Information Institute, accessed December 7, 2021. https://www.law.cornell.edu/supremecourt/text/461/574.

10. *Green v. Connally*. 330 F. Supp. 1150 (1971). Justia US Law, accessed December 7, 2021. https://law.justia.com/cases/federal/district-courts/FSupp/330/1150/2126265/.

11. Balmer, Randall. "The Real Origins of the Religious Right." *Politico Magazine*, May 27, 2014. https://www.politico.com/magazine/story/2017/07/16/the-john-birch-society-is-alive-and-well-in-the-lone-star-state-215377.

12. Horton, Alex. "Trump says he's an anti-abortion champion like Reagan. History says not really." *Washington Post*. May 19, 2019. https://www.washingtonpost.com/history/2019/05/19/trump-says-hes-an-antiabortion-champion-like-reagan-history-says-not-really/.

13. Dukakis, Andrea. "50 Years Ago, Colorado Passed Nation's First State Law Liberalizing Abortion." Colorado Public Radio, April 28, 2017. https://www.cpr.org/show-segment/50-years-ago-colorado-passed-nations-first-state-law-liberalizing-abortion/.

14. Holzberg, Melissa and Ben Kamisar. "Poll: Majority of adults don't support overturning Roe v. Wade." NBC News, September 29, 2020. https://www.nbcnews.com/politics/2020-election/poll-majority-adults-don-t-support-overturning-roe-v-wade-nl241269.

CHAPTER 36

1. Maremont, Mark and Jonathan Randles. "NRA CEO LaPierre Allegedly Told Travel Agent to Hide Certain Stops on His Private Jet Flights." *Washington Street Journal*, April 8, 2021. https://www.wsj.com/articles/nra-ceo-lapierre-allegedly-told-travel-agent-to-hide-certain-stops-on-his-private-jet-flights-11617929414.

2. "GOP Senators Spend Independence Day in Moscow." NPR, July 6, 2018. https://www.npr.org/2018/07/06/626664156/gop-senators-spend-july-4-in-moscow.

3. Hennigan, W. J. "The Strange Case of the NRA-Linked Russian Charged with Being a Kremlin Agent." *Times*, July 16, 2018. https://time.com/5340362/mariia-butina-arrest-russia/.

4. Harte, Julia and R. Jeffery Smith. "Constitutional Sheriffs: The Cops Who Think the Government Is Our 'Greatest Threat.'" NBC News, April 18, 2016. https://www.nbcnews.com/news/us-news/constitutional-sheriffs-cops-who-think-government-our-greatest-threat-n557381.

5. Robertson, Lori, Robert Farley, D'Angelo Gore, and Eugene Kiely. "Trump's Mixed Record on Gun Control." FactCheck.org, August 8, 2019. https://www.factcheck.org/2019/08/trumps-mixed-record-on-gun-control/.

6. Bipartisan Background Checks Act of 2019. H.R. 8, 116th Cong. (2019-2020). Congress.gov, accessed December 7, 2021. https://www.congress.gov/bill/116th-congress/house-bill/8.

7. Robertson, Lori, Robert Farley, D'Angelo Gore, and Eugene Kiely. "Trump's Mixed Record on Gun Control." FactCheck.org, August 8, 2019. https://www.factcheck.org/2019/08/trumps-mixed-record-on-gun-control/.

CHAPTER 37

1. Daniller, Andrew. "America's immigration policy priorities: Divisions between—and within—the two parties." Pew Research Center, November 12, 2019. https://www.pewresearch.org/fact-tank/2019/11/12/americans-immigration-policy-priorities-divisions-between-and-within-the-two-parties/.

2. Reagan, Ronald. "Remarks Announcing the Formation of the Statue of Liberty—Ellis Island Centennial Commission." Ronald Reagan Presidential Library and Museum, May 18, 1982. White House, Washington D. C., United States of America. https://www.reaganlibrary.gov/archives/speech/remarks-announcing-formation-statue-liberty-ellis-island-centennial-commission.

3. Reagan, Ronald. "Reagan's Farewell Speech." PBS, January 11, 1989. https://www.pbs.org/wgbh/americanexperience/features/reagan-farewell/.

4. Moore, Mark. "Stephen Miller calls Bush immigration policy a 'betrayal.'" *New York Post*, February 17, 2019. https://nypost.com/2019/02/17/stephen-miller-calls-bush-immigration-policy-a-betrayal/.

5. Allen, Mike. "Talk radio helped sink immigration reform." Politico, August 20, 2007. https://www.politico.com/story/2007/08/talk-radio-helped-sink-immigration-reform-005449.

6. Min Kim, Seung and Carrie Budoff Brown. "The death of immigration reform." Politico, June 27, 2014. https://www.politico.com/story/2014/06/how-immigration-reform-died-108374.

7. "The Cost of Immigration Enforcement and Border Security." American Immigration Council, January 20, 2021. https://www.americanimmigrationcouncil.org/research/the-cost-of-immigration-enforcement-and-border-security.

8. Gonzalez-Barrera, Ana and Jens Manuel Krogstad. "U.S. deportations of immigrants research record high in 2013." Pew Research Center, October 2, 2014. https://www.pewresearch.org/fact-tank/2014/10/02/u-s-deportations-of-immigrants-reach-record-high-in-2013/.

9. Dreier, Peter. "Most Americans Are Liberal, Even If They Don't Know It." *American Prospect,* November 10, 2017. https://prospect.org/power/americans-liberal-even-know/.

CHAPTER 38

1. Saez, Emmanuel and Gabriel Zucman. "The Rise of Income and Wealth Inequality in America: Evidence from Distributional Macroeconomical Accounts." National Bureau of Economic Research, October 2020. https://www.nber.org/system/files/working_papers/w27922/w27922.pdf.

2. Horsley, Scott. "After 2 Years, Trump Tax Cuts Have Failed to Deliver on GOP's Promises." NPR, December 20, 2019. https://www.npr.org/2019/12/20/789540931/2-years-later-trump-tax-cuts-have-failed-to-deliver-on-gops-promises.

3. Hobson, Jeremy. "Trump Said Tax Cuts Would Be 'Rocket Fuel' for the Economy. Analysis Shows They Haven't." WBUR, May 31, 2019. https://www.wbur.org/hereandnow/2019/05/31/trump-tax-cuts-economic-impact.

4. Paletta, Daiman and Max Ehrenfreund. "Trump's treasury secretary: the tax cut 'will pay for itself.'" *Washington Post*, April 20, 2017. https://www.washingtonpost.com/news/wonk/wp/2017/04/20/trumps-treasury-secretary-the-tax-cut-will-pay-for-itself/.

5. Jackson, Brooks. "Trump's Dubious $4,000 Claim." FactCheck.org, October 23, 2017. https://www.factcheck.org/2017/10/trumps-dubious-4000-claim/.

6. Horsley, Scott. "After 2 Years, Trump Tax Cuts Have Failed to Deliver on GOP's Promises." NPR, December 20, 2019. https://www.npr.org/2019/12/20/789540931/2-years-later-trump-tax-cuts-have-failed-to-deliver-on-gops-promises.

7. "Distributional Analysis of the Conference Agreement of the Tax Cuts and Jobs Act." Tax Policy Center, December 18, 2017. https://www.taxpolicycenter.org/publications/distributional-analysis-conference-agreement-tax-cuts-and-jobs-act.

8. Federal Reserve Economic Data (FRED). Economic Research Federal Reserve Bank of St. Louis, accessed December 7, 2021. https://fred.stlouisfed.org/.

9. Ibid.

10. Ibid.

11. Ibid.

12. Editorial Board. "You Know Who the Tax Cuts Helped? Rich People" *New York Times*, August 12, 2018. https://www.nytimes.com/interactive/2018/08/12/opinion/editorials/trump-tax-cuts.html.

13. Frank, Robert. "The wealthiest 10% of Americans own a record 89% of all U.S. stocks." CNBC, October 18, 2021. https://www.cnbc.com/2021/10/18/the-wealthiest-10percent-of-americans-own-a-record-89percent-of-all-us-stocks.html.

CHAPTER 39

1. "Efforts to appeal the Affordable Care Act." Wikipedia. Wikimedia Foundation, last modified November 23, 2021. https://en.wikipedia.org/wiki/Efforts_to_repeal_the_Affordable_Care_Act.

2. Stolberg, Sheryl G. "G.O.P. Faces Risk from Push to Repeal Health Law During Pandemic." *New York Times*, June 22, 2020. https://www.nytimes.com/2020/06/22/us/politics/republicans-health-care-coronavirus.html.

3. Levitan, Sar A. and Robert Taggart. "The Great Society Did Succeed." *Political Science Quarterly* 91, no.4 (1976-1977): 601–618. Accessed December 7, 2021. https://doi.org/10.2307/2148796.

4. Glied, Sherry A., Stephanie Ma, and Anaïs Borja. "Effect of the Affordable Care Act on Health Care Access." The Commonwealth Fund, May 8, 2017. https://www.commonwealthfund.org/publications/issue-briefs/2017/may/effect-affordable-care-act-health-care-access.

5. "Premium Growth Has Slowed for Employer-Provided Family Health Coverage." Center on Budget and Policy Priorities, 2018. https://www.cbpp.org/premium-growth-has-slowed-for-employer-provided-family-health-coverage.

6. Hamblin, James. "Some American Say They Support the Affordable Care Act but Not Obamacare." *Atlantic*, October 1, 2013. https://www.theatlantic.com/health/archive/2013/10/some-americans-say-they-support-the-affordable-care-act-but-not-obamacare/280165/.

7. Dropp, Kyle and Brendan Nyhan. "One-Third Don't Know Obamacare and Affordable Care Act Are the Same." *New York Times*, February 7, 2017. https://www.nytimes.com/2017/02/07/upshot/one-third-dont-know-obamacare-and-affordable-care-act-are-the-same.html?_r=1.

8. Norris, Louise. "12 ways the GOP sabotaged Obamacare." HealthInsurance.org, July 26, 2019. https://www.healthinsurance.org/blog/12-ways-the-gop-sabotaged-obamacare/.

CHAPTER 40

1. Strauss, Valerie. "Texas GOP rejects 'critical thinking' skills. Really." *Washington Post*, July 9, 2012. https://www.washingtonpost.com/ blogs/answer-sheet/post/texas-gop-rejects-critical-thinking-skills- really/2012/07/08/gJQAHNpFXW_blog.html.

2. Freedberg, Louis. "Democrats and Republicans in Congress spar over need for more federal education aid." EdSource, June 15, 2020. https://edsource. org/2020/democrats-and-republicans-in-congress-spar-over-need-for- more-federal-education-aid/633765.

3. "Governor Stanley Response to Decision in Brown v. Board of Education." Document Bank of Virginia, accessed December 7, 2021. https://edu.lva. virginia.gov/dbva/items/show/207.

4. Simms, Angela, and Elizabeth Talbert. "Racial Residential Segregation and School Choice: How a Market-Based Policy for K-12 School Access Creates a 'Parenting Tax' for Black Parents." *Phylon* (1960) 56, no. 1 (2019): 33–57. https:// www.jstor.org/stable/26743830.

5. Harris, Douglas N. "Are the education proposals of the Democratic presidential candidates really that liberal?" Brookings, June 26, 2019. https://www.brookings.edu/blog/brown-center-chalkboard/2019/06/26/ are-the-education-proposals-of-the-democratic-presidential-candidates- really-that-liberal/.

6. Freedberg, Louis. "Democrats and Republicans in Congress spar over need for more federal education aid." EdSource, June 15, 2020. https://edsource. org/2020/democrats-and-republicans-in-congress-spar-over-need-for- more-federal-education-aid/633765.

7. Leachman, Michael, Kathleen Masterson, and Eric Figueroa. "A Punishing Decade for School Funding." Center on Budget and Policy Priorities, November 29, 2017. https://www.cbpp.org/research/ state-budget-and-tax/a-punishing-decade-for-school-funding.

8. "Table 3 Grade breakdown." BMC. Evolution: Education and Outreach, accessed December 7, 2021. https://evolution-outreach.biomedcentral.com/ articles/10.1186/s12052-017-0066-2/tables/4.

CHAPTER 41

1. Lavelle, Marianne. "Climate Activists Plot How to Turn Anti-Trump Rage into Anti-Trump Votes." Inside Climate News, April 18, 2017. https://insideclimatenews.org/news/18042017/climate-change-peoples-climate-march-environmentalists-donald-trump/.

2. Meyer, Stephen M. "The Economic Impact of Environmental Regulation." Accessed December 7, 2021. http://bechtel.colorado.edu/~silverst/cven5534/Economic%20Impact%20Environ.%20Regulation.pdf.

3. *Do Regulation Kill Jobs?* Edited by Cary Coglianese, Adam M. Finkel, and Christopher Carrigan. University of Pennsylvania Press, 2015. https://www.upenn.edu/pennpress/book/15183.html.

4. Berman, Eli and Linda T. M. Bui. "Environmental regulation and labor demand: Evidence from the South Coast Air Basin." *Journal of Public Economics 79*, no. 2 (2001): 265-295. Accessed December 7, 2021. 10.1016/S0047-2727(99)00101-2

5. Morgenstern, Richard D. "Jobs and Environmental Regulation." Resources for the Future, May 6, 2015. https://studylib.net/doc/11331917/jobs-and-environmental-regulation-richard-d.-morgenstern-...

6. Semuels, Alana. "Do Regulations Really Kill Jobs?" *Atlantic*, January 19, 2017. https://www.theatlantic.com/business/archive/2017/01/regulations-jobs/513563/.

7. Staples, Louis. "Ben Shapiro's historic comments about climate change have gone viral again because of how idiotic they are." Indy100, June 2, 2019. https://www.indy100.com/news/ben-shapiro-climate-change-video-sea-level-comedian-8939886.

8. Walker, W. Reed. "The Transitional Costs of Sectoral Reallocation: Evidence from the Clean Air Act and the Workforce." *Quarterly Journal of Economics* 128, no. 4 (2013): 1787-1835). Accessed December 7. http://faculty.haas.berkeley.edu/rwalker/research/walker_transitional_costs_CAA.pdf.

CHAPTER 42

1. Thompson, Derek. "Busting the Myth of 'Welfare Makes People Lazy." *Atlantic*, May 8, 2018. https://www.theatlantic.com/business/archive/2018/03/welfare-childhood/555119/.

2. Mishel, Lawrence. "Vast majority of wage earners are working harder, and for not much more." Economic Policy Institute, January 30, 2013. https://www.epi.org/publication/ib348-trends-us-work-hours-wages-1979-2007/#:~:text=Key%20findings%20include%3A,4.5%20additional%20weeks%20per%20year.

3. Levin, Josh. "The Welfare Queen." *Slate*, December 19, 2013. http://www.slate.com/articles/news_and_politics/history/2013/12/linda_taylor_welfare_queen_ronald_reagan_made_her_a_notorious_american_villain.html.

4. Lybarger, Jeremy. "The Price You Pay: Of the wealth and times of woman you know as the welfare queen." *Nation*, July 2, 2019. https://www.thenation.com/article/archive/josh-levin-the-queen-book-review/.

5. Roberts, Steven V. "Food Stamps Program: How It Grew and How Reagan Wants to Cut It Back; The Budget Targets." *New York Times*, April 4, 1981. https://www.nytimes.com/1981/04/04/us/food-stamps-program-it-grew-reagan-wants-cut-it-back-budget-targets.html.

6. "Helms Sings a Song of 'Dixie'; Moseley-Braun Looks Away." *Los Angeles Times*, August 6, 1993. https://www.latimes.com/archives/la-xpm-1993-08-06-mn-20952-story.html.

7. Pear, Robert. "Poverty Rose to 15% in '82, Highest Level Since Mid-1960's." *New York Times*, August 3, 1983. https://www.nytimes.com/1983/08/03/us/poverty-rate-rose-to-15-in-82-highest-level-since-mid-1960-s.html#:~:text=The%20national%20poverty%20rate%20rose,in%201981%2C%20the%20bureau%20said.

CHAPTER 43

1. Dionne, E. J. Jr. *Why the Right Went Wrong: Conservatism—From Goldwater to the Tea Party and Beyond.* New York: Simon & Schuster, 2016.

2. "O'Neil says Cheney told him, 'Deficits don't matter.'" *Chicago Tribune*, January 12, 2004. https://www.chicagotribune.com/news/ct-xpm-2004-01-12-0401120168-story.html.

CHAPTER 44

1. Gold, Hadas. "Report: Trump asked Gary Cohn to block AT&T-Time Warner merger." CNN Business, March 4, 2019. https://www.cnn.com/2019/03/04/media/att-time-warner-trump-gary-cohn/index.html.

2. Rampell, Catherine. "Trump decries 'cancel culture'—but no one embraces it more." *Washington Post*, July 4, 2020. https://www.washingtonpost.com/opinions/2020/07/04/trump-decries-cancel-culture-no-one-embraces-it-more/.

3. Schmitt, Eric. "Promotion in Jeopardy for Army Officer Who Challenged Trump on Ukraine." *New York Times*, June 18, 2020. https://www.nytimes.com/2020/06/18/us/politics/vindman-impeachment-promotion-trump.html.

4. Pengelly, Martin. "Trump administration drops efforts to halt Michael Cohen's tell-all book." *Guardian*, July 31, 2020. https://www.theguardian.com/us-news/2020/jul/31/michael-cohen-trump-tell-all-book.

5. Campbell, Colin. "Donald Trump tells his fans to 'knock the crap out of' any protestors about to throw tomatoes at him." Business Insider, February 1, 2016. https://www.businessinsider.com/donald-trump-crap-protesters-tomatoes-2016-2.

6. Gjelten, Tom. "Peaceful Protestors Tear-Gassed to Clear Way for Trump Church Photo-op." NPR, June 1, 2020. https://www.npr.org/2020/06/01/867532070/trumps-unannounced-church-visit-angers-church-officials.

7. Kranish, Michael. "Trump long has relied on nondisclosure deals to prevent criticism. That strategy may be unraveling." *Washington Post*, August 7, 2020. https://www.washingtonpost.com/politics/trump-nda-jessica-denson-lawsuit/2020/08/06/202fed1c-d5ad-11ea-b9b2-1ea733b97910_story.html.

8. Boot, Max. "Conservatives have a 'cancel culture' of their own." *Washington Post*, July 10, 2020. https://www.washingtonpost.com/opinions/2020/07/10/conservatives-have-cancel-culture-their-own/.

9. Sonmez, Felicia. "Missouri county GOP rescinds invitation to Sen. Roy Blunt to protest emergency declaration vote, report says." *Washington Post*, March 18, 2019. https://www.washingtonpost.com/politics/missouri-county-gop-rescinds-invitation-to-sen-roy-blunt-to-protest-emergency-declaration-vote-report-says/2019/03/18/d27de7ae-49bc-11e9-93d0-64dbcf38ba41_story.html.

10. Caputo, Marc. "Scaramucci disinvested from Florida GOP fundraiser for bashing Trump's 'racially charged' attacks." Politico, July 18, 2019. https://www.politico.com/story/2019/07/18/anthony-scaramucci-florida-gop-fundraiser-1419204.

11. Hasan, Mehdi. "Donald Trump is the king of cancel culture." *Washington Post*, June 30, 2020. https://www.washingtonpost.com/outlook/2020/06/30/cancel-culture-trump-mcenany/.

12. Wise, Justin. "Cruz vows never to buy Nike products again after 'Betsy Ross flag' sneaker cancelled." *Hill*, July 2, 2019. https://thehill.com/homenews/senate/451369-ted-cruz-vows-never-to-buy-nike-products-again-after-company-cancels-betsy.

13. Link, Taylor. "Fox News viewers boycott Keurig after it pulls ads from 'Hannity.'" Salon, November 12, 2017. https://www.salon.com/2017/11/12/fox-news-viewers-boycott-keurig-after-it-pulls-ads-from-hannity/.

14. "The Dixie Chicks backlash begins." History.com, last modified March 9, 2021. https://www.history.com/this-day-in-history/the-dixie-chicks-backlash-begins.

15. Morenz, Emily. "Beatles 'More Popular Than Jesus'—Really? Meaning of Lennon's Infamous Quote." Groovy History, March 4, 2021. https://groovyhistory.com/beatles-more-popular-than-jesus-lennon.

16. Orrell, Brent. "What the conservative version of cancel culture looks like." American Enterprise Institute, July 23, 2020. https://www.aei.org/articles/what-the-conservative-version-of-cancel-culture-looks-like/.

CHAPTER 45

1. "The Polarization of the Congressional Parties." Legacy. VoteView.com, last modified January 30, 2016. https://legacy.voteview.com/political_polarization_2015.htm.

2. Dionne, E. J. Jr. *Why the Right Went Wrong: Conservatism—From Goldwater to the Tea Party and Beyond*. New York: Simon & Schuster, 2016.

CHAPTER 46

1. Millhiser, Ian. "A brief, 90-year history of Republicans calling Democrats 'socialists.'" Think Progress, March 6, 2019. https://archive.thinkprogress. org/a-history-of-republicans-calling-democrats-socialists-777bcd2b7a6d/.

2. Ibid.

3. Ubel, Peter. "How Truman's Medicare Efforts Were Foiled by Red Baiting." *Forbes*, January 15, 2014. https://www.forbes.com/sites/peterubel/2014/01/15/ how-trumans-medicare-efforts-were-foiled-by-red-baiting/.

4. Millhiser, Ian. "A brief, 90-year history of Republicans calling Democrats 'socialists.'" Think Progress, March 6, 2019. https://archive.thinkprogress. org/a-history-of-republicans-calling-democrats-socialists-777bcd2b7a6d/.

5. "Goldwater's 1964 Acceptance Speech." WashingtonPost.com, accessed December 7, 2021. https://www.washingtonpost.com/wp-srv/politics/daily/ may98/goldwaterspeech.htm.

6. Albert, Victoria. "National Republican Congressional Committee Compares Democrats to Stalin." Daily Beast, March 1, 2019. https://www.thedailybeast. com/national-republican-congressional-committee-compares-democrats-to-stalin.

7. Marr, Chuck and George Fenton. "Corporate Lobbying Campaign Against Biden Tax Proposals Is Inaccurate, Unpersuasive." Center on Budget and Policy Priorities, September 10, 2021. https://www.cbpp.org/research/federal-tax/ corporate-lobbying-campaign-against-biden-tax-proposals-is-inaccurate.

CHAPTER 47

1. Rosser, Ezra. "We're all for supporting states' rights, except when it comes to the poor." *Hill*, September 11, 2017. https://thehill.com/blogs/pundits-blog/ state-local-politics/350078-were-all-for-supporting-states-rights-except-when-it.

2. "State legislation in protest of federal law in the United States." Wikipedia. Wikimedia Foundation, last modified September 27, 2021. https:// en.wikipedia.org/wiki/State_legislation_in_protest_of_federal_law _in_the_United_States.

3. Stratford, Michael. "Trump endorses states' rights—but only when he agrees with the state." Politico, April 2, 2018. https://www.politico.com/ story/2018/04/02/trump-states-rights-education-sanctuary-drilling-492784.

4. Bean, Lydia and Maresa Strano. "Part One: State Preemption Unleashed" in *Punching Down: How States are Suppressing Local Democracy*. New America, last modified July 11, 2019. https://www.newamerica.org/political-reform/ reports/punching-down/part-one-state-preemption-unleashed/.

5. Hertel-Fernandez, Alexander. *State Capture: How Conservative Activists, Big Businesses, and Wealthy Donors Reshaped the American States—and the Nation*. Oxford University Press, 2019.

CHAPTER 49

1. Dionne, E. J. Jr. *Why the Right Went Wrong: Conservatism—From Goldwater to the Tea Party and Beyond*. New York: Simon & Schuster, 2016.

2. "Category: Political compromises in the United States." Wikipedia. Wikimedia Foundation, last modified April 14, 2021. https://en.wikipedia.org/ wiki/Category:Political_compromises_in_the_United_States.

3. Serwer, Adam. "We Can Finally See the Real Source of Washington Gridlock." *Atlantic*, April 1, 2020. https://www.theatlantic.com/ideas/archive/2020/04/ republican-party-discovers-virtues-stimulus/609244/.

4. Cochrane, Emily and Sheryl Gay Stolberg. "$2 Trillion Coronavirus Stimulus Bill Is Signed Into Law." *New York Times*, March 27, 2020. https://www. nytimes.com/2020/03/27/us/politics/coronavirus-house-voting.html.

5. Lee, Taeku and Mark Schlesinger. "Signaling in Context: Elite Influence and the Dynamics of Public Support for Clinton's Health Security Act." John F. Kennedy School of Government. Harvard University, May 2001. https:// research.hks.harvard.edu/publications/getFile.aspx?Id=18.

6. Moorhead, Molly. "Mitt Romney says 47 percent of Americans pay no income tax." Politifact. The Poynter Institute, September 18, 2012. https://www.politifact.com/factchecks/2012/sep/18/mitt-romney/ romney-says-47-percent-americans-pay-no-income-tax/.

7. Dionne, E. J. Jr. *Why the Right Went Wrong: Conservatism—From Goldwater to the Tea Party and Beyond*. New York: Simon & Schuster, 2016.

8. Riotta, Chris. "GOP Aims to Kill Obamacare Yet Again After Failing 70 Times." *Newsweek*, July 29, 2017. https://www.newsweek.com/gop-health-care-bill-repeal-and-replace-70-failed-attempts-643832.

9. Fieldhouse, Andrew and Josh Bivens. "The congressional GOP has smothered a more rapid economic recovery." Economic Policy Institute, January 18, 2013. https://www.epi.org/blog/congressional-republicans-smothered-rapid-economic-recovery/.

CHAPTER 50

1. Saad, Lydia. "The U.S. Remained Center-Right, Ideologically, in 2019." Gallup, January 9, 2020. https://news.gallup.com/poll/275792/remained-center-right-ideologically-2019.aspx.

CHAPTER 51

1. Cohen, Donald. *Dismantling Democracy: The forty-year attack on government, . . . and the long game for the common good.* February 21, 2018. https://www.inthepublicinterest.org/wp-content/uploads/DonaldCohen_DismantlingDemocracy_2018.pdf.

2. Mariantes, Karl. "Vietnam—The War That Killed Trust." *New York Times.* January 7, 2017. https://www.nytimes.com/2017/01/07/opinion/sunday/vietnam-the-war-that-killed-trust.html.

3. Hacker, Jacob S. "Don't Dismantle Government—Fix It." *American Prospect*, April 1, 2016. https://drive.google.com/file/d/15aN67EutYu2Y66E0lgV_g80ivtcAlZka/view.

CHAPTER 52

1. "Remarks by the President at a campaign Event at Roanoke, Virginia." The White House President Barack Obama, July 13, 2012. https://obamawhitehouse.archives.gov/the-press-office/2012/07/13/remarks-president-campaign-event-roanoke-virginia.

ABOUT THE AUTHOR

 **BILL IS THE COFOUNDER** of Fight for a Better America, an organization that invests in key battleground districts and states throughout the US, with the goal of either flipping them blue or maintaining a Democratic incumbent. Through his travels with the organization, he has made hundreds of contacts with folks in local civic and Democratic clubs throughout the country—primarily in California, Pennsylvania, New York, Florida, and New Jersey—and organized hundreds of volunteers on the ground. He's had thousands of conversations with voters and prospective volunteers about the issues that affect them most. A New York City native, Bill Kuhn grew up in a political household. His mother was a key fundraiser for the Democratic Party, most notably for Walter Mondale during his 1984 presidential run against Ronald Reagan. His stepfather served as a lawyer on the judiciary committee during President Nixon's impeachment, and as a White House counsel to President Clinton. Politics and the Washington experience were the air he breathed during his formative years. Bill graduated from Georgetown University with a BS in finance and holds graduate degrees from Columbia University (MBA) and Hunter College (MEd). He began his career in investment banking and capital markets (Citi, Collins Stewart, Bank Otrikitie in Moscow), but ultimately came to the realization that his interests better aligned with education and policy. He became a dean and teacher of mathematics and economics at a high school

while pursuing special education research at Hunter. The transition has spurred a new outlook on life for Bill, and he has developed a passion for improving education and addressing inequality in our country. Bill lives in New York City with his wife.